BOBBY
TAMBLING

To Brian
I hope you are
a blues fan, and you
enjoy the book

Best Wishes

Bobby Tambling

202

BOBBY
TAMBLING

GOALS
IN LIFE
MY AUTOBIOGRAPHY

Sport Media Ⓢ

To Val, my rock.

By Bobby Tambling
with Richard Godden

© Bobby Tambling

First Edition
Published in Great Britain in 2016.
Published and produced by: Trinity Mirror Sport Media, PO Box 48,
Old Hall Street, Liverpool L69 3EB.

Edited by: Chris Brereton
Publishing Director: Steve Hanrahan
Commercial Director: Will Beedles
Executive Editor: Paul Dove
Executive Art Editor: Rick Cooke
Senior Marketing Executive: Claire Brown

ISBN: 9781910335376

Photographic acknowledgements: Bobby Tambling, PA, Mirrorpix
Front cover image: Press Association
With thanks to Paul Dutton

Printed and bound by CPI Group (UK) Ltd, Croydon, CR0 4YY.

CONTENTS

THANKS

I have so many people to thank for the incredible life I have led.

First and foremost, my family.

My wonderful partner Val, as I wouldn't be here today without her, as well as my fantastic sons, Gary and Glenn, their wives Moira and Val, and my gorgeous grandkids. I am so grateful to have them all living so close to me.

I must also mention Jamie, Val's son who came into my world at only three years old and is like my own, and his lovely wife Ayesha. I am so proud of them all. All Val's family have been fantastic through the years and I am very fond of her brothers, Ger (Boo), Buzz, Adrian and Tom.

Adelaide, initially Val's friend, but now a wonderful friend to us both and her hubby Lar have both been terrific.

A very special thank you must also go to Derval, who is like a little PA to me, and has been a wonderful help with this book, as well as all my close friends, especially Barry and Megan Bridges, Christine and Don Slyne, Dave Johnson and Steve Forbes.

Richard Godden, who encouraged me to write this book, also deserves huge praise. He has been a tremendous support, always at the end of the phone, always taking my calls, sometimes too many times in one day.

A big thank you also to Roman Abramovich, who has supported us old boys of Chelsea. He, more than anyone, has appreciated that we weren't the big earners of today's football world and has ensured we are remembered.

Thanks as well to Bruce Buck, Chelsea's chairman, who shares Mr Abramovich's ideals and is always there for us and also David Barnard, the club secretary, especially for arranging the replacement of my England caps.

Chris Brereton, Paul Dove and Steve Hanrahan at Trinity Mirror also deserve a mention for helping the book come together so painlessly.

The Chelsea stewards were particularly fantastic when I was wheelchair bound and all the staff behind the scenes at Chelsea deserve a lot of praise, none more so than the wonderful Gary Staker. I have a gorgeous memory of being out with him and his Dad for this fantastic Italian meal, which I will forever hold dear.

Eddie and Pat Barnett who were the ticket managers for years at Chelsea until they retired are fantastic and, of course, so is Emma Wilkinson, who does such tremendous work for Chelsea.

In addition to these, I must thank all the girls who work behind the scenes to make the ex-players annual lunch such an event and all the staff at the hotel, especially Nick, who always looks after me and Val so well.

I cannot stop thanking my wonderful doctors, Carl, Gerry, John and their lovely wives who have become such great friends and all the terrific staff of the CUH who have been superb with me. I must also make a special mention to the Chelsea Supporters Clubs in Ireland (Ennis, Dublin, Cork, Limerick, Waterford and Kerry).

ACKNOWLEDGEMENTS

The Norwegian Chelsea family, especially Tsalve and Hansen and their lovely wives have become wonderful friends and I love meeting them at the home games at the Bridge as I do the American Chelsea family, especially the terrific Beth Wild and Michael Neat.

Dave O'Connor from Suit Distributors, all at Crosshaven AFC and Carrigaline AFC and Andrew and Conor of Simply Suits have also been wonderful friends over the years.

Another thank you has to go to Frank Lampard, who has been such a great support to me and Val. When my illness was at its worst and there was big financial pressure on Val, Frank stepped in and did an interview with me for The Sun, which helped us enormously. I have said it before, I couldn't have asked for a better person to beat my record.

Lastly a special thanks to the Chelsea fans, you are my backbone and the reason I have been so fortunate to play professional football and have such an amazing career.

I could fill this book with thanks as there are too many to mention and I apologise to anyone I have left out, I have been so blessed to have met so many wonderful people along the way.

Bobby Tambling, August, 2016

"It's not about me, it's about the team."

How many times have I heard that over the past nine months? Almost 50 years have passed since Bobby last kicked a ball in anger for Chelsea and still he refuses to take any of the glory which comes with the territory of being a club legend.

From the moment we first discussed the book, you made me feel part of your team – along with Val and Derval, who have both been a great help – and it has been an absolute pleasure working with such a generous and humble man. You deserve this.

I'd like to thank all at Trinity Mirror Sport Media, in particular Chris Brereton, who came in at the 11th hour and polished a few rough edges.

My colleagues in the publications department at Chelsea have also been incredibly supportive, most notably David Antill, whose input throughout the process has been invaluable.

This book may never have even got off the ground had it not been for Emma Wilkinson, who approached Bobby in the first instance and talked up my credentials as a writer and as a person. I hope I lived up to the billing!

There have been a few crucial cameos. The ever-accurate statistics provided by Paul Dutton add weight to the words of a truly great goalscorer; David Kostis and Murray Summers helped to fill in a few blanks with their impressive programme collections. And Caroline Mabey – no more printing, I promise!

I also owe so much to Steve Mackenzie and John D Taylor, whose belief gave me the confidence to pursue my writing dream. As JDT always says, it beats working for a living...

The biggest thank you of all is reserved for my family. To my mum, Pauline, brother, Nick, sister-in-law, Sinead, my two nephews, George and Arthur, and my beautiful Hannah – I'm looking forward to spending more time with you all and less time glued to a laptop. Thanks for always being there.

Finally, I'd like to dedicate my efforts in this book to my father, who passed away just a few days after I began working on it. I hope I have made you proud; it's all I ever wanted.

Richard Godden, August, 2016

FOREWORD

I'm going to start with an admission: when I signed for Chelsea I didn't have a clue who Bobby Tambling was. I don't think I'm alone there. Until recently, when people thought of Chelsea from the 1960s and Seventies it was all about the likes of Peter Osgood, Alan Hudson, "Chopper" Harris, Peter Bonetti, Charlie Cooke and obviously David Webb for his winner in the 1970 FA Cup final. They were the Kings of the King's Road, the "sexy football" team of that era.

To me, that anonymity is testament to Bobby's low-key personality and how he is as a bloke. Here is a guy who, for the best part of 50 years, held the record for scoring more goals for Chelsea Football Club than any other player, but it's only in the past few years that the wider footballing world has come to acknowledge that achievement because he kept himself out of the limelight, enjoying his life in Ireland without milking the acclaim.

Football, and team sports in general, take all sorts: you have the people with bigger personalities which smack you in the face more, then there are those who just get on with their job and go home to their families. Obviously, I didn't know Bobby back when he was banging in goals for Chelsea, but it's clear he was just a regular bloke who was happy to work hard, do his job for the team and get on with it.

I know what that era of football was like because my dad, although he's a bit younger than Bobby – and he'll be so pleased with me getting that in there! – was involved at that time. You hear the notorious stories of all the drinking and team bonding that went on, particularly with the Chelsea team at that time, and I think you need characters to keep you in check. From what I can gather, Bobby was one of those sensible guys and I'm sure some of his old mates will be grateful he was around to help them out on certain nights!

My dad played in a pretty famous West Ham team, packed full of big names, and it was the same over at Chelsea. It was a great era for London football and Bobby played his part in it, so it's wonderful that he has started to get a bit of recognition for his achievements, especially when you look at the stats and the sheer number of goals he scored for Chelsea.

Had he done that today, with the wall-to-wall coverage available to supporters, and netted 202 goals for a club the size of Chelsea, it would be a different ball game. I'd be sat here writing about a £50million player. The best thing I'd say about Bobby is that there is no bitterness about that. He's very pleased with the career and life he has had, he hasn't sat around cursing the fact he missed out on the fame and money which would have come his way had he played in this era.

On the day I signed for Chelsea, I took a look at the list of the club's all-time leading scorers and didn't even get as far as Bobby's name. I looked up Gustavo Poyet, who had scored 49, and Dennis Wise on 76, and that was it. Those two guys had just left Stamford Bridge and were held in high regard by Chelsea supporters. I'd tried to make a bit of a name for myself at West Ham as a goalscoring midfielder, so I knew that was my game and what I wanted to bring to the table. I thought I could have a decent crack at 70 to 80 goals; if I stayed for 10 years, I might get there.

If you had asked me to guess who held the record for most goals, I'd probably have said Kerry Dixon. I'd grown up with him banging them in for Chelsea. Bobby was well off my radar, and it's fair to say he probably didn't fancy my chances of getting there, either.

There's a great quote from Bobby talking about when I signed for the club. He said: "I thought Frank was a typical West Ham poser. But, boy, did he prove me wrong." I'm glad he added the second part! I actually think Bobby has been quite kind to me with that comment, I'm sure a few others had plenty to say about me being worth £11million at that time. I was never a poser and, actually, I think at West Ham we were under the impression the Chelsea lads were posers! They've all proved me wrong, I hasten to add, and now Chelsea has become the love of my life as far as football is concerned.

I didn't actually meet Bobby until I'd been at Chelsea for a few years, although I couldn't put an exact date on it. When I joined there was a bit of an issue between Chelsea and a few of the legends, and I don't think the club was embracing all of the ex-players and making them feel comfortable at the club. I'd like to make a point of praising the brilliant job that Roman Abramovich has done bringing the old boys back into the fold, because it's been huge for the club. When you're talking about an era when matches weren't regularly televised and there certainly wasn't anything like social media, the new generation could easily forget about them. What's important at a club like Chelsea is that we have the history – a great history, despite what others might say, and we've created plenty more in recent times as well – and incorporating those ex-players in what the club does around matchdays and at events is what a great club should be like. You always think of Manchester United doing it very well and now Chelsea are there, too. Roman Abramovich made great strides to do that.

As the years went by and the club made more of a push to get the old boys involved, I met Bobby and just remember the gentleman's air he had about him. Some ex-players you meet don't have that softness about them, and I mean that in a good way. He was so nice in his manner and very supportive of me and the club. He just loved Chelsea and being a part of it.

Whenever I'd see him at games or events, he was always egging me on towards the record, and Kerry Dixon was the same as well. Bobby had so much faith in me and I don't think I really believed I had a shot at it until around 2010, when I got to the mid-100 goal mark. I'd had a couple of good years and scored something like 27 goals that season – who am I kidding, I know it was exactly 27 – and I passed Peter Osgood and Roy Bentley on 150 when I scored four against Aston Villa. It was at that point when I realised I had a chance. When I passed those two legends at the same time, and I was scoring freely, that's when I started to look up at it. I really wanted to beat it.

Just like Bobby, I never have to research any of my goal milestones or anything like that because we both have that striker mentality, even though we didn't play as out-and-out strikers. I blame my dad. Or perhaps a better way of putting it is that I credit my dad for it. As a young midfielder, he would sometimes criticise me for being content to pass the ball around from within the centre circle.

"If you're going to make real strides, you need to get in the box and score goals," he told me. It gave me a real desire to do it. And do you know what? That's the way it should be, whether you're a midfield player, a winger, a striker. I've played with strikers who don't quite have that desire, and they don't get the goals they should. A great goalscorer like Bobby, anyone who scores that many goals, is going to have that desire. And you remember things, because goals become your life in football. 'Goals in Life' is an appropriate title for this book as far as Bobby is concerned.

The beauty about Bobby is that most forwards who score that amount of goals are pretty selfish both on the pitch and in life off the pitch – it's a certain trait which you almost have to put up with when it comes to a great goalscorer who wants all the glory. With Bobby, he must have had that desire on the pitch, but you never sense it off the field. I just don't see that in him as a person. My bond with Bobby became so strong when I was getting closer to the record, when he was unselfishly supporting me all the way. For me, that is what Chelsea Football Club is all about. The togetherness. We're a family. Bobby epitomises that.

I recall the club honouring him with a special recognition award, which I was due to present, but it was at a time when he was very unwell and he wasn't able to attend, so Val and her brother collected it on his behalf. I was so pleased for him to be honoured in that way and it was lovely when, a year later, his health had improved and he came over to London to return the favour for me. As I say, Bobby didn't always get the recognition his achievements deserved and he was never sticking his neck out for it, so this was such a wonderful thing for him. I love the fact the club and others are now giving him the recognition he deserves for such a great career.

During his illness, it was really hard to see him in such poor health, but the real difficulty was felt by Bobby and those closest to him. It's a credit to him that whenever I saw him, no matter how poorly he was, he held himself with such class and good humour. What a fighter he is. No desire for any sympathy, just hold your head high and act like nothing was going on, even though you could see he was struggling. That's a sign of the man. And he came through it.

I remember seeing him at one point and thinking he was really struggling, but obviously I didn't say anything to him. Then you jump forward a year and it was the old Bobby again.

We all talk about this nice, lovely fella, but underneath all that is a steely determination, a tough core, and he needed it to come through that period in his life. He's also got an incredible family. I know how important Val is and how strong she remained throughout the whole ordeal. In those circumstances, you rely on the people close to you.

Speaking about Val, there's obviously something about scoring goals for Chelsea which attracts us to Irish ladies – I don't know if that's good or bad! It certainly helped increase the bond between us because, whenever we get together, the girls have got some common ground and Bobby is always telling us to come over to Ireland, which we really need to do as soon as I pack up and I've got a bit more time on my hands.

One story which jumps out about Bobby actually concerns Val. Now, John Terry won't thank me for telling this, but I remember the four of us having a chat and we were joking about the goal record and what have you. Suddenly, Val says to John: "Now, listen, you can do us a big favour here. The next time we get a penalty, you're the captain, so you take it off Frank."

John reminded her about Moscow and we all had a good laugh about it. I know both her and Bobby were supporting me all the way. Mind you, if she'd said it to Didier Drogba I might have been in trouble, because he wouldn't have wasted any time grabbing the ball next time!

It was strange that as I got closer to his record, Bobby's health seemed to get better. It was such a boost for me to see his improvement. He wasn't able to come over too often and suddenly I'd see him again and he was looking much better; he was walking again and he had this brightness about him. It was fantastic to see the strength of the man. As soon as the Aston Villa game finished after I'd broken the record, I called him up and we had a good chat.

I'm so glad Bobby has come back to the fore. Because he keeps his head down and doesn't go searching for that sort of thing, it was a long time in coming, but it's great for him and his family that at this stage of his life he can enjoy the limelight. It's long overdue. Suddenly, people realised Chelsea had this prolific goalscorer. But there's so much more to Bobby than goals. He is a gentleman of football and Chelsea Football Club. If you want an ambassador, someone who shows what this club means and who transcends the generations, he is the man.

Other players may have taken the headlines back then but, Bobby, you are the main man as far I'm concerned. It's an absolute privilege to call you my mate.

Frank Lampard, May, 2016

1

THE
DREAM

21 September, 2013
Chelsea v Fulham, Stamford Bridge

"There's only one Bobby Tambling – one Bobby Tammmmmbling!"

The words cut right through me; tears stream down my face. I realise just how lucky I am.

A few months earlier I was knocking at death's door, with the title of Chelsea's record goalscorer coming to the grave with me. Some say football is a matter of life or death; Bill Shankly thought it was even more important than that.

But clearly I didn't share that opinion.

I valued my life far more than I did that goalscoring record. Against all odds, I won the biggest match of my life, beating Martorell's ulcer on penalties after snatching a last-gasp equaliser.

This terrible, debilitating illness had left me a shadow of my former self and fighting just to stay alive, stealing years from my life. Lying there in my hospital bed, accompanied by my beautiful wife, who has been to hell and back throughout this horrible ordeal, I could finally see light at the end of the tunnel. Writing about my life brought laughter to the room and, more often than not, tears to my eyes. Some of the stories had seemed so far away when I thought about them in the past, little more than distant memories. But once you get it down on paper it suddenly comes back to life. It seems real again.

Never in a million years did I dream I would be able to see the most wonderful football supporters again, let alone walk around a pitch that I had the pleasure of sharing with some of the best friends anyone could ever wish for. But here I am. Reborn. Those three words ringing around the stadium: "One Bobby Tambling!"

What a life I have been privileged to lead.

A lot of the autobiographies I've read have been filled to the brim with scandal and score-settling, but I've not set out to do that in my book.

If that's your thing then I suggest you stop reading now, and if I have caused offence to anyone I've written about then I apologise unreservedly. It was not my intention.

This is supposed to be a book about how I've lived out my dreams on the field, representing the greatest football team the world has ever seen.

I became a Chelsea fan the day I signed for the club. I loved the kit, the stadium, everything. In fact, I think I became a fan the day I met Jimmy Thompson. He was the perfect man to get me to sign for the club – he made me feel special. Then, the first time I walked through those big gates at Stamford Bridge I was smitten. I've felt the same way every time I've been back over the past six decades.

A lot of people know me as the man whose goalscoring record Frank Lampard surpassed on that fateful afternoon at Villa Park. I often said I'd be dead before he broke the record, and little did I know how close I was to being right. I'm glad I'm not! When he finally broke it I actually felt a sense of relief. Relief that people would stop asking me that same bloody question!

A couple of decades earlier it had looked as though Kerry Dixon would beat my record. He left abruptly, nine goals shy of my tally, and I was relieved he was gone. Not because I don't like the bloke – quite the opposite, in fact. Rather, I was disconnected from the club and this record was my footprint at Chelsea. A lot of people probably only knew of me because of that fact and the youngsters especially didn't really know anything else about me. The older ones may have seen me play, but the younger ones just knew me as that name in the matchday programme. So people might say, "Have you heard of that Bobby Tambling?" and they'd reply, "Yeah, he scored goals at Chelsea."

But stick me in a line-up of blokes and they wouldn't know me from Adam. Then Frank started chasing the record and it put me back on the Chelsea map. Half the people probably didn't realise I was still alive! Now I feel as if I'm part of the family again.

I came out of the underground for the FA Cup game against Scunthorpe in January 2016 and met up with Tommy Baldwin.

We were having a chat, always pleased to see each other, and I'd spoken to a guy who was with his wife and a youngster. They said, "Oh, we can't believe we've seen you." And I said, "Well look, here's Tommy Baldwin. He's another legend." The fella was in a different world, like he'd gone back in time. After the game, I walked back to catch the train back to Portsmouth and these two youngsters, both in their mid-twenties, went dopey because they'd bumped into me! I was amazed. They didn't say, "Are you Bobby Tambling?" it was "You are Bobby Tambling!"

Later on I was stood on an empty platform and from across the tracks someone started shouting: "There's only one Bobby Tambling!" I was thinking how weird it was that I could travel almost unrecognised when I was playing for Chelsea but now I'm noticed a lot more.

When you finish, you think that's the end of it. If someone said after I'd left the club that in 50 years time people would still be looking for me to sign something I'd have told them to stop being so silly.

I feel the same way about the fans as they do about me. They always say how much they appreciate what I've done for them, but it should be the other way round. During my playing career, football was kept alive by the spectators.

I'm in no doubt about that. There was no sponsorship, no advertising, no television deal – it was those who paid on the gate who generated revenue. So, actually, I feel I owe you something. It might not have been you specifically but it would have been someone like you years back.

I've had several people associated with Chelsea, from different periods, tell me that I don't owe the club anything, but I do. They've given me such a wonderful life. To have spent so many years at the club and achieved so much, then to be received the way all of us old boys are today, I just cannot thank them enough. It was such a brilliant time. A dream.

I'm sometimes spellbound at how people feel the way they do about us old boys. I always thought we were just entertainers, but then you get someone in their sixties telling you: "You're the reason I watch Chelsea." Did we really have that much influence on people? I'm just an ordinary guy who was lucky enough to play a sport I loved from the age of seven or eight.

I'm so glad the club has enjoyed the success it has over the past 20 years, otherwise a lot of supporters would probably have been cursing me and my team-mates for turning them into Chelsea supporters!

Why do you think I moved to Ireland when I did?!

I can understand players being remembered – this era especially but in my day the likes of Peter Bonetti and Ossie – because they won cups. You're always going to remember the most successful sides. Funnily enough, you talk to people about the Sixties and although we never won much, we symbolised a change in Chelsea's fortune and style. People would say, "What an exciting team." We never won many trophies, but people loved us.

It could be because we were just like them – we were supporters, but instead of being in the stands we were on the pitch. We were no different to them, and they could see it. We mingled with them, travelled with them and so forth. We were ordinary guys who just happened to be better than them at football!

Or just luckier than them, perhaps...

My story really started in the small seaside town of Hayling Island where, as the light of day used to fade, you could hear the excited cheers of a group of lads playing the final minutes of what was the most important game of their lives. Until the next day, that is…

No goal posts were in sight, only the coats and bags of a few eight-year-old boys were piled up, and this makeshift football stadium would be the foundation for the hopes and dreams of these wannabe footballers.

The same scene would be playing out across the country, whether it was on grass, mud, concrete, whatever. All that was needed was a ball. The rest was an added bonus.

The dream was exactly the same for each of these youngsters: to follow in the footsteps of their boyhood hero and become a professional footballer. Mostly, these dreams would fall by the wayside.

This, however, is the story of one lad who lived his dream; the happiness that came with that, allied with disappointments along the way; the fine line between success and failure and how luck plays its part in defining each and every one of us.

Back in those early years, that dream started to develop between the coats and school bags which formed a crucial part of the pitch where I would imagine myself as my hero: Stan Mortensen.

As there wasn't much football on television in those days, and most of us didn't have our own set anyway, most boys would pick their favourite player based on what they saw in the flesh, or perhaps in an FA Cup final, which was one of the few matches to be televised.

I'd read about Stan in football magazines and books and was already a fan by the time I watched him in the 1953 FA Cup final between Blackpool and Bolton.

THE DREAM

I watched the whole game outside a local electrical shop because we didn't have a television set at home, but I may as well have been playing at Wembley as I kicked every ball that day.

Bolton were leading 3-1 and Blackpool's hopes of winning the famous trophy for the first time lay in tatters before the most incredible turnaround saw them win it 4-3 with virtually the last kick of the game.

Despite Stan becoming the first player to score a hat-trick in an FA Cup final at Wembley, a record which still stands today, the game was dubbed "The Matthews final" as the great Stanley Matthews set up several goals and finally lifted the trophy after losing two previous finals with the Tangerines. He was 38 at the time!

Recently, his FA Cup winner's medal was auctioned for £220,000, which is more than any of the 1966 World Cup winner's medals have sold for. Stan truly was a magician – but, as a goalscorer, Mortensen was the one for me.

For some reason, I remembered Stan being called the "Lion of Vienna" after a particularly brave performance for England against Austria, but it turns out that was actually Nat Lofthouse, who also played in that 1953 FA Cup final. In my defence, it was more than 60 years ago.

I had the pleasure of meeting him later in life. I was in the England camp and as I opened a door to go out into the corridor he was there. My hero, in front of my very eyes. I panicked.

"Uh, Mr Mortensen, I'd, erm, just like to let you know that you were my hero," I blurted out, my face reddening by the second. Now, when people tell me I was their hero and call me Mr Tambling, I correct them: "It's not Mr – I'm just Bobby."

As kids, we spent nearly all our spare time in the park, kicking a ball around and each taking our turn in a different position and giving a running commentary on the action.

"Stanley Matthews has got the ball out on the right wing, that's a great cross to Mortensen, he must score.. oh, how has Mortensen missed that?!"

No prizes for guessing who I was.

I couldn't keep count of how many cup finals I played in or the caps I won for England in that park. Dreams!

At home, there was always talk of sport. I come from a big family, with five brothers and two sisters, although the family seemed to be split into two halves as the four eldest children had left home while the youngest four were still at school. Although my father never really played any sport or had any interest in it, all of us boys turned out to be good all-round sportsmen.

Dad was a poultry keeper on a local farm and mum was the one who looked after the family's needs. On a Saturday or Sunday night she would love to sit down and listen to all of the stories from the games that had been played by her boys. It must have been hard for her to keep up as there was usually three or four games being relayed to her on a blow-by-blow basis, all at the same time as we fought to have our stories heard. It was a madhouse of sport. Hearing these stories just made you want to be part of all that fun and excitement.

My parents were brilliant and our house was always full of fun and laughter. It was a great place to grow up and I've got so many fond memories from my childhood.

Dad's lack of football knowledge was clear for everyone to see. I remember saving up all my pocket money from helping him out every evening putting the hens in their huts so I could buy my first pair of Adidas football boots which had the new screw-in studs. They cost me £5, which might seem like a bargain to any youngsters reading this, but believe me, that was a lot of money in those days.

I was so proud when I brought them home and my brothers seemed to be just as happy that I had these brilliant new boots. Then dad asked how much I had paid for them. When I told him they'd cost a fiver he went mad, telling me what a waste of money it was. "What good would they be for you?" he asked. Many years later we would have a good laugh about what a waste of money it really was.

He offered up a similar response when I was late coming to help him out one evening. I would always cut it fine, leaving the game at the last possible moment at which it was physically possible to run to the farm, but this one particular game was a nail-biter and I just couldn't let my team down.

Dad went mad when I told him why I was late. He came out with a classic: "A lot of good football will do you. You're not going to earn a living from kicking a ball about!"

I received plenty of encouragement from the rest of the family, even if dad thought I was nuts, but I will tell you one thing: there wasn't a prouder man than my father when I realised my dream of playing professional football.

We would often bring up these little stories, all in good fun, and I would tell him he nearly put me off trying to become a footballer. Perhaps his attitude drove me on to try even harder, as I realised what he was saying was true in most cases.

The park was really only the start of things for me but I never forgot the skills I picked up in those early days and they certainly had some bearing on my football career.

My brother Mick and I would spend hours playing in the street with our mates. A tennis ball was all we had to play with and to this day Mick is adamant it made us both good strikers of a football because the sweet spot was that much smaller. He makes a good point, but I wouldn't draw the line at striking. All of our football skills were honed using a tennis ball, so when we actually played with a proper ball it seemed so much easier.

Fifty yards up the road from where we lived there was a cul-de-sac with a few houses on either side. The road was in sections, so we used to play through them, with a goal at each end. I remember it like it was yesterday. Lunchtime was half-time! We'd all go off to get something to eat and then meet up again for the second half.

We played for hours and hours. There was no such thing as, "I'm going indoors to watch the telly", and there certainly wasn't any such thing as video games to distract us. Get out and play ball – what else would we do?

Past the road was a field and if there was no cattle or anything like that we'd go out there and play. We were competing with cows for the right to play football! We'd play three goals and in, with everyone taking it in turns between the posts, and we would pretend to be our heroes. The problem – and I'm sorry if you're reading this, Catty, because you did as much as anyone to change this – was no one tried when they were in goal because none of our heroes were goalkeepers. We all just wanted to get back out on the pitch as soon as possible.

My first involvement with a team came at school, as I'm sure it did for so many young boys. Our school was only small, probably the smallest in south-east Hampshire, and the team was always bottom of the league. Even so, everybody was proud to play in the side and represent our school. This was a valuable lesson.

I was put in the team as a 10-year-old, with legs resembling matchsticks, whereas most of the lads were about 15. They needed to call on younger lads just to be able to put out a team most weeks!

Mick was our captain and I was so proud to be playing in the same team as him. He played inside-right and had two great feet. There was no doubt in my mind he was the best player on our team.

We used to take some real beatings from some of the bigger schools in the area, but it never dented our enthusiasm for the next game. The experience taught us some great lessons about fighting uphill battles and how to never give up. That proved invaluable for me in my professional years, but it was equally important to take that into life itself.

The bigger the defeat, the harder we worked in the next game. For a team that was bottom of the league, you wouldn't believe the enthusiasm of all the players in such a dire situation.

Despite our predicament, we managed to pull off a huge upset in our first tie of the cup competition. Winning that match alone was a feat in itself. There was no such thing as coaching or training – we were a self-taught group and all of our practice came from kickabouts with each other and our mates.

When we won our next cup tie as well, the semi-finals beckoned and suddenly we had the whole school behind us. It was a wonderful feeling and we made sure we spent all our spare time with a football in tow. That was the only way we could prepare, because we certainly didn't have any tactics. Just a huge desire to play the game we loved and, most importantly, to enjoy ourselves.

Well, that desire took us all the way to the final, where we would face the biggest school in the area. Not only had they already wrapped up the league title, they were also prolific trophy winners over the years and brushing aside the team propping up the table would surely prove no trouble whatsoever on their way to winning the Double.

I'm telling you this story because there are a lot of lessons to be learned from what happened and how many emotions can be felt in sport by how quickly things can change for both better and worse.

There was massive excitement within our school and we knew everybody would be at that game supporting us. It was to be a first taste of fan power, and I'd be a liar if I said I didn't want more of that in the future.

The final was mentioned from the stage at every assembly, which made the whole team so proud, and we worked every day after school to make sure we didn't let anybody down.

Two days before the final, we had finished our kickabout and were just mucking around as young boys do; perhaps a little overzealously, but that's what being a kid is all about. Then, disaster struck. I fell and landed awkwardly on my wrist. One trip to hospital later and my worst fear was confirmed: it was broken and I would have to sit out the final.

Words simply cannot describe how devastated I was; heartbroken doesn't even begin to cover it. What made it worse was everyone trying to cheer me up when they saw the disappointment etched across my face. I know they were only trying to help, but it just made me feel even worse.

On the day of the game, as upset as I was, there was no way I was going to sit around sulking. The rest of the school was behind the team and I would be no different. The game itself was a classic case of the underdog taking the overconfident favourites by surprise. The team chased every lost cause, working their socks off for each other and taking so much heart from the support they received from the crowd. Our lads seemed to lift themselves, whatever was thrown at them, and the game looked destined for extra-time with the two teams locked at 1-1. Then, with just minutes to go, came the perfect ending: Mick popped up with a brilliant goal. We had won the cup!

The feeling of winning against all the odds was immense. I'd never heard anything like the cheer the lads got when Mick led them up to get the cup, it truly was beyond my wildest dreams.

By this point I had tears in my eyes, just as I do now recalling this story. Some of it was down to happiness, of course, but it was also tinged with sadness at missing out on such an unbelievable occasion. That was all lifted from me when I got the call to go up and collect a medal for my efforts in the earlier rounds. I was so proud.

That day, and indeed the whole season, fuelled my desire to make my dream come true. All that happened at the age of 10. The joy, the excitement and even the disappointment left me with no doubt: this was what I wanted to do with my life.

Even to this day, Mick and I talk about winning the cup and how it fed our love for the game. I always argue that Mick was by far the better player out of the two of us. As I've already mentioned, he had two great feet and was a tremendous athlete. He had so much heart, too, and never knew when he was beaten. What a great role model he was for me to follow. He played local football for years, but I often wondered why he didn't play at a higher level.

The dream of fame and fortune as a professional footballer might be what drives some boys on nowadays, but for me it was only the first part of that which was applicable. No thought of money ever crossed my mind, it was all about playing football for a famous team. I didn't even have a clue what sort of money footballers were on in those days.

Compared to today, there was nothing like the organisation or coaching in youth football. If you had a teacher at school who cared enough to spend his own time helping you out, you were among the lucky few.

School football was certainly about to get a lot easier for me, but not before it was so very nearly taken away from me. By now you will know what a football fanatic I was as a kid and how it occupied almost my every waking thought. Well, back in my day you had to take the 11-plus exam and, if you passed this, your next port of call would be a grammar school. So far, so good. There was just one problem: we didn't have any of those on Hayling Island, so you'd have to go off the island to either Portsmouth or Petersfield for the nearest one. Neither of them played football, they were both rugby schools. Can you imagine little old me trying to play rugby?!

Rugby in those days seemed to be for rich kids only. People who grew up to become doctors played rugby at school, whereas football was a game for everybody. The message in my mind was crystal clear: to go to a grammar school was to be avoided at all costs.

Obviously, I didn't tell my parents about this, but I honestly don't think they'd have been bothered anyway. I didn't even think I had a chance of passing it and, lo and behold, when they read out the list of people from the class who had got through my name was not one of them. I was absolutely delighted. Then, shock upon shock, she said that three extra places had become available and they were going to pick the next five best students to resit the exam, with the top three going through – and my name was read out. How could this have happened? Now, I know what you're thinking – it must have been the top five out of six for my name to be on there. And the odd one out was off sick the day of the exam.

When it came to the resit, I made sure I wouldn't be in the top three. I was fairly handy at maths and I knew if I messed it up then that would seal my fate, so I deliberately put the wrong answers in. When the three names were read out, I was delighted once again. It must have been quite a picture to see me sat there with a big smile on my face while the others were sick as pigs. It just shows you how, even at that age, I was so determined to play football. To follow my dream.

I didn't even want to consider what could have happened if I'd gone to the grammar school. A mate of mine, a fella called Steve Forbes – who gives me a lift up to the Bridge when I stay in Hayling with my brother – told me he had the same thought process as me when it was his turn to sit the exam a few years later. He went one further by missing the exam full stop. They arranged for it to be sat again and he missed that as well. He was the same as me, he didn't want to be stuck playing rugby. I don't know if I started a trend. I hope not – I wouldn't want to be looked at as a bad role model. Steve didn't make it as a footballer, so perhaps he shouldn't have followed my example.

After the 11-plus episode, I went to a bigger school on the mainland which had the best football team. We were winning every match comfortably, securing league titles and cups along the way. How things change. With that, doors started to open for me. It just goes to show that no matter how talented you are, being in the right place at the right time is so important.

Suddenly, when I was 13, I was playing for my local area's Under-15s side, then it was on to the county side. Along with school football, this was very important for my development as clubs would send their scouts along to pick out the next starlet to sign. If you got picked to play for your national team, then you were certainly in the spotlight.

That's what happened to me when I got called up to the England Under-14s to play in Norwich. By now, I was on the radar of plenty of scouts, and I knew the next year would be telling for me. It would be my final 12 months as a schoolboy footballer and I knew I had to impress sufficiently to get signed for a club.

I was having a good season with Hampshire, which saw us beat all-comers in the Home Counties and led to me being called up to England's Under-15s side. Among my team-mates were Bob Wilson, who was to become Arsenal's goalkeeper for many years, and Nobby Stiles, a future World Cup winner.

At this stage, I would like to thank all the teachers who did so much for me, who gave up their own time to help me improve and to enjoy what was a wonderful time. For all the teachers who start so many lads on the road to so much enjoyment, whatever level of sport they reach, I hope they realise what a wonderful job they are doing.

Before we left school we had a visit from the careers mistress, who interviewed all those leaving. She would ask what industry we were looking to go into and find out if there was any way she could help. It was my turn to go in and see her. "Robert, what are you going to do?" she asked.

"I'm going to become a professional footballer," was my short and sweet answer.

She smiled a smile that many a young lad would have seen over the years. "Nearly every boy I have seen this week has had that very same dream," she said, adding: "So, what are you really going to do with yourself?"

I thought for a moment. "Live my dream," I replied. It was at that moment I told her I had a contract to join Chelsea. How that came about is another story altogether.

2

JIMMY THOMPSON

I've named this chapter after one of the most influential men in the history of Chelsea Football Club: Jimmy Thompson.

Football is full of funny characters, but no one came close to Jimmy. He was one of the first people I met in the professional game and he was clearly one of the most successful in the scouting business. He was Chelsea's chief scout and, when you look at the talented players he took to the club, it's hard to argue. Jimmy Greaves, Terry Venables, Barry Bridges, the Harris brothers and many more all signed for the Blues under his watch.

Before I divulge a bit more information about Jimmy, I want to tell you a few stories which show just how fickle football and the clubs within it could be, but also how there were good people in the game and, in Jimmy's case, how funny they can be.

With England schoolboy honours came interest from clubs via their scouting network. Once the calls came, my parents were honest enough to admit they didn't have enough knowledge on the subject. They knew I needed help to sort out the first step in what we all hoped would be a long career, so they would ask one of my older brothers to sit in on the chat to make sure my best interests were looked after.

When I think back to those conversations with scouts, I realise just how fickle football and clubs could be, but also how funny this game can be and what nice guys are to be found within it.

Wolves were the biggest team in England at the time and they were very keen on signing me. We spoke at length and I was impressed with them. I went off to Plymouth to play for England schoolboys against Eire and we thrashed them 9-3. I scored three of the goals playing centre-forward and Wolves couldn't have been on the phone any quicker.

"Come and have a look around, see what you think of the club and then we can sort out the contract," the scout told me.

Before I had a chance to go up there, there was another England game, this time against Scotland at Wembley. We were victorious again, this time only winning 2-0, but I didn't have a particularly good game.

This time there was no phone call right away. A week must have passed before they rang to inform me that they were no longer interested in signing me. Obviously, I was disappointed, but I accepted their decision and had no time to mope around as there was another England game to focus on.

We went over to Belfast for a game against Northern Ireland and I was back on form, scoring twice in a 3-1 win. By the time we arrived home, Wolves had phoned again. There had been some sort of mistake and in fact they did want to sign me after all.

I turned them down. It was not a difficult decision to reach. Having spoken with my parents and older brothers, who had all been around the block, we all agreed this was a club to avoid.

With the phone continuing to ring with callers from far and wide, I made the decision that I didn't want to join a club that was too far away from home. London was my cut-off point and I was sticking to it.

I received a really positive phone call from Reading manager Harry Johnston, who used to play for Blackpool. That alone made me keen to speak with him. I was also aware that he had signed a few of my team-mates from the county side, so he was using this to try and persuade me to join them.

We had a long chat, but I told him I had set my sights on a bigger club. Harry was a gentleman and he was very understanding of my situation. He offered me some useful advice.

"Don't sign for a club too close to home," he said. "You'll just end up with all of your family and friends trying to give you advice and that may end up hindering your budding career. I'd also advise you to consider a club that likes to give youngsters a chance – and Chelsea certainly have a very good youth scheme."

The first part of his advice ruled out one team: Portsmouth. He needn't have worried. In all the time I had spent living and playing football just around the corner from them, I never received so much as a phone call. I was to learn much later that they were convinced I would join them. As they say, if you don't ask, you don't get.

Things were falling into place. The two clubs with the best reputation for bringing through young talent and giving them a chance were Manchester United and Chelsea. The latter had shown big interest in me.

All of my brothers were a great help to me when it came to considering which club to join, but Ray used to follow Chelsea and he was the one really pushing for me to go there. In fact, he came with me on my first visit and he was convinced it was the best club for me to join. He wasn't wrong.

Jimmy Thompson had been on my case for two years. He was in regular contact with me throughout this time and I really liked him. It was hard not to – he was incredibly funny, with a bit of devil in him. As friendly as he was and as much as he made me laugh, I always had the sense he was plotting something. He probably was. Some of the best young talent in the south of England were convinced to sign for Chelsea by Jimmy, and each of them had a funny story to tell.

He was the original Del Boy. Terry Venables once told me about the time he met Jimmy at Waterloo Station. It's a big station, so Terry asked where they should meet. Jimmy said underneath the clock. So, Terry gets there, stands under the clock, but there's no sign of Jimmy. All he can hear is a strange noise, which seems to be coming from this fella hiding beneath a newspaper. "I can't be seen talking to you!" That was Jimmy to a tee. I won't say he was a conman, but he was a character.

He would arrive at the door completely unannounced,

bringing a sense of fun and always armed with outlandish stories. He was a typical cockney geezer and he would have a trilby hat perched on one side of his head and his appearance and demeanour was that of a street dealer.

He was so cheerful and there was absolutely nothing serious about him. "I've come here to do you a favour today, young man," he'd say, followed by a chuckle.

He was good at convincing you that it was all about what he could do for us, not what we could do for him.

One night he arrived at the house clutching the form which he told me would make me a Chelsea player. In those days, schoolboys were not allowed to have anything to do with professional clubs until they left school. I knew that, so there's not a chance that Jimmy wasn't aware of that. When I pointed this out to him, his response was to laugh it off.

"Listen, Bobby, I know what the rules are and we are not going to break any of them," he insisted. "I'm just going to give you this form, you can sign it and then keep it somewhere safe for when you've finished school."

I was slightly puzzled by this. The form would be in my hands, which meant it had absolutely no worth to the club regarding my future with them. He was playing mind games with me, but it worked. I signed the form and stashed it away.

A few nights later, there was a knock on the door. Jimmy had returned, but this time he had company: Ted Drake. After being messed about by Wolves, I was really impressed that the manager of Chelsea Football Club was here in person to come and meet me.

Ted was the complete opposite of Jimmy. He just looked like a gentleman, I can't think of any other way to describe him, and he spoke very well. But his role in this meeting was very clear: he was to be the bad cop to Jimmy's good cop.

"Could you get the form for me please, Bobby," he said.

I looked over at Jimmy, who was vigorously shaking his head and pulling all sorts of funny faces. How I didn't burst out laughing I will never know. Eventually, I offered a half-hearted response.

"I'm sorry, Mr Drake, but I don't know what you're talking about. I didn't sign anything."

"Look, I know Jimmy would have got you to sign the form," he said, knowing full well I had just lied through my teeth. "You've done nothing wrong here. It's just Jimmy's enthusiasm to make sure you join us, but I know you're going to be a Chelsea player, so let's do things properly."

He was dead right. They had played me well. I had taken a big old bite of the bait they had offered up and now they were just reeling me in. I retrieved the piece of paper with my signature on it and handed it over to Ted.

"Jimmy tells me you want to stay on at school until the summer, is that right? Well, you stay on and play your games for England schoolboys and then we'll sign you up in the summer and you can come to us for the start of the new season."

What a double act. I was a Chelsea man right from that moment, and I have never regretted that decision. I was Chelsea then, Chelsea now more than 50 years later, Chelsea till I die. Becoming part of the Blues family has had a huge impact on my life and I thank my lucky stars that Jimmy Thompson found me and had faith in my ability.

Even though it was a done deal, Jimmy came down to visit me a couple of times. I think it was a combination of him wanting to keep me sweet, but knowing Jimmy I am sure he was also making sure I hadn't been approached by any other clubs.

On the second of his visits he beckoned me to come outside. "I've got something for you in my car – you'll be well pleased with this," he chirped.

Now, signing on fees for kids were not allowed at that time, but in the dressing room of the England schoolboys team there had been plenty of talk about these visits from scouts and the brown envelopes that were handed over. In my head, I'm already wondering how much he's going to give me and what I could spend it on.

We headed outside and walked over to where Jimmy's car was parked. He opened the boot and all I could see was a golf bag maybe half-full, if that, with clubs. Perhaps he plays golf, I thought to myself.

"There you are," he said, handing over this second-hand set to its proud, new owner.

Jimmy told me I'd be needing need them because all the pros played golf. I had to laugh. I was just happy signing for Chelsea and my dream starting to become a reality.

I'd never played golf until I was given those clubs, but when I got to Chelsea I realised Jimmy was dead right. Most footballers did play golf – and they still do. That's one of the few things in football that hasn't changed since my day.

There has never been another character quite like Jimmy Thompson, though. When I arrived at Chelsea I realised how good a job he was doing when just about every lad, many of whom went on to play a huge part in the club's future, had a story to tell about how Jimmy had signed them.

I wish someone would write a book about him some day.

3

REALITY

Dreaming about playing football for a living and then actually doing it was a massive reality check for me. Coming from the sticks, a place which had probably never produced a professional footballer, well, that was it – I thought I was the bees knees when I came up to Chelsea. It took less than a month for me to beg to go back to Hayling!

The change from being a country boy to living in London was massive, but I was quite fortunate when I rocked up to my digs in Wimbledon that the two other youth-team players staying there were in exactly the same boat.

We got on really well from the off, me and the two Barrys: Bridges and Smart. We were all country boys – Bridgo from Norwich and Smarty, who had played in the same England schoolboy team as me, from Suffolk – and Mr and Mrs Johnson, the couple we were staying with, couldn't have been any nicer to us.

It's important at this point to differentiate between joining Chelsea as a young player today compared to the 1950s. We were ground staff lads, learning our trade while helping out whichever way we could around the stadium. One week out of every four was spent doing this and I'd always try to make sure I was on dressing room duty. That largely meant clearing up after the first team and making sure their boots were nice. It was a good way of getting to know the senior players at the club, as long as you picked your moments. If you came along to clean the dressing room before the lads were finished, that was it – you were straight in the bath.

I also learned another important lesson very early on: never, ever get stuck working next to Terry Venables. If you were sweeping the terraces and Venner was alongside you, prepare to work twice as hard because he was a lazy bugger! The first-team boys would be training and he'd be leaning on the broom watching them play while we all worked.

Venner was just one of the many great lads who were in and around the youth team at that time, which made settling in all the easier. But, despite that, and the arrangement for us to travel back home one weekend every month, I was feeling terribly homesick.

I went in to see the manager about this and told him I wanted to go back to live in Hayling. We talked it over and he suggested I could go home every weekend. I think he had dealt with so many boys he knew just what to do.

And it worked for me. After a few months I had settled down and was going home like we had first arranged.

REALITY

Living in digs with Smarty and Bridgo was proving to be such great fun. We were finding out so much about ourselves, what with leaving home for the first time and living in the city, and we decided to learn how to dance. The reason? It was the best way for us to get girlfriends, although Smarty didn't seem to need much help as he always seemed to have a girl on the go.

Me and Bridgo were a bit different. I picked up a girl in about the second or third year, who turned out to be my future wife! I met her in Hayling when she was visiting on holiday. Bridgo was gutted. "I'll never be married, you'll all be married before me," he moaned.

Well, you can guess what happened – he was the first to be married. I remember going out on his stag night, which was on the evening before his wedding as was customary in those days. Anyway, we were up town and I don't know how we got home.

The next day I was playing in the reserves at Charlton. I thought: "Christ, I ain't half going to be in trouble here. I'm not even going to be able to move."

Well, you'd have thought whatever I was drinking was petrol. I was all over the place, I couldn't stop running! I had a brilliant game, even if I say so myself. "Perhaps I should have done that more often," I thought to myself. Then the day wore on and I felt worse and worse. Ah, that's why I didn't do it more often.

Anyway, back to the dancing. There was a Victor Silvester dance studio and the three of us went in there to be greeted by a lady who asked us if we wished to join the group or have our own private lesson. We were so embarrassed we went for the latter, which shows how young and naive we were because the main class would have been full of girls!

There were footprints painted on the dance floor to act as a guide and, I must say, I was quite good when no one else was around to get in my way. In reality, none of us were much cop. In fact, I can still hear the frustration in the lady's voice as she screeched: "Quick, slow; quick, quick, slow."

Whenever Bridgo does his impression of her it still gets me every time. We were at the wedding of Val's son, Jamie, and we'd had a good drink and were among the last to leave. The music suddenly came back on and Bridgo grabbed me. "This is how we used to do it," he said, leading me on a merry waltz. "Quick, slow; quick, quick, slow."

Smarty was the only one who had a car and for the life of me I cannot remember what it was, but he was ever so proud of it. We only had a small window in the room we shared and he was always clambering onto the bed so he could catch a glimpse of his pride and joy.

Obviously, Bridgo and I would use this as a stick to beat him with. If either of us woke up before Smarty we would be straight up at the window. "Smarty, you'd better get yourself up here. Your car's been nicked!"

He'd bolt straight up to look for it. Well, you know where this is going. One time, we looked – and it had actually gone. "Yeah, yeah, of course it has." He was in for quite a shock.

I haven't seen Smarty for many a year. He didn't really get a chance to do much at Chelsea with Peter Bonetti at the club and left after a little while to return to Suffolk.

While we were together, the three of us had such fun we didn't call what we were doing work, even though you realised there were so many good young players at the club it was going to be hard to make it as a pro. One thing we had to help us was our training ground, the Welsh Harp at

REALITY

Hendon. Across the lake stood Wembley Stadium, the Mecca of football and the venue in which so many of my dreams were played out.

The training ground provided a great laugh. It was full of Londoners who all seemed to be jokers and there was humour injected into everything we did. I'm talking about people like Terry Venables, Mike Harrison and Allan Harris, and then there were the older boys: Jimmy Greaves, Peter Brabrook, David Cliss. That I've listed Greavsie in that category shows you just how young our squad was.

Mind you, we had to have a sense of humour, because even something so simple as kitting yourself out proved to be a struggle. Each player was given one set of training gear. When it got wet and muddy, which you'll be surprised to hear was quite a regular occurrence in England, the only way to dry it out was to hang it on a clothes horse which was next to a big wood-burning stove. Those who finished training first would get the best place to dry their kit. You'd think this wasn't exactly conducive to getting players to stay out on the training pitch for some extra practice, but the smart ones worked out that you could spend time honing your technique and still have dry kit to change into the next day. How? Just make sure you were first into training and you had your pick of the training gear, whether it was yours or not. I'll leave it to your imagination as to the state of the kit left out for those who were late arrivals into training.

It might seem like I'm having a moan, but I actually consider this sort of thing to be an important part of the development of young players. We were left in little doubt that we were on the bottom rung of the ladder at the football club and it simply

51

made us doubly determined to get out of the youth team and among the senior players in the first-team squad.

It was far from glamorous, but it was the first steps of our future lives. Thinking about it later, the laughs, wind-ups, friendships, the feeling in the dressing room, but most of all the love for Chelsea, was to hold the club in good stead for many years to come.

For all of the camaraderie within the group, one man above all others stands out from my youth-team days – a man who did more than any to put us, and then keep us, on the right path to stardom.

Dickie Foss was in charge of the youth set-up at Chelsea for donkey's years and, if I've given too much credit to Jimmy Thompson in the previous pages of this book, then I really cannot say enough about Dick and his impact on this football club.

He was a very straight and honest guy who didn't waste time or words. He put many of us right, don't you worry about that. He would sit next to you on the coach back to the Bridge and ask if you were happy with the game. On one occasion, I had scored a hat-trick and we had won by seven or eight, so I told him I was very happy indeed. Then, he spent the next five minutes going over things I could improve on! He kept your feet well and truly on the ground and you could never get carried away as the most he would offer up was a "well done" or "you played well today". But, even then, it always was as a team.

Lessons were obviously learned in the week you spent working on the ground, but it was nothing compared to what was being drilled into us during the three weeks per month that were spent with Dick. One thing you learned early on was that you had to work hard and listen to what was said to you. We hardly had our feet on the first rung of the ladder to the top. We had a lot to learn and, even then, you had to be lucky to get a chance to show what you had.

The set-up at Chelsea was like a well-oiled machine thanks to Dick and that was borne out by the results. Not only did a large proportion of the juniors go on to represent the first team, but we also won most of the competitions we entered, many by very big scores. It was easy to see why. The players being produced by the club during the Fifties and Sixties was matched only by Manchester United. However, one trophy continued to elude our grasp: the FA Youth Cup.

For those accustomed to seeing Chelsea's Under-18s running away with the competition seemingly every year in recent times, it was a different story when I joined the club. We had never won the competition and it was apparent that Dickie saw it as his Holy Grail. He wanted to win it so badly.

When Jimmy Greaves was in the youth team everyone thought it was Chelsea's big chance to finally win the trophy. Jimmy was already scoring goals for fun in the first team, so you can imagine just how prolific he was playing against kids his own age.

They reached the final of the competition in 1958 and, although I wasn't yet involved, both of my housemates were in the team. Wolves provided the opposition – perhaps I would have been playing for them had things worked out differently – and Chelsea blew them out of the water in the first leg at Stamford Bridge, winning 5-1. Surely it was simply a case of turning up for the second leg and that was it?

Well, as Jimmy Greaves would say in later years, football is a funny old old game. The second leg proved that. Incredibly, Wolves went one better and beat Chelsea 6-1. It was an incredible shock and we all wondered how Dickie would take the defeat and whether he would be able to get over the disappointment of having not one, but two hands on the trophy and somehow seeing it slip out of his grasp.

It's a sign of his character that just two years later, with a completely new side, he finally did it. His Holy Grail. What's more, we did it in some style. And that's an understatement. We won eight of our 10 games, scoring an incredible 46 goals and conceding just four.

You'd be forgiven for thinking there were a few nerves when the final was in the balance after the first leg against Preston North End finished 1-1 at Stamford Bridge, with Bert Murray scoring our goal. I don't think we were the fancied side, in all honesty, and many thought we'd missed our big chance. Dickie's faith never wavered, though, and that filtered down to the team. We put in a brilliant performance up at Deepdale and I scored a hat-trick as we won the game 4-1. We'd done it!

Every player was immensely proud to have been a part of the first Chelsea side to win the Youth Cup, but I think I speak for all of the lads from that team when I say the victory was for Dickie. Everyone wanted so badly to win the trophy for the man who made them. I'm sure he had a tear in his eye as he thanked everyone for the effort they had put in. He went around and shook every player by the hand. I don't think I'd heard him say this many words in all the time I worked with him!

When he finally reached me, I'm sure he said something like: "Not bad for you at the end."

REALITY

I thanked him for everything he had done for me, and added: "I know, I know – I should have done better."

"No," he said. "It showed you listened. You couldn't have thanked me in a better way than by scoring a hat-trick."

Several players from that side went on to sign professional contracts, and the likes of Peter Bonetti, Allan Harris, Ron Harris, Terry Venables, Bert Murray and myself went on to play our part in Chelsea's first team through the Sixties. All of those lads are still very good friends of mine down to this day, but more about them later. While most of us would enjoy long and successful careers with the first team, that wasn't the case for one lad who had been a star throughout that cup run.

Of the 46 goals we scored, Gordon Bolland had contributed 15 of them. He scored four times in each of the first two rounds as we beat West Thurrock Athletic 10-0 and Colchester United 9-1 respectively and then got a hat-trick in the third round against Ford United. But the striker only managed two first-team appearances before being released by the club in 1962, as injury and a lack of playing time put paid to his chances of making it as a Blue.

Nothing guarantees success. You see players with great skills fail to make the grade, while others who may not be as talented succeed because of the hard work they put in. One thing which is so important is having the right attitude. Being willing to learn and teachable right through your career will help keep your boots on the pitch. Above all else, be lucky!

I never forgot the lessons I learned under Dickie Foss during those years in the youth set-up. It gave me and my team-mates the perfect grounding in the game and taught us so much, both on and off the field, as to what it would take to make it in the pros.

It must have given Dickie great pleasure to see all the players that had played for him go on to perform so well for the first team early in the Sixties. By my count we had eight former youth-team players appearing regularly at Chelsea at one stage. All, I am sure, would say they couldn't thank him enough.

A year before the victorious Youth Cup final, I was given quite the unexpected surprise. One week I was playing up at Welsh Harp, nothing but a carefree junior, and the next I was to receive the biggest shock of my short time at Chelsea.

4

JUST A KID

As I was learning my trade under Dickie Foss in the juniors, I looked at the other players at the club, the left-wingers in particular, and I must admit the first team looked to be way off into the distance. Frank Blunstone, Micky Block, Mike Harrison – all great left-sided players and all ahead of me in the pecking order.

I certainly wasn't disheartened by this. I was still only a kid, just 17 years old, and most of these guys in front of me had probably forgotten more about football than what I had learned so far. But in the back of my mind I knew that Ted Drake was never afraid to give youth a chance. Having attracted most of the cream of the crop from schoolboy football for a number of years, Chelsea was teeming full of bright, young starlets eagerly awaiting an opportunity to make their name. Jimmy Greaves, Peter Brabrook, David Cliss and Mel Scott were among those already in the first team.

One Saturday in February 1959, I had a particularly good game for the juniors. I can't remember the opposition, but we won 8-1 and I scored five of them. On the same day, Bridgo had done well for the reserves, finding the back of the net and receiving some positive feedback for his performance.

The following Thursday, the pair of us were called in to Ted's office. Neither of us had a clue what it was about. We hoped it was related to our recent performances and perhaps we were due a pat on the back.

It turns out there had been a spate of injuries and illness within the squad, which had resulted in four left-wingers being sidelined for West Ham's visit to Stamford Bridge at the weekend. Ted explained the situation and said he was considering playing the two of us in the first team.

It was tough to keep a grin from breaking out across my face, but I wasn't getting carried away. I knew what football was like, and in the back of my mind was this nagging feeling that one, or maybe even more, of the wingers would shrug off their injury to leave me waiting in the wings once again.

After training the next day, we eagerly rushed into the dressing room just as the team was being pinned on the wall. I scanned the names on the list, working my way to the bottom, and there I was:

9 BARRY BRIDGES
10 JIMMY GREAVES
11 BOBBY TAMBLING

JUST A KID

I couldn't believe it! Talk about a stroke of good fortune. Four players in my position all ruled out of the same game. "Lucky" must have been my middle name. This was my big chance. Could I take it?

That night in our digs was full of excitement. The telephone must have been in use for just about the whole evening between myself and Barry phoning home and telling our family and friends the exciting news. They hardly believed me. I could hardly blame them. From playing for the juniors one week in front of one man and his dog to Stamford Bridge and 50,000 supporters. Some jump, eh?

I could hardly sleep for excitement, but the nerves didn't kick in until Ted started his team talk. Even walking through the gates at Stamford Bridge, all I could think about was how this was the moment I had dreamed of since I was a little boy.

I'd pulled on the famous Chelsea strip many a time for the juniors, but this time it felt different as I tugged the shirt over my head in the first-team dressing room that I knew like the back of my hand, having spent more time cleaning it than I cared to imagine. It felt like a symbolic moment. I was ready. Or, at least I thought I was.

I don't know what Bridgo was thinking, but as we were sat there listening to the manager go through his instructions for the game and what he expected from each of us, panic began to set in. Having been so confident and excited beforehand, suddenly I was a bundle of nerves as self-doubt began to creep in. How on earth am I going to be able to do half of what he is asking of me? Luckily, there was a good bunch of senior lads in the side who were able to calm my nerves. Seeing smoke billowing out of one of the toilet cubicles gave us all a good chuckle and when I realised it was Reg Matthews, our experienced goalkeeper, puffing away on a fag, a sense of calm returned to me. I'd later learn that nerves before a game were a regular occurrence, and you needed them to give you that edge. If the butterflies weren't flying around your stomach, something was wrong.

Walking out in front of over 53,000 supporters was a moment I will never, ever forget. This is what dreams are made of. They can come true.

Was I overawed? Yes, no doubt about it. I'm not sure the same could be said of Bridgo. Just nine minutes into the game, he went on a barnstorming run, brushing aside three West Ham defenders in a manner which reporters likened to Ted Drake in his pomp. He looked certain to score, but somehow Ernie Gregory clawed away his left-footed shot.

I had barely had a kick by the time Vic Keeble gave the visitors the lead a few minutes later, but I never allowed my head to drop. Enthusiasm goes a long way in football and I knew if a chance came my way I was going to take it. Little did I know it would arrive only moments later.

The ball came to me just outside the box and I took a touch, which allowed the defender to close me down, but still I was able to get the shot away in the nick of time. The ball squeezed into the net at the near post and time seemed to stand still as the crowd erupted. I was running and punching the air, dancing a jig of delight with Bridgo, who was the first player to catch up with me. If only our dance teacher could see how far we had come.

We were dancing again a few minutes later when Bridgo wrote his name after mine among Chelsea's debut goalscorers, powering home a header from a Greaves free-kick, but when West Ham equalised the game looked to be petering out into a draw. As pleased as we were with our first Chelsea goals, they would have been even more special if we could grab a winner. Fortunately, within our ranks we had the greatest goalscorer of the lot and Greavsie scored a late winner to seal what the Daily Mirror described as "a classic worthy of the day's best attendance".

The rest of the day was a blur. In the dressing room after the game I seem to recall everybody joking about our win bonus of £4, which was about half our wage. I didn't want to leave, I wanted this moment to last forever, but I'm so glad I did. As we prepared to head home we were met by a crowd of people looking for autographs. We happily signed away. Was this really happening?

Straight after the game, I rang my mum and dad. They were thrilled for me, as you can imagine any parents would be. I was on such a high and went out with some other friends and had a few pints. I thought I was King Pin after scoring on my debut and spent the night reliving the moment. By the end of the evening, I'd say my friends were starting to yawn, but I was so proud of myself. My dreams were becoming reality.

The next morning, Barry and I went rushing out to buy a copy of every single newspaper. We read all of the articles about these two wonderkids who were going to be the next stars for Chelsea Football Club and nothing could wipe the beaming grins off our faces.

As we were making our way through each story, enthusiastically reciting every mention of our names, a call came up from the landlord.

"Bobby, phone call for you."

"Hello?"

"Oh, hello there," began the voice on the other end of the line. "I'm Desmond Hackett. I don't know if you've heard of me, but I write for the Daily Express."

I'd spent many a morning reading articles by Desmond.

"Hello Desmond, lovely to hear from you," I said, attempting to maintain some level of composure while inwardly I was doing cartwheels.

We had a lovely chat for half an hour. He was asking me all about the game and I was giving him the most thorough answers I could come up with. I was absolutely delighted to be doing the interview. Then he broke it to me.

"Bobby Tambling, you really are a bloody idiot, aren't you? This is Peter Sillett!" He burst out laughing. "It's a good job it's me and not the manager."

That was a common wind-up in our day and one which I was more than happy to carry on after being on the receiving end. It was incredibly embarrassing, but it was just part of the initiation to the first-team squad and it made it all the more enjoyable when you were able to catch someone out yourself.

That was the thing about being on the ground staff, we would mix with the senior players while cleaning their boots or the dressing room. It really helped youngsters make the step up to the first team, although I'd have perhaps preferred not to have ended up in the bath a few times for being cheeky! Still, it made for a happy dressing room and one which I hoped to be a part of for a long time.

However, my run in the first team proved to be a short one, for just a week on from my debut I found myself back in the juniors. Mr Drake was in no hurry with young players and he helped so many slowly find their feet without getting carried away with themselves.

Even though the Daily Mirror headline boomed: "Boy Bridges Is Here To Stay – Says Drake" after the manager told their reporter that Bridgo would be "leading the attack next week and I don't see what's to stop him continuing", a 3-1 defeat at home to Burnley the following Saturday was the last first-team action he would see that season.

We both had plenty to learn, but one thing was certain – after that tiny taste, we were desperate for more.

5

LEARNING FROM THE BEST

My introduction to first-team football had been short and sweet, but I didn't sit around moping and cursing those in front of me in the pecking order. I went back down to the juniors, gave it my all in every game and kept scoring regularly to keep myself in the manager's plans.

Although I didn't play another first-team game that season, I wasn't too disappointed. I knew I'd have to be patient. I was still only a kid, very raw, and with so much to learn. Besides, how could I be too upset when I knew I had an end-of-season tour to look forward to? These trips were always among the highlights of my year, whether it was with the juniors or, later on, the first team. As well as getting to see parts of the world you might otherwise have missed out on, we would always, without fail, have a bloody good time.

With the juniors, we'd go to the Netherlands at the end of every season to play in two tournaments, which we invariably ended up winning. The first was in the Hague and then we'd head to Amsterdam to conclude the tour. We'd stay in each place for about a week and the most important thing was to gain experience playing against European teams – while having a great time!

The first time I went to the Hague I got a taste of exactly what these tours were all about when we organised a night out early in the trip. You'd always have a few lads who were in their final year of youth-team football and some of them would know by then if they were going to have a chance of making it at Chelsea or if they were being released. If it was to be their last tour, they would make sure it went with a bang.

Now, I wasn't really a big drinker, so when the older boys went up to the bar and asked me what I was having, I told them I'd have whatever they were drinking: rum and blackcurrant. I'd never had it before, but it tasted lovely and I couldn't get enough of the stuff. What's more, it didn't seem to be having an effect on me. How naive I was. At the end of what had been a brilliant night until that point, I got up from the table and suddenly I realised I may have been more than a little bit tipsy. I thought I'd kept my composure as I made my way over to the door. The next thing I know, I'm waking up in my bed with a stinking headache and total bewilderment as to how I got there.

The lads later filled me in. As I went to leave the establishment, I fell straight through the open door and onto the pavement outside. I went out like a light. Luckily, I was surrounded by a good group of fellas, even if they had been the ones who got me in that state, and they got me back safely. Sometimes you've got to learn things the hard way.

We'd always do things together as a group, which helped to build a bond between us that would get stronger and stronger by the year, and at least once on every trip we'd go to the swimming pool together. That was one thing I never looked forward to and the lads always had a great laugh about it because I was the only one who didn't know how to swim. Yes, you've read that correctly: the guy who grew up by the sea and spent many a summer day in my childhood messing around at the beach, couldn't swim.

I decided to face my fear in the Hague, where they had a massive water slide which the lads dared me to go down. I could see how much fun they were having, although that was tempered somewhat by me being terrified that I wouldn't be able to stand up when I went into the water, and I convinced myself the water wasn't particularly deep.

I climbed the ladder to get to the top of the slide and once I was up there I started to have second thoughts, so I shouted down to the lads to make sure they were ready for me just in case it all went wrong. Down I went... "Wooooohoooooo," I yelled as I jumped down the slide and went whooshing down, feeling a huge rush of adrenaline. "They were right," I thought to myself, "What fun!"

Then I hit the water. The panic hit me as soon as it happened and I couldn't find the surface with my feet. It must have been some sight for anyone watching as my head bobbed in and out of the water, each time punctuated by my cry for help. Bert Murray swam out to get me, but I was in a real panic. He managed to drag me far enough along so that I could stand up. As I sheepishly made my way over to the side of the pool to climb out, the lads didn't know whether to laugh or not.

This old lady came rushing over. Glaring at me, she pointed over to the slide and then at the pool. "You not in here," she said, while directing her finger down to the other end of the pool, which was occupied by a bunch of kids splashing around. It was, of course, the shallow end. "You in that end." And with that she took off.

If the lads weren't laughing before, they were now. There was plenty of slaps on the back reserved for Bert, too, and I lost count of the amount of times the word "hero" was bandied about. It took me a while to live that one down, but I promised myself that I would learn to swim to avoid any embarrassment in future.

On the football field, I was getting the best education a young forward could hope for by playing and training alongside one of the greatest goalscorers in the history of the game. Many people might look at the 1959/60 season as a disappointment for me, seeing as I only played four matches in September, but what they don't realise is how much I was learning from Jimmy Greaves.

Chelsea at this time was now a mix of older players coming to the end of their playing days and raw, promising young players full of running but not a lot of experience. Greavsie seemed to be slap bang in the middle of this; still in his teens, he already had 50 goals in the First Division to his name. He was a carefree youngster with the natural ability and smarts to make any defender look like an amateur. What a talent he was, and here I was, a lad of 17, with the best seat in the house.

For those who never had the privilege of seeing Greavsie in action, I honestly don't think it would be an unfair comparison to liken him to Lionel Messi. If he received the ball anywhere in the opposition half, you knew a goal could be just around the corner as he had that ability to weave his way through defenders as though they were statues. And, like Messi, you'd rarely see him put his foot through the ball. His shots were like an artist stroking his brush across the canvas, and he'd pick out the bottom corner with unerring precision. It was a joy to watch him.

I remember being sat up in the old North Stand for one of his best goals in a game against Wolves, who were one of the top sides at that time. The players looked like Subbuteo men, we were that far away, and Micky Block hit it from the halfway line with his left foot, just drove it high to the edge of the box. Jimmy was facing the ball and as it came to him he volleyed it over his shoulder with his left foot. It was unbelievable. I just wish it had been done today, with all the different camera angles, because it was a goal you wanted to watch again and again. I'm pretty sure he scored five that day. That's what he was capable of.

The only time I ever saw Jimmy shirk a challenge was in a game against Bolton once. Their back four were all massive, no-nonsense defenders who could kick the living daylights out of you. And the referee usually let them. Most of their surnames began with H, too: Hartle, Higgins and Hennin, with Edwards the odd man out, although I'm sure his middle name must have been Hardasnails.

Anyway, Ron Tindall and Jimmy were both taking a bit of a kicking from these guys, and when Reg Matthews, our goalkeeper, went down injured, you have never seen two centre-forwards run back to their own goal so quickly. The race was on to see who could get the goalkeeper's jersey! Ron won – he was the designated keeper anyway – and I've never seen Jimmy look so disappointed.

Our team that season was a good, honest side, but it wasn't so well organised. Football in those days was more man against man, 10 little battles taking place all over the field. The team which won most of these battles usually won the game – but, if you had Greavsie, then he could win it on his own. He'd win his battle four or five-nil!

We relied heavily on Jimmy. With someone that good, you rest everything on him. You think: "Oh, Jimmy will score, just give him the ball." Let's be honest, his record for Chelsea was unbelievable. He scored 100 league goals before he'd turned 21, which is a record that stands to this day. I won't say he was like a machine, because that makes him sound boring, but when it came to goalscoring I've never seen someone that reliable.

As I said, I only played four games that season, but watching Jimmy in action was worth so much more than that. Frank Lampard wrote about it in his foreword, and it's true: any goalscorer has to have that desire within them to score goals. I think it's a burning desire in you, I don't think it can be coached. It's what I call a natural goalscorer – where others react, we anticipate. The difference is split seconds, but that's all it takes.

That's the difference between a defender getting his toe to it and poking it clear or the centre-forward getting to it.

I put myself in that category, Frank's certainly in there, too, and Kerry Dixon is another. But Jimmy was the best of the bunch. Even with him in the side, Chelsea still came perilously close to dropping into the Second Division. Something would have to change, and I knew an opportunity for me would be just around the corner.

6

DOC'S ORDERS

When you've got a striker like Jimmy Greaves who scores 41 goals in a season and you end up mid-table and nowhere near the title, there is something wrong. That's league-winning form from a centre-forward, which means the rest of the team wasn't pulling its weight. If we could have defended better, Chelsea would have been a danger to any team.

I'm sorry to bang on about Jimmy so much, but I just think he is one of those players whose name isn't mentioned enough when it comes to the legends of Chelsea Football Club. His record speaks volumes about just how good he was: 132 goals in

169 matches. And that was at the very beginning of his career in a side which was pretty average! When he left us at the end of the 1960/61 season, he wore the captain's armband and scored all four of our goals against Nottingham Forest. Who was writing his script? It was as if he was saying: "I'm leaving now guys, try and live up to that." Thanks, mate!

I was utterly bemused that the club was allowing him to leave. I know AC Milan is one of the most illustrious names in the world of football, but he was our superstar, a player we could try to build a team around. Instead, all of a sudden you'd hear the same thing every time one of our young forwards scored a goal: "He's the new Jimmy Greaves." And, for me, that was a huge worry. As much as it was a massive compliment to be compared to Jimmy, I knew he'd left an almighty set of boots to fill. It was beyond just about any player in world football to replace him, so I could have done without that huge weight on my shoulders.

The new Jimmy Greaves? I was nothing like him, almost the polar opposite, in fact. He was all skill, a top-class individual footballer who could win a game almost on his own. I was a product of the team and I relied on them immensely. Jimmy didn't need to rely on anybody. Just give him the ball and let him do the rest. I've often said I was an old banger compared to the Rolls Royce that was Jimmy Greaves. People laugh, but I reckon it's spot on.

It was around this time that I bought my first car, which was a Ford Cortina estate. I won't tell you how many times it took me to pass my driving test, but it was too many. Was it more than three? No. Was it less than three? No! I was always a bit nervous when I was driving, and it showed in my tests. The first guy who tested me was a real bully, shouting at me when I did even the slightest things wrong. It's no wonder I failed. Then, the second time, I was caught out by being too eager. I don't know if they still do this, but back then the instructor would have a clipboard and tell you to perform an emergency stop when he whacked it against the dashboard. I watched him constantly out of the corner of my eye, and he must have moved his hand up to scratch his nose or something because the next thing I know I've slammed my feet down on the brake and clutch and nearly sent him flying through the windscreen. I'd been driving fairly decently up to that point. "What the bloody hell did you do that for?!" Better to be safe than sorry. We may as well have just driven back to the test centre then.

I suppose one of the things that I hadn't got on top of was what they call "clutch control". After I'd figured it out I sailed through everything. With it being my left foot, I probably should have mastered it sooner!

After I passed, I bought a Cortina, which is a very modest car. That's always been my style and the only thing close to a flash car I've ever had was a brand new Ford Corsair. It was smart and a GT. You put your foot down and it sat you back in the seat. None of us at Chelsea were really flashy flash, though. I don't think Ron Harris even drove when I was at Chelsea. I think his wife might have dropped him into training or he travelled in on the train. Most of us used public transport a fair bit and it was pretty rare you'd be recognised. Good thing, too. Venner was always messing about when he'd travel back from training with Ken Shellito because they both lived out in the East Ham area. Venner's stop was first and he'd say: "All right darling, I'll see you tomorrow", and then give him a kiss and get off the train. Nowadays that's nothing out of the ordinary, but in those days Ken would have a good few stops having people staring at him. That was typical Venner.

Cars weren't really a big thing for us, it didn't worry me that I didn't have one at first. I think we all mainly had a Ford or Vauxhall. When Tommy Doc joined he made sure he had the biggest and best, mind. He was bloody mad. I remember driving to the training ground in Mitcham. There was a heck of a queue of traffic and Doc pulled out around them, there's a bus coming down the road, a set of lights that have turned red so we couldn't get through anyway, the bus was coming toward us and Doc just pulled over the other side of the road to park and then the bus went through. He was a good driver, but a little bit crazy behind the wheel.

Anyway, back to our old Rolls Royce. I was lucky to have played some games with him as a young lad, when I would work the left flank and he played the old inside-right position. It didn't take me long to figure out that the whole team both expected and relied on Jimmy scoring a goal. Mostly, he would oblige. Pundits, players and supporters wondered what would happen to us after he was gone. The majority suggested it would be a struggle and, boy, were they proved right. Although Bridgo and I both did a decent job of replacing Jimmy, it was taking two players – and our two most prolific players at that – to even match his individual goal output. Throw in the fact it was a younger, less experienced team which failed to tighten up at the back and you've got a recipe for relegation there.

It's funny – take one of the greatest goalscorers in English football out of any side and it wouldn't take a rocket scientist to tell you they are going to struggle. But the biggest issue was keeping the ball out at the other end. I was actually doing a pretty good job of replacing Jimmy's goals in the early part of the season, racing to 11 after 13 games, but a young side was lacking the necessary consistency to put any sort of run together. We beat Man United early in the campaign with a side filled with eight players who had come up from the youths, but then lost 5-2 against Cardiff City. That was the story of our season: a few good days but the majority bad.

There was an interesting addition made to our squad in February 1961, one which would have huge ramifications for the future of the club. With so many young players struggling to get going, an experienced head was brought in as player-coach: Tommy Docherty. Larger than life and with big ideas, I can remember Tom's debut well as I scored a hat-trick in a 6-1 win over Sheffield United. He only made another three appearances. The next thing we knew he had replaced Ted Drake as manager.

Like Ted, he was struggling to find the right mixture of youth and experience and our season was going the way most people feared it would. But things were moving in the right direction for a new Chelsea to emerge, as hard as that was to see at the time as we lost one game after another. Tommy made it clear what was expected of us all: either work with him or move on. I think most made their mind up pretty quickly and it's no surprise that faith was placed in the young players, despite the patchy results.

Doc decided to throw all his eggs in the youngsters basket and there were so many of us trying to make a name for ourselves, to become part of Chelsea's history. We were extra keen to follow what we'd been taught and in our new coach, Dave

Sexton, we had one of the greatest teachers we could hope for.

Football in the 1950s was more off-the-cuff stuff and defenders weren't so much in a system. It was just full-back against winger, centre-half and centre-forward, that sort of thing. I wrote before that it was just 10 different battles going on among the outfield players. Under Dave's tutelage we were to discover there was far more to it than that.

They say you can't teach an old dog new tricks and we made it easier by being so willing to learn all the time. We were dead eager to become better players and learn on the training ground. We worked for hours trying different things and working on various routines with Dave. I can honestly say he improved every player by a good 50 per cent. Even now, the FA use some of his coaching methods, which goes to show just what a visionary he was.

Dave was a great studier of football in general. When he first came, the first thing he said was that he loved the Hungarian side of the Fifties, who played a different style to almost everyone else. They played with a deep-lying centre-forward, years before all of this false nine talk. They were doing it 50 years before Barcelona! The discipline of the defenders, making sure they took care of their man, meant the false nine would create gaps in the middle of the defence for other players to take advantage.

While we were learning on the job, the season was reaching its conclusion and we were struggling badly. We knew we had to put a run of wins together, but it never happened. In our final 11 matches we didn't even win once and five draws simply was not good enough to keep us in Division One. The Second Division beckoned, just a few years after Chelsea had won the championship for the first time in the club's history. While ulti-mately the season ended in disappointment, think of the long-term gains. Five of the eight or nine youth players who featured regularly would go on to play for England in the mid-Sixties.

One thing that stood out for me in that dismal run at the end of the season was the attitude of the supporters. They did everything in their power to keep us in Division One, cheering us on and always turning out in great numbers. That just made relegation an even bigger disappointment. Of course, we were disappointed for ourselves, but even more so for those great fans.

Life off the pitch was far from a disappointment for me, though.

A few years earlier I had met a young lady named Kath Saunders, who was from Croydon, and we quickly settled down together. It was just the done thing in those days, although I can imagine most youngsters reading this couldn't imagine anything worse than settling down with their partner at the age of 17! By the age of 19 I was a married man. Most would – and many did – say I was too young, but I was happy. I was living the football life, which is one of the best lives a young sports-mad lad could have. But off the field I was just a normal guy. Sure, there was a spotlight on us footballers and people held us up as heroes, but nothing like what you see today. You'd find us on the back pages of the papers and that was it. We led private lives and had no image to live up to. I don't envy the lads of today having their every move scrutinised.

Kath and I would go on to have three children: Gary, Sharon and Glen. All little treasures. My wife had been a Jehovah's Witness before we met and we often talked about the future our children would have. I took a study with Kath's brother about the future and beliefs of the Jehovah's Witness and, 10 years later, I joined their faith.

I was still thinking about what to do when we had a home game against Wolves, who we had toured the West Indies with the summer before. I was in our dressing room getting ready for the game when the doorman came over to tell me that someone wanted to see me and that he thought the guy was a Wolves player. It was Peter Knowles, who asked straight away if I was a Jehovah's Witness because he was taking a study. Peter was to cause an uproar by giving up football to become a Jehovah's Witness, which led to people wanting to know why I was still playing. I informed them that everyone could make their own mind up with what they did. That was the closest my private life ever came to being scrutinised during my time as a footballer.

For 20-odd years, I believed that was the way I wanted to live, but deep down there were doubts whether I could carry out their belief. I know that I could not make that call for my children and as time went on I came to doubt why was I doing something I couldn't carry out, I became weaker in the faith and stopped doing things I should have.

7

NEW DAWN

After the darkness comes the dawn. One of the biggest disappointments of my football career was followed by a season which remains one of the happiest years of my life.

One of my favourite Chelsea songs is Carefree, because that word perfectly encapsulates life in the Sixties. After the Second World War, it felt like the next decade or so was spent getting over it, which is entirely understandable as it is something I hope people never have to live through again. I'm old enough to remember rationing and how families had to cope with that. My siblings and I actually revolted in our household – we said we weren't getting enough butter. Our parents taught us a lesson by giving us the amount we were supposed to get, which ended up disappearing within a day! "Okay, we'll take what we were getting before."

Suddenly, life was all about enjoying yourself, about doing what you wanted and just getting back to some form of normality. The music was all about excitement. I loved Elvis, but I truly adored The Beatles. In my early married days, if I was in the house on my own of an afternoon, I'd stick the Beatles LP on and have the volume up as loud as I could bear it. People used to tell me they could hear it 50 yards up the road!

That's how we played our football, too, and I think that's what attracted the fans to us. We weren't fully carefree on the pitch because we did play to a system, but we thoroughly enjoyed it and that really shone through. It must be the same if you're seeing someone on stage. If they're going through the motions, you can pick up on that. But if they're enjoying what they are doing... That's how we played, with a smile on our face. And, if we got knocked down, we picked ourselves up and tried again. It was a joy to play.

When we went down, it would have sunk a lot of young people. But we came back with such a zing. For the club, it lifted everybody's spirits. It could have been the Chelsea team for the next decade or so, with the core of the side all 21 and 22-year-olds. Obviously that didn't happen, for reasons I'll explain later on, but we and the fans didn't know that at the time.

You wouldn't have guessed it by the way we went about our business that season, but it actually started with a fair bit of discontentment within the squad. It was the first pre-season with Doc at the helm and, to put it politely, some of the older lads were struggling to take to him. I'm not talking about Tommy as a bloke, rather his methodology and coaching style. It was a long way from what they'd been used to under Ted Drake, and everyone was expected to give their best in every single session, right from the get-go.

An example of this came one morning early in pre-season training when we were doing some road work to prepare us for the hard slog ahead. You had to run a small distance, walk for a bit, then run again and so on. It was hard, but it was to ease us into what was coming later in pre-season. As early as this you could see trouble was just around the corner.

The younger players were up the front, doing what was asked of them, but most of the older players were slowly becoming detached from the rest of us. It was a hilly bit of road out near Ewell and we eventually reached the point where we were to turn around and run back. We stopped to catch our breath, but only half of the squad seemed to be there. Tommy looked back down the road and there were the others, labouring up the hill. He was waving frantically at them, urging them to get a move on – I'm sure he used some pretty colourful language – and it took plenty of self control for the rest of us not to fall about laughing when they waved back at him and slowly carried on about their business.

We were told to make our way back to the training ground and the pace was fairly hot with so many young players in that squad all trying their best to impress the manager. Most ran all the way back, others not far behind, and then some returned at their own pace. It was clear for everyone to see: some players were going to give their all to make sure their fitness was up to standard, while others weren't willing to put in the hard yards. By the end of that week there were plenty of blistered feet.

After that episode, Tom was very forthright in letting people know what he wanted. He told everyone it was in their own hands if they wanted to play for Chelsea and if anyone wanted away then he would help them find a new club. Some chose to go down that path, but thankfully a few of the older players opted to stay and fight for their place in the team. They worked really hard to keep up with us youngsters in the fitness stakes.

The club had a really potent mix of youthful talent and wise, old heads, combined with an innovative coaching staff who were eager to prove themselves. People like Frank Blunstone, John Mortimore and Frank Upton would prove how valuable experience can be, and little Tommy Harmer joined us early in the season. He only played five games that season, but I honestly cannot speak highly enough about the impact he had on our squad. What a player, and an absolute gent, too.

Everything was geared to start with a bang and we threw ourselves into anything that was thrown at us by the coaching staff. Tommy pushed us as hard as he could and Dave Sexton was showing why he was so highly regarded as a coach. Not only did he help each and every one of us to improve our skill levels, he was getting us to play together as a team, which is the most important thing in football. By the time the season started we were already champing at the bit. We came out ready to make a big impression and, boy, did we.

Tommy had also decided to name a new skipper in place of Andy Malcolm as the pair of them had fallen out, and Andy was soon to be heading across west London to join Queens Park Rangers. What a surprise when he said it was to be me! There wasn't a big deal made about it at all. He told me they were an easy lot to handle and that me and him would get on just fine as long as I didn't come to him asking for bigger bonuses on behalf of the squad! That was Tom to a tee – nothing complicated, just straight to the point and with a bit of good humour thrown in.

He was right, of course, to say I'd have no problems handling the group in my new role. We all got on so well, with the majority coming up through the ranks together, and the additions he made to the squad were all good characters. Eddie McCreadie was one of them, a young Scottish full-back who had joined towards the end of the relegation season. We didn't know too much about Eddie when he signed, but it quickly became apparent he had that rarest of talents for full-backs of that era: he could attack just as well as he could defend. In fact, Eddie was adamant he was brilliant at just about everything, whether it was golf, cricket, snooker, whatever.

We all loved a game of golf, and I'm a firm believer that you can go out onto a golf course with the weight of the world on your shoulders and leave it all behind while you concentrate on not making a mess of the next 18 holes. It's great for team bonding as well, because when you regularly play together it becomes very competitive and, at the same time, a great laugh.

We used to play at Wimbledon Park, which had a decent-sized course that wasn't particularly long or difficult, and that summer we had a golf day for all the lads. The way Eddie had been going on about it, you'd have thought Jack Nicklaus himself was joining us on the course, and when he got to the course decked out to the nines and with a brand new set of clubs, we all decided this was one of those days when you keep your wallet in your pocket. How wrong we were! All the gear, no idea is the phrase which springs to mind.

To be fair, I wasn't much better, although at least I stuck to using the second-hand clubs I'd been given by Jimmy Thompson, and Bridgo was as useless as me. Johnny Hollins, on the other hand, was one of those fellas who made you green with envy with a golf swing as smooth as silk. It's a good thing he's such a nice bloke, otherwise I'd have really hated him!

There was complete harmony within the club and we started the season perfectly. Everything we worked on in pre-season was paying off. The defensive shambles of previous seasons looked to be a thing of the past as we kept three clean sheets in a row, our overlapping full-backs were proving to be an absolute menace at the other end and we were averaging three goals a game in those early fixtures.

We were still a work in progress, though, and there were defeats in games we should have been winning, while my own form was proving to be a bit of a concern in the early weeks of the season, even if the lads were praising my captaincy seeing as I kept winning the toss every week. The problem was that I was struggling to find the back of the net, but that all changed when we played against Portsmouth on their own patch, which felt like a bit of a local derby for me seeing as I grew up just down the road from there. I always took great satisfaction in scoring against them and to this day I will never understand why I was never visited or even received so much as a phone call from the club while I was banging in the goals for my school.

Tommy Harmer was playing a very big part in our promotion drive and he was a tremendous presence in the dressing room. It wasn't just his experience and his skill, but the help he offered to everyone in the group. I remember being impressed when I went back to the training ground in the afternoon to do a bit of ball work and he was there to join in and help me out. He would tell you to drive the ball at him; his ball control was always immaculate. Then he'd say "harder", and it didn't seem to matter how hard you kicked it at him, he'd always bring it down. Then he would work on his free-kicks, chipping the ball up and over the wall with ease. He just loved playing football and always had a smile on his face. That enthusiasm and work ethic could only rub off on a young lad like myself.

Those goals seemed to kick off what was one of the best runs of my career. Having scored three in the opening 10 games, from the next 11 matches I was on target no less than 22 times, including one hat-trick against Derby and four goals in the second half against Charlton. It was against the Rams that I scored possibly the strangest goal of my career. I'd netted a brace and was obviously eager to take home the match ball as I chased down a pass to the keeper and fell just as he went to kick the ball, which cannoned off my back and spun right up in the air, over his head and into the back of the net. They all count.

That win over Derby took us to the top of the table and my goals ensured we were sitting handsomely at Christmas time and looking down on all the other teams in Division Two. Surely nothing could stop us achieving our goal of promotion. Then, it happened… snow, snow and more snow. After our win at Luton Town on Boxing Day we didn't play another league game until the beginning of February.

The big freeze not only put a stop to the English football season, it stopped us right in our tracks just as we'd built up a head of steam. With no sign of the weather improving, Doc took us to Malta so we could continue training, and he also arranged for a couple of friendly matches.

Malta is a lovely country, don't get me wrong, and it was great to finally get back on the pitch. But when your focus is on getting the club back up to its rightful place in the First Division, you just want to keep ticking off the league games and keep your momentum going. We had the brakes slammed on us through no fault of our own and Lady Luck certainly wasn't smiling on us at that point.

When we got back from Malta we played an FA Cup replay against Tranmere on a pitch that was as dangerous as anything I'd played on in my career. It was completely frozen and everyone was sliding all over the place, but despite the best Bambi on ice impressions you've ever seen, we somehow managed to win the game. That was on 30 January and we didn't play in front of our own fans again until the beginning of March.

The only matches we played in February were both in Wales. Swansea Town, as they were known then, and Cardiff beat us. When we finally played again at Stamford Bridge, against Huddersfield, it went the same way. In fact, we lost our first five league games in the new year and were rocking badly. We were knocked out of the FA Cup. Stoke City and Sunderland had wiped out our lead, our confidence was shot and we were like an old wreck.

As much as we tried to put a brave face on it, Doc recognised that the team needed a shot in the arm and he delved into the transfer market to sign Derek Kevan, who was a big target man. As good a goalscorer as Derek was, we just didn't play in a style which suited his game, but we started to win a few more games to keep ourselves in the hunt. Going into the run-in, the two promotion spots were still up for grabs between Chelsea, Stoke and Sunderland. Adding to the intrigue, we still had games against both of them.

The Potters were first up at Stamford Bridge, where more than

66,000 fans crammed in to see what was surely a title decider. I believe that's the biggest crowd for a Second Division game in this country and most of us had never played in front of so many supporters before. I honestly cannot speak highly enough of the fans that season as they stood by us even when things weren't going well. Unfortunately, the great Stanley Matthews had a wonderful game, despite Ronnie Harris living up to his nickname and doing his best to chop down the Wizard of the Dribble at every opportunity. We lost 1-0, and with it went our hopes of the title. Now we'd have to go to Sunderland and come away with a win if our dream of promotion was to become a reality.

That Saturday, the wind swept through Roker Park and it was clear this was going to be a day for scrapping rather than trying to play them off the park. The Doc pulled off a masterstroke by lining up with Frank Upton and Derek Kevan in the forward line. We didn't call Frank a tank for no reason. I also, as I like to remind Ron Harris, played the biggest part in the victory by continuing my run of success in the coin toss and electing to play with the wind behind us in the first half. How ironic that after playing such a big part in our downfall that season, nature would lend us a helping hand when we needed it most.

We knew we had to take advantage of the wind by getting a goal in the first half to give us something to cling to, and it duly arrived from a corner kick. With our team loaded with big players, I swung the ball right into the mixer and hoped one of them would be able to get their head to the ball. It missed them all, but there was little Tommy Harmer, the smallest man on the pitch, to get a touch on the ball and send it into the back of the net. It came at Tommy about waist height and – how can I put this politely? – he used a part of his anatomy usually associated with another type of scoring to knock the ball in. As I said before, they all count!

With a lead to hold onto, the second half took place almost entirely in our half of the field. All our defenders and Catty in goal were heroic, and Tom's selection of the big boys up front worked a treat as they dropped back into midfield, which they had to as Catty could only reach about 30 yards up the field with his kicks into the wind.

Sunderland had only been beaten at home once up until that point, but we changed that. Even so, for all the excitement and joy in the dressing room afterwards, the train journey home included several reminders from Tommy that the job was only half done. Three days later we were to host Portsmouth and, again, nothing but a win would do.

There were 54,000 fans at Stamford Bridge to make sure we did exactly that and we were geared up, that's for sure. Portsmouth were an experienced team but with tiring legs, so we were out to make sure we didn't get a nasty shock. Within a minute of kick-off there was a huge sigh of relief throughout Stamford Bridge as Derek Kevan chose the perfect time to score his first goal for the Blues. Nothing was going to stop us now.

I said Portsmouth were an experienced side before kick-off – well, that goal turned them into an ageing side. It gave us the impetus to run them ragged and they were caught out time and time again by the pace of the Blues. By half-time it was 3-0 and we were on our way back to the First Division. Frank Blunstone, Venners and four goals for myself completed the scoring in an incredible 7-0 win. But it didn't matter who got the goals, we were as one: manager, coaches, players and fans.

I'll never forget that feeling of elation when the final whistle blew. The fans came streaming on to the pitch to carry us off the field, literally making us feel 10ft tall!

We went back into the dressing room briefly, where we enjoyed a few cups of champagne. Well, most of us did; Doc swigged straight from the bottle, he was definitely going to enjoy himself. We donned our dressing gowns and headed out to the directors' box to salute the supporters who had cheered us on throughout a spectacular season. Doc cupped his hands around his mouth and shouted out: "I promise that we'll give you a team to be proud of." Even when it looked like it was unravelling before us, you never left our side. We all wanted to live up to that promise.

When we returned to the dressing room for another drop of champers, Joe Mears came in and told us he had an announcement to make on behalf of the board of directors. As a thank you for achieving promotion, they were sending us on holiday for a week in the south of France. What a treat!

When I look back at that night when we beat Portsmouth 7-0 at Stamford Bridge, those dreams of a young boy in Hayling seemed as though they had come true. There are so many stories from this season, enough to fill two books, containing every emotion you can possible think of.

Looking back on it all, I ask myself: did we make an impression on Chelsea fans? In every way the answer would have to be yes, so much so that even to this day people who saw and remember those times say what a great time it was to be a supporter and what a wonderful team we had.

We were a new Chelsea, a proper team. We played a very fast, attacking style of football; we could break out of defence quickly down either flank, we moved the ball quickly from defence to attack in a couple of passes. We were also well organised as a team, and not just in set-piece situations. It showed in everything that we did that we had been together, most of us, for a few years. We worked like clockwork.

That would be used as a stick to beat us with in later years, when we failed to achieve what people felt we were capable of. Some called us robotic, lacking superstar quality.

They may well have been right. But, at last, Chelsea had a team the fans loved, but more importantly they had a team that loved the fans. We won promotion because we played for the club we loved, for fans who had known us as boys – we won it for each other.

Through the next few seasons our emotions would be put through the mixer on a regular basis, with the end result nearly always the same – so close and yet so far. But, while success is measured by the trophies that are won by the club over the years, it doesn't tell the full story. Think of all the supporters who began their love affair with Chelsea at that time.

When you start playing you are really going out to enjoy yourself. It's a life of fun and enjoyment, but you don't realise the effect it has on people who are watching. Speaking to fans over the years, you start to realise what an impact you had on people while you were making your dream come true.

8

RIGHTFUL
PLACE

Whenever a side is promoted from the second tier up to the Premier League, the first thing everyone seems to mention is money. You hear the play-off final being dubbed "The richest game in football" and it's almost as if the prestige of playing at the highest level of English football is an afterthought. For us, promotion was simply about restoring Chelsea back to its rightful place. Everybody was excited about the new season and we couldn't wait to see if we could take that confidence from the previous campaign into our return to Division One.

However, 11 games into the season, it was pretty clear that

the one player suffering from a crisis of confidence was me. Although we had started okay as a team, I simply could not score for love nor money. The worst part of it was that I couldn't put my finger on what was going wrong. As a goalscorer, it's always magnified when you're going through a bad run because the statistics don't lie. When the goals dry up, the longer the run goes on the more you worry about it. So, you start to try a little harder, and then things get even worse. You start overthinking everything, snatching at chances you'd have usually buried nine times out of 10. The pressure starts to build in your own mind, regardless of what your team-mates and the manager say to try to put you at ease. Shooting practice becomes the most important part of every training session and you'll ask everyone – coaches, team-mates, even next door's cat – for their opinion. Your confidence ebbs away, but you cannot give up. That's the easy way out.

Often, what you need is a big challenge to reinvigorate you, and for me that came against Stoke City. The Potters were never one of my favourite teams to play against. Eric Skeels always picked me up and he invariably came out on top. Well, lo and behold, a game against Stoke was exactly what the doctor ordered for me to break my duck, against the best goalkeeper in the league, no less. That's right, I scored an own goal past Catty as we drew 3-3! I took a good bit of ribbing over that one. But, as I told the lads, my goal drought couldn't go on much longer – if I could beat the best, surely I could beat the rest? Of course, it was just a little joke, but actually I convinced myself it was something I could take confidence from.

Then it happened. In the week, I was called aside by Tommy. "Here we go," I thought. "That's me out of the team." And what could I say to that? We weren't winning many matches and the man relied on to score goals couldn't hit a cow's arse with a banjo. How could I possibly argue with him?

Clearly, I had underestimated Tom, because he told me had no intention of dropping me from the team. He had faith in me, and to hear that from your manager makes you feel 10ft tall. However, he brought me straight back down when he told me he thought it would help me find my feet in front of goal if I gave up the captain's armband. Personally, I didn't think the captaincy had affected me, but I was willing to try anything that would help me get some goals. He felt it would be a weight off my shoulders. I was just happy to still be in the team.

It proved to be a wise decision from Tommy as I scored twice in our next game against Ipswich Town, which we won 3-1. Off the mark at last – perhaps it was just a cursed armband, as poor Ken Shellito, my replacement, was to find out when he went down with an injury soon after the Ipswich game which kept him out for the season. Filling the gap he left was not going to be easy. I was sorry to lose the captaincy, but perhaps it was for the best. I was proud to have captained such a fine club and to have done so during our promotion campaign.

Our season was full of ups and downs, but we seemed to be settling down and moving through it without too much trouble. One of the highlights was a brilliant win over Spurs in an FA Cup third-round replay, which was played in front of 70,000 fans. What a great night. But the FA Cup was not a competition I would enjoy too much luck or success in throughout my career and that was proven in the next round when we lost to Huddersfield.

Two games in particular stick out from the rest of the season.

One was at Highbury in March when we took on Arsenal. The ground was very heavy with a lot of mud, but we went out and beat them 4-2 with all of the goals scored by me. I loved the mud, but I loved playing against Arsenal more. My record against them was brilliant on an individual level, obviously aided by those four goals, but as a team we barely lost to the Gunners during my time at Chelsea.

The other game was a trip to another north London giant, Tottenham Hotspur, but it wasn't memorable because of my own personal glory, although I did score both of our goals in a 2-1 win. In a lovely gesture from Tommy Docherty which showed just how highly we valued the fella, little Tommy Harmer, who had barely played all season, was brought back into the team and given the captain's armband on his return to the club where he had made his name as a player. I found an old report from The Times about this game and the headline summed up Tommy perfectly: "Harmer an intellectual among the herd."

I'm going to quote part of the article as, for me, it describes exactly what I thought of Tommy as a footballer and in a far more eloquent manner than I could ever dream of expressing it.

"Within a matter of 20 seconds, Harmer had put his delicate stamp upon an otherwise rugged, frantic match. In a flash, the little man rubbed his magic lamp. He saw the opening almost before it existed. Always it was Harmer – looking like a boy among men – who truly lit the stage. There were stretches across the sunny afternoon where he seemed to have disappeared down some trapdoor as the battle swirled around. But this was an illusion. He was always quietly moving around, directing,

Above: What a dapper lad
Right: Tasting school success

Howzat:
A keen eye
for the ball,
whatever
the game

Competitive: Showing a drive to win on
the pitch during my youth, above and being
presented with a cricket bat, right

A family affair: Mick, Beryl, Peter, Ray, Ivy, Bobby, Bill and Don and Mum and Dad in front

England calls: My Three Lions debut, with goalscoring great Jimmy Greaves and manager Walter Winterbottom, November 1962

Bubble trouble: It might look like a cuppa but I was joining the Doc in sampling some champagne after we clinched a return to Division One with a win over Portsmouth, above, while Frank Blunstone lends me a hand during that season, November 1962, below

Promotion party: Leading the revelry at the Bridge in 1963, having scored four against Portsmouth

What's up Doc?: Chelsea manager Tommy Docherty, above right, chats with, from left, Barry Bridges, Graham Moore and myself during a training session at Ewell in Surrey, 1962

1st GOAL Bobby is stumbling . . . Arsenal players surround him . . . but he manages to stab the ball home.

2nd GOAL It's in the net — Tambling has put us back in the lead from Bert Murray's corner.

Awesome foursome: My four goals against Arsenal were thankfully caught on camera in a 4-2 league win on 14 March 1964 and got special treatment in the Chelsea programme

3rd GOAL Once again Arsenal players are on all sides, but the result is the same . . .

4th GOAL Arsenal 'keeper Furnell is once more stranded as Tambling strokes his final goal.

Bobby Tambling

Poster boy: Looking the part in blue as I posed for a picture, left, and in the white away kit but still doing the business, hitting five goals in a 6-2 win against Aston Villa in Division One on 17 September 1966, below

International call-up, but still down to earth: I may have joined the England squad, (above, front row, fourth from the left), but for many years I could also travel to my "day job" on public transport without drawing too much attention, as the photo on the right from February 1963 shows

CHELSEA: FOOTBALL LEAGUE CUP WINNERS 1965

Back row, left to right: J. Hollins, A. Young, P. Bonetti, M. Hinton, J. Boyle and skipper Ron Harris. Front row, left to right: A. Murray, G. Graham, T. Venables, B. Bridges, R. Tambling and J. Fascione.

League of our own: Being part of Chelsea's first ever League Cup win was something I shall always cherish

Getting the ball rolling: It was a dream start as I opened the scoring in the first leg of our triumphant League Cup final against Leicester City but Eddie McCreadie stole the show with a goal he constantly reminded us about!

OUR INTERNATIONAL LINE-UP

Standing: T. Docherty (Scotland), A. Murray (England Under-23), K. Shellito (England), R. Tambling (England), P. Bonetti (England Under-23), T. Venables (England), M. Hinton (England Under-23), R. Harris (England Youth), H. Medhurst (Trainer, England Under-23).
Seated: P. Osgood (England Youth), E. McCreadie (Scotland), G. Graham (Scotland Under-23), J. Boyle (Scotland Youth), J. Hollins (England Under-23).
Trophies: Football League Cup (left) and Glasgow Charity Cup.

International pedigree: The quality of our 1965/66 squad is shown through their representative colours, we oozed class and character all over the pitch

RECORD BREAKER!

("Daily Telegraph" photograph)

BOBBY TAMBLING makes Chelsea history as he scores our first goal – a penalty, above – in last week's 3-0 win against Spurs. That goal was Bobby's 151st in first-team competitive matches for Chelsea, beating the previous record of 150 by Roy Bentley, now manager of Reading. Here are their respective goal figures:

ROY BENTLEY (1948-1956)		
Season	League	F.A. Cup
1947-48	3	2
1948-49	20	5
1949-50	17	3
1950-51	8	5
1951-52	12	5
1952-53	12	—
1953-54	21	—
1954-55	21	1* 1
1955-56	14	
Total	128	1 21

150

BOBBY TAMBLING (1959 to date)				
Season	League	F.A. Cup	League Cup	Fairs Cup
1958-59	1	—	—	—
1959-60	1	—	3	—
1960-61	9	—	—	—
1961-62	20	2	—	—
1962-63	35	2	—	—
1963-64	17	2	6	—
1964-65	15	4	—	2
1965-66	16	5	1	—
1966-67	10	—	—	—
Total	124	15	10	2

151

*F.A. Charity Shield

Congratulations, Bobby! Those 151 goals have come in a total of 254 appearances. He is close to another all-time Chelsea scoring record, needing five to pass Roy Bentley's total of 128 in League football.

Chelsea FC 1965-66

Back: John Hollins, Marvin Hinton, Peter Bonetti, John Boyle, Ron Harris, Ken Shellito.
Front: Barry Bridges, George Graham, Terry Venables, Bobby Tambling, Jim McCalliog.

Friends for life: Each and everyone of my team-mates at the Bridge in the 1960s brought their own strengths and qualities to the club. They were wonderful, wonderful days

Standing tall: The immense pride I felt in captaining Chelsea back to the top flight in 1963 remains with me to this day

pointing, soothing and changing the tempo, taking a hand in affairs when it really mattered…he was the little Napoleon of the battlefield."

Tommy's "delicate stamp" in the opening 20 seconds was to tee me up for the opener, and he was also heavily involved in my winning goal on the hour. I've always said what a great lad he was! Joking aside, I had so much respect for Tommy. Respect isn't something you can just ask for, and that's the same everywhere you go – you have to earn it. There are many ways in which you can do that and you respect different players for a whole lot of reasons. John Boyle, Tommy Baldwin, Nobby Houseman, Bert Murray – all of these guys earned respect for the way they worked and fought for Chelsea. They were not the big stars who received the praise and the headlines; because of where and how they played, they were not the stars, they were the guys who would give the team their all in every single game. They simply did not know how to play any other way. They all had skills, sometimes more than other players, but it wasn't really picked up by the press. But without a doubt the side couldn't perform as well as it did if these players were not part of it.

Nobby was a very quiet player around the the dressing room, so much so that you hardly even knew he was around. But on the training ground his skill stood out as good as anyone else. Slowly, everybody began to appreciate what a good player he was. John Boyle wasn't spectacular but, boy, could he get around the pitch. He did the easy thing and the right thing when he was on the ball, and when he didn't have it he would fight like his life depended on getting it back. A real worker, he deserved everything he got out of the game. He worked his socks off improving himself with skills that were to bring reward to the team.

Bert Murray and Tommy Baldwin would have been a perfect pairing if they played in the same side, but Tommy didn't join us for another couple of seasons. The former was a winger who spent much of his time learning how to put a cross into the right position for someone to dart on to it – and that's what Tommy practised until he could do it blindfolded. They would look like easy goals, but hours of work from the two players involved. One would depend on the other to get the right result. Dave Sexton had us all practising these movements. The wide man playing the cross didn't have to look up and try to pick out a player, his job was to hit the area where there was no player, which was between them and the goalkeeper. The forward had to learn how to lose his man and the oldest trick in the book was to make out to go to the far post and then nick back to the near post. It was all about timing and being decisive with your movements. Tommy was excellent at this, as was Barry Bridges.

Someone who came along a lot later than these two was Frank Lampard. Once Frank was in the opposition's half he thought like a forward and he did what all good strikers do – he antici-pated what was going to happen because he practised doing that until it became second nature. And then he practised some more. The difference between reacting and anticipating might only be a split second, but if you're on the right side of that split second then you've got a much better chance of scoring. They say practice makes perfect and that's why certain players are very good at things like free-kicks. Someone like David Beckham wasn't just born with it, it came from hard work.

Some people would argue we were a predictable side, and we

might have been to some extent. But I thought we had a good mix. We had speed throughout the framework of this team and at the back we had arguably the best goalkeeper in the league, the man we nicknamed the Cat. What a sight it was when he was flying across the goal or coming out to catch crosses. Top class.

In our full-backs we had two complete opposites. Ken Shellito was class. He never looked rushed, positioned himself well and was a great user of the ball. Ken liked to get forward and with the new tactic of overlapping our winger, he would always have the quality to find someone with his cross. Sadly, Ken was to endure a nightmare with a knee injury that in the end was to bring what looked a very successful career to a very abrupt end. If we all had dreams to fulfil, this was the other side of the coin – a nightmare you wouldn't wish on an enemy let alone a good friend and team-mate. Ken was pure class and we would miss him badly, although I'm glad to say he developed into a very good coach and remains a good friend of mine despite the fact he lives on the other side of the world.

Eddie McCreadie was really quite the opposite, all energy, very fast, great tackler, hard as nails – and that was only in the five-a-sides. If looks can be deceiving, Eddie was the perfect example. He was smallish in build and actually looked quite fragile, but he lacked for nothing. Tackles would fly in down his side of the field, he won headers against far bigger lads and he was super fast, so if he ever missed the first tackle he was always quick enough to get a second one in. Like Ken, he overlapped the winger every time he had the chance. There was many things to like about Eddie, but his enthusiasm for the game was infectious.

I've got a good story which shows just what kind of a man Eddie was. When we played Stoke in our promotion season, so much was at stake, as you'll know by now. Stanley Matthews, at something like 48, was up against Eddie, which would be a no contest for our Scottish whippersnapper, one would think. But Eddie played Stan with too much respect. Later, when asked why he had done it that way, he replied: "I didn't want to be known as the man who kicked Stanley Matthews out of the game. Football is a sport – it should be played by sportsmen."

In the middle of defence we had John Mortimore and Marvin Hinton, who made for a good pairing with qualities which complemented each other. They were both reliable, but old fashioned, big centre-forwards would give us more trouble than most. John also had a fantastic nickname: Purse. Frank Blunstone still calls him that and it all stems back to his first day at the club, when he went to pay for something and pulled a coin purse out of his pocket. It's amazing how it stuck, but Frank still laughs his head off whenever he remembers that. As for Marvin, he was known as Lou.

We had some great nicknames for the lads. Everyone thinks of Ron Harris as Chopper, which is what he wants to be called, but to us he was always Buller because every time he opened his mouth a load of bulls**t came out! He was such a quiet lad back then and it's incredible to think of how he has become a fantastic after-dinner speaker and host at Chelsea.

Eddie McCreadie was Clarence. There was a TV programme about a lion, a real one, that was cross-eyed and, as you'll have gathered by now, Eddie's eyes weren't the straightest. That's why he got away with so many of his passes – you never knew which way he was going to pass it. Frank Upton was the Tank.

He'd shake your hand and you'd count your fingers afterwards. I think he enjoyed the fact he could see you wincing! If you weren't watching him when he walked past you in the dressing room he'd dig his fingers into your gut or ribs.

Frank was part of our midfield with Terry Venables, John Hollins and Graham Moore, sometimes Buller, too, as he was a real Jack of all trades. Graham isn't someone you hear about too often, but he looked like Garth in the old newspaper comic strips, if that helps you to picture him. We used to call him that, too. He was a good-looking guy and him and Venner used to make a good comedy double act. The part Terry played had a peculiar accent which he was very good at and Graham would always play dumb. If any girls were around at the pub, Terry would loudly whisper in this stupid voice: "He likes you". Graham would just sit there nodding away, not saying a word.

When I think of Venner I'll often picture him pretending to dig away in the boot room while singing the Bernard Cribbins song Hole in the Ground. "There I was, a digging this hole," he'd sing away. And he obviously fancied himself as a singer, but he'd have us in fits of laughter. It didn't matter where or what we were doing, Terry would always have us laughing. I often wonder if the cracks appeared in our harmonious dressing room because he and Tommy Doc were both vying for centre stage. But more on that later.

Offsetting all of this was the baby-faced John Hollins, who was everyone's mate. He didn't look old enough to be out of school and I remember picking him up for training for the first time and assuming he was a schoolboy because he certainly didn't look old enough to be playing for our first team. Then you saw him go. What an engine this boy had on him, but there was so much more to him than energy. He had the lot and would go on to prove what a fine player he was for Chelsea. He would be your second pick in five-a-side, but only because Ron Harris was always the first. That's a good sign of where you stood in the squad, although I suspect Ron was being chosen as it meant you stood less chance of being kicked by him if he was on your team! I'm doing him a bit of a disservice as he was a far better footballer than many give him credit and one of the finest man-markers of his era.

Coming forward we had two wide players who would have been a credit to the wing-backs of today: Burt Murray and Frank Blunstone. These two earned the respect of not only the crowd but all of the team for the work they did in making the style and pattern of the side work so well. They would attack wide, both could go past their man and cross the ball so accurately that it became our trademark. But that was only half of what they did for the team. They worked back to cover the full-backs who became so valuable to us in making forward runs.

Finally, Barry Bridges and myself made up our attack-minded team. Bridgo was lightning quick and no defender wanted to see him running in behind them. He scored many of his goals by getting onto crosses coming from our attacking wide players and it seemed the tighter the chance the better he finished them. Both of us were running men who liked nothing better than the ball into space behind the defence. We had players who could supply exactly what we were after.

As a team, we played to our strengths. We were exciting to watch, all action, fast and strong. As I said before, perhaps over time we became a little predictable, but people enjoyed the action and we eventually enjoyed a fine return to the First

RIGHTFUL PLACE

Division that season. We only lost one game out of the final nine, leaving us in a more than respectable fifth place at the end of our first season back in the top flight and only seven points off the title. Chelsea Football Club was back on the map and our best was yet to come. Exciting times.

9

ON TOUR

Some of my most cherished memories from my time as a foot-baller came at the beginning and end of every season when we went on tour. Nowadays, every Tom, Dick and Harry can travel and see the incredible sights the world has to offer, but back in the 1960s you had to be in an incredibly privileged position if you were to be afforded such an opportunity. We saw places all over the world, places we had seen in the cinema and thought we could only dream of visiting.

There was a big difference between a pre-season tour or a trip to extend what had already been a long, hard campaign. The latter was always very relaxed and easy to enjoy the other delights on offer, but they could often drag on a bit as we went away for up to a month at a time, sometimes even longer. Pre-season was a different kettle of fish, but that wasn't a problem. It was all about getting fit and the club made sure we usually went somewhere to focus solely on football. The location would typically be away from busy towns and cities, sometimes miles away from the local villages or even any shops.

We had a place like that in Sweden. Miles from the town, it was. It was the training camp used by Brazil in their victorious 1958 World Cup campaign. So if it was good enough for them, then it would be just grand for us. It wasn't luxurious – in fact, it was like a long log cabin and somehow it was able to accommodate all of us, albeit two to a room with minimal furniture. There was good food, training pitches and plenty of different routes for our cross-country runs, which were invariably led by Catty. That's right, the goalkeeper was the fittest man in the squad. That's not to say the rest of us were slackers, rather that Peter was an incredibly fit man. Morning and early afternoons we all gave our utmost on those runs, grateful to get back for a session on the pitch so we could work on our skills before enjoying a lively game between the players. The time we spent there was to get us ready for the new season and you had the wonderful feeling of anticipation at what was around the corner.

All of that hard work became an afterthought when we departed for our end of season tours, which helped you to relax and ease yourself out of the hard work of the campaign just past. If I was to try and name all the countries we visited I think I would need an atlas to aid me, but I'll do my best to give you some idea of where we went.

Let me start with Australia. What a place. The game was only just beginning to take off Down Under, although it was still years before they were to make any sort of impact at a World Cup, and people were really happy to see English clubs in the flesh. We were just pleased to relax on the beach, although some of our opponents were keen to make sure we earned that rest. The beaches all seemed to have pure white sand and I am always reminded of that whenever I see an advert for Bounty bars. It was obviously not as hot as it can get in Australia, since we were there in winter time, but the weather was still nicer than what we could expect back home. One day we were all sat around topping up our sun tans when we noticed this fella walking towards us with four or five ladies floating around him. As he got closer, one of the lads piped up: "I think that's James Bond!"

"No, it can't be. Don't be silly. Is it really him? Why don't you go and find out?"

Off he went for a bit of snoop and, a few minutes later, he was back with some interesting news. "It's definitely James Bond, all right. But I tell you what, he's a right prat!" That was all the coaxing we needed to give him a bit of stick, but he certainly had plenty of back-up with those ladies in tow. He was living the life of James Bond for real – even down to the Vodka Martini he was drinking – so, for all the stick we gave him, I don't think it bothered him one little bit.

We always enjoyed a spot of fishing on tour, even though no one other than Charlie Cooke seemed to have the faintest idea what they were doing, and the West Indies offered plenty of opportunities for that. On one occasion, Frank Upton, the brute that he was, decided to take a different approach than the usual rod and tackle when he saw a shoal of fish swimming through a stream in a beautiful little cove we had uncovered.

He picked up a stone and threw it straight at the fish. You won't believe me, but one suddenly floated up to the surface! Frank skipped with joy, which was a rare sight indeed for such a big, tough fellow, and he had his shoes and socks off in seconds to wade in after his catch of the day.

We were all watching this from above when suddenly he stopped and yelled out in agony. He had stepped on something and it quickly became apparent it had very sharp needles on its back. He was a yard or so away from the fish so we called out to let him know it was coming round, as he had only managed to stun it with the rock. He managed to grasp it just as it looked like it was going to swim away. Frank suddenly forgot how much pain he was in. "That's my dinner tonight!" he shouted out triumphantly.

When we got back to the hotel, Frank's foot was really starting to swell up. He could hardly walk on it. But there was no way that was keeping him from his dinner. "Was it worth it, Frank?" one of the lads asked him.

"Too bloody right!"

He finally gave in and went to see the doctor the next morning, who pulled this needle out.

One of the lads would always get in a spot of bother on every single trip, without fail. In Bermuda, it was Eddie McCreadie. Despite his terrible eyesight, Eddie decided it would be a good idea to explore the place by moped, without a helmet. Off he went with Boylers in tow, both of them speeding along on these little death traps, and I'm sure it seemed like a good idea until the two of them returned and didn't say a word to anyone. Eddie was covered in cuts and grazes all over one side of his face and his arms and legs. He'd obviously come off, but Boylers kept schtum, obviously sworn to secrecy by his pal. It had really shaken a tough guy like Eddie and, unsurprisingly, no one else hired a moped on the rest of that trip.

Even the weather could be against us. After we'd clinched promotion to Division One we headed over to Spain in good spirits, starting off in Las Palmas. It wasn't as sunny as you'd expect, but actually that made for perfect conditions for a six-a-side game on the beach. A half-time break for beers made for a particularly boisterous match, although a few of the lads were moaning about not being able to get a sun tan.

Some of the team hadn't made the trip, Peter Bonetti being one of them, so Errol McNally was the only keeper with us. Errol was a Northern Irish lad who hadn't been with us long, but he was good fun and clearly looking forward to getting a chance to show the manager what he could do. However, that evening he hadn't appeared for dinner. Bert Murray asked me if I had seen him and I began to wonder if something was wrong. "Go up to his room and have a look for yourself," Bert said.

When I got to his room I noticed the door was ajar and I could hear laughter, so I poked my head around the door so I could have a peak. Errol was laid out on the bed with his arms apart and his legs spread, covered in white cream, while two lads just laughed their heads off. He wasn't moving at all and he certainly didn't see the funny side of it. Despite the lack of sun, or so we thought, Errol's pale Irish skin hadn't been able to cope with it. He had a bad case of sunburn and the cream was Harry Medhurst's idea to try and calm it down.

While it was all a big joke to us, no one had put two and two together yet – Errol's sunburn was so bad he wasn't able to play in the first match, and we didn't have another goalkeeper in the squad. Bert took the gloves and, thankfully, it was only for the one game. It seems Errol wasn't the luckiest of chaps. He was at the club at the same time as one of the best goalkeepers Chelsea and England has ever seen, and on the rare occasions he did manage to get on the field – nine times in competitive matches – he never won a game, losing five and drawing four.

We also had a diving competition on this tour, which became a common occurrence provided wherever we were staying had the facilities, and it was judged by the non-swimmers. So, that was me.

The lads were always competitive, trying to invent new dives, and this was where Dave Sexton came into his own. It wasn't just his football tactics which were innovative. One dive he came up with involved him running to the end of the board, springing up and landing on his bum before bouncing back up and diving in. It looked clever and easily won him first prize, not to mention a few envious glances from the lads who decided they'd try it out for themselves. Poor Frank Upton gave it a go and instead of landing on his backside he missed the board and whacked his back.

Frank was also convinced he could teach me to swim. It was as if I was his own personal project and by the end of the trip he was adamant I was ready to swim a length. Foolishly, I told him I had this cine camera and asked him if he minded shooting some footage of me trying to swim. We were all set up and he told me to dive in at the deep end and swim away. Well, I dived in and started to do the front crawl. I was moving! I managed two or three strokes, but they were all under water and when I came to the surface I managed to keep going while splashing water everywhere. I finally reached the other end and as much as Frank was killing himself with laughter, along with the other lads, he was so pleased I'd managed to reach the other end.

It wasn't all fun and games, mind. One trip to South America included a tournament in Venezuela. We watched with intent as the local team and Setubal, a Portuguese side who we were due to face next, played against each other. One thing stood out right away: they had a left-winger who was lightning quick. Ronnie Harris was our right-back at that time and all the lads were giving him plenty of stick about this lad, saying how good was and that we'd never seen someone that quick. Even quicker was Ron's response: "Let's see how fast this fella is without any legs."

Someone must have warned this winger about Ron, or maybe his hardman reputation travelled far and wide, because every time he got the ball he played it first time to one of his teammates. After about 15 minutes or so the goalkeeper took a goal kick which was heading Ron's way. He could see the winger out of the corner of his eye and he moved to control the ball but made a horrible mess of it and the ball bobbled to this poor fella. The winger's eyes lit up as he finally had a chance to get the better of Ron with him off balance. Ron had other ideas. His poor touch was deliberate, or so he told us, and he was perfectly poised to launch into a tackle. It was fair – they always were with Ron, according to him – but he put everything behind this tackle and left him in a crumpled heap. He wasn't badly hurt, but Ron didn't have to worry about him for the rest of the game.

Venezuela seemed to be a really nice place, but at that time the students were having some problems with the government and there was a lot of trouble around the campus. I'm talking serious trouble, gunfire and so forth. We kept a very low profile that week.

Those tours were great to keep the team spirit high, whether it was a joke on one person or whatever. We could all laugh them off, it was just a joke after all, and any one of us could be caught out at any time. We all learned to laugh at ourselves as much as at anyone else.

Usually the pre-season tours were a bit more serious, but one in particular I recall being funny for all of us. We had endured an incredibly difficult fortnight in Germany, working hard morning and afternoon, but the time had come to move to our new base in the Black Forest, so we all boarded the coach for the long journey. Perhaps in view of where we were headed, conversation turned to horror films and what we were all scared of. All of a sudden, the sky went really dark and we were hit by a thunderstorm. That was all the encouragement we needed to start hamming up the stories.

There were all sorts of predictions made for the hotel and what the staff would be like, with Frankenstein's monster cropping up a lot. Well, when we pulled off the road at our hotel, we all burst out laughing. The hotel was exactly what you'd expect from a horror movie. It was a tall, old-fashioned building with shutters on all the windows. It looked genuinely scary. Everything seemed to be just like people were saying on the coach and it was a good job it was two to a room. I don't think anybody would have gone to bed that night if they were on their own.

As we all drifted off in the direction of our rooms, Venner said to Catty and I: "Fellas, did you notice anyone looking particularly nervous? I'm sure Eddie is really spooked by this place."

He decided we needed to catch him out, so we started plotting. They were all simple things: taking the bulb out of his light, rustling up a bit of string to dangle from the doorway to hit his face when he walked in. I'd noticed the curtains were set quite a bit forward from the dormer windows, so we decided we'd put a pillow in someone's pyjamas so that when Eddie pulled the curtain back it would fall on him. I had a pair of black pyjamas which were perfect for this particular job.

Off we went to dinner, but afterwards we left the card players to it and decided to partake in a more devilish game of our own. When we had finished, content we'd got everything just right, we had no idea nature was about to give us the final piece of a puzzle that would scare most right-minded folk.

After a little while, we heard an almighty crash, followed by banging, shouting and God knows what else. I went out into the hallway and noticed it was coming from the floor above, so I shouted up to ask if everything was okay. The response, in a thick Scottish accent, was along the lines of: "If I catch the person responsible I'll do them some serious damage!"

The next morning was hilarious. At breakfast, Eddie gave us the lowdown on what had gone on the previous evening. There were plenty of tricks but no treats! Apparently, he had seen the funny side of it all until the moment he found himself unable to sleep because of the horrid weather outside. A branch was knocking against his window and he decided it was going to keep him up all night so he got up and walked over to the window. As he pulled back the curtains, the pillow fell on him and that was it – he bolted out of his room and started banging on the door next door, which just so happened to be occupied by Terry and Ken Shellito. He jumped into bed and wouldn't move the rest of the night!

That morning, Eddie was keeping an eye out for a pair of black pyjama bottoms. Thankfully I was wise to him and had already chucked them out – I wasn't going to be owning up to that one. And he took it fairly well because I think the shock would have given me a heart attack! If you're reading this now, Eddie, I'm so sorry, but that was just the way of the dressing room. Jokes and wind-ups were all part of a day's work and it helped keep our spirits up.

One of my last tours with Chelsea was in 1969, when we finished the season with a trip to Mozambique for two games against their national team. While we were relaxing outside one of the many cafes which populated the town centre where we were staying, this huge fellow walked past us. When I say huge, I mean absolutely massive – he must have been more than 8ft tall and he was struggling just to walk upright. Marvin Hinton joked that it would be just his luck that this guy would be playing centre-forward for Mozambique. We later found out his name was Gabriel Estêvão Monjane, who would one day go on to be judged as the world's tallest man. Other than celebrity spotting, we were really struggling for entertainment and, when we had a whinge about this to the hotel manager, he set us up at a country club where there was a lovely golf course. When we got there, they fixed us up with a huge hamper, complete with a few bottles of wine, and provided us with clubs and our own caddies. "I could get used to this," I thought to myself.

Then, one of the lads had a bit of a brainwave. "Are there any snakes out there?" he asked his caddy, to which the response was what nobody wanted to hear.

"Yes, sir. Lots. Some of them are even deadly."

He delivered all of this information with a broad smile on his face, but I can tell you now that I didn't see the funny side of it.

I had grown up with a fear of snakes. When I was a kid, we'd often pass the time messing about, as kids do, and we'd run over to the side of the railway where there was this marsh which flooded in the winter and then resembled a swamp in the summer. I'd be there mucking about with my older brothers, playing chase or something silly like that, and then everyone would freeze. "SNAKE!" There were adders in there and I was always terrified of seeing one. Then, I was picking primroses one day and I got my hand in there, and around the plant was this curled up adder! That is as close as I ever wish to get to a snake as long as I live.

Back on the golf course, I told my caddy he could play everything out of the rough. He didn't have to wait long for his first shot. I noticed he had no shoes or socks on and I could see the scars that had been left on his feet and ankles. I knew my golf skills weren't the only enemy confronting him today, but he was obviously a handy player as he chipped a lovely shot right at the hole.

A few holes later, I noticed one of the caddies up ahead getting a little excited and there was a bit of commotion. The others couldn't get to him quickly enough and there was a lot a chatter as we reached where he was standing. It soon became apparent what had caused the excitement. Lying there in the middle of the fairway was this brightly coloured snake which was about 4ft long, quite thick and very dead! Someone had obviously taken a dislike to him and clubbed him over the head. "Was it a poisonous snake?" one of the lads enquired. The caddy laughed. Of course it was. I think they were enjoying scaring us, especially as it meant they were likely to get a few more shots.

I love to tell people about this round because it was the first time I've been around a golf course and taken less than 60 shots. It's just a shame the caddy added 40 or so to that...

Those trips brought the boys together and made us a tighter, stronger unit, ready to fight for each other on the pitch and who knows what extra percentage those tours gave us as a squad and as a club.

However, as we found to our cost on one particular occasion, time away from the Bridge did not always help us out. In fact, a trip to Lancashire one night had far reaching consequences for the club Chelsea were and the club they were hoping to become.

10

ONE NIGHT

One night. That's all it took. One stupid mistake to undo years of hard work. On our fateful trip to Blackpool, more than just a curfew was broken. The feeling of togetherness which had developed among a group of lads who had been brought together by Chelsea Football Club, forming friendships which would last a lifetime, was suddenly ripped apart over one silly little incident. Things would never be the same again.

The 1964/65 season should have been the start of a beautiful, successful era for Docherty's Diamonds. Before our players were to become front page news, more and more column inches in the sports pages were being dedicated to us. From a group of youngsters with a lot of enthusiasm and energy, a team of well-drilled young men began to emerge. In an earlier chapter,

I spent some time highlighting the quality running through our squad and I make no bones about that team's ability and spirit. I'm not saying we were the finished article; a bit of fine-tuning was needed, small adjustments here and there, but not the radical overhaul that was on the horizon.

And over what? Something trivial that got completely blown out of context. People were wrong and mistakes were made, but a better handling of the situation could have repaired the damage. It happened at a time when we should have only been getting stronger.

With a quality player like George Graham joining us, that's exactly what happened at the start of the season. We were pretty much a team of youth graduates, sometimes up to nine of the team having been made in Chelsea, but with the odd sprinkling of quality from elsewhere. It was a super team to play in and we started the campaign with a bang, winning regularly and the goals flying in from all corners. By the end of November, we'd won 15 matches and three players, myself included, had already hit double figures. We were far from predictable and everyone was getting in on the act. George, Barry and myself worked well as a frontline and we were also getting goals from set-pieces. George was a very good header, he got up very well, and Barry was great at getting on the end of crosses. I was handy around the box and often on hand to put the finishing touch on our incisive passing moves, of which there were many as we were so quick on the counter-attack.

There were goals from all over the pitch and so many different scorers that the lads who hadn't scored by now were getting stick from all the others. Another name appeared on the scoresheet, one which Chelsea fans would become more than familiar with over the years: Peter Osgood. He scored twice on his debut at Workington and it was clear he was blessed with plenty of talent. He looked right at home in the team, but the form of others meant he'd have to bide his time to get a proper run.

The fans were absolutely loving it, and who could blame them? Not only were we a winning team, but we were exciting to watch, too. We were attracting massive crowds: around 50,000 for league games against Arsenal and Spurs and more than 60,000 for cup games against the latter and Peterborough.

It really was a huge season for all of us and, looking back at it now, it's easy to see why we were such a popular side. But it wasn't any good just being popular – we wanted to be a successful side, so we had to finish the job. We'd made it to the final of the League Cup, the semi-final of the FA Cup and were still in the running for the league. What a season so far. Could we finish the job? The simple answer to that question is no. Those final 13 games of the season proved to be more than just unlucky for us – it was the beginning of the end for a very good side which had room for improvement, for sure, but could have been one of the all-time great sides.

We lost in the league against Manchester United, a 4-0 drubbing away from home, which put a massive dent in our title hopes but was far from a critical defeat. In fact, it didn't seem to have too big an impact as we rebounded by winning the first leg of the League Cup final against Leicester. Back in the early years of the competition, the final was played over two legs. Nowadays, people point to the competition as the weakest of the domestic trophies and they say it lacks prestige, but there's a final at Wembley at the end of it. We didn't even have that.

The first leg was a strange old game, but it highlighted how Doc's willingness to think outside the box could sometimes pay off in the most spectacular manner. When Bridgo was ruled out of the game through injury, the obvious thing to do would have been to give the No.9 shirt to Ossie, who was champing at the bit. But, no. Doc decided the best man for the job was our left-back, a man who had always dreamed – and told anyone who would listen – that he was made to play as a centre-forward. Well, if you think I've told the story of a boy whose dream has come true, wait until you hear what happened to Eddie McCreadie.

To the best of my knowledge, I don't recall ever seeing Eddie playing as a centre-forward for Chelsea before this game. In a five-a-side match in training, perhaps, but other than that he was a left-back and that was that. Typically, he was all-action, making runs and challenging for every ball in an evenly matched game on a wet and fairly heavy pitch. We'd twice taken the lead through first me and then Terry Venables, only for Leicester to peg us back each time. Then, with 10 minutes to go, came the moment Eddie had been waiting for his entire life. He had the ball in our half of the field and the visitors looked to have over-committed in the attacking third as they were short at the back. That was all the encouragement Eddie needed. He set off on a run, taking it past one man and then another, both of whom turned to chase him. Once he was past the halfway line, Eddie came to the last defender and knocked the ball around him and set off for goal. We were trying to keep up with him to give him some support – Eddie was a quick bugger at the best of times, let alone when he had a wonder goal in his sights – and I was racing down the middle. But that night Eddie had only one thing on his mind: scoring.

ONE NIGHT

As Gordon Banks slowly edged out to narrow the angle for the shot, with two defenders chasing like mad to catch up with him, I was free as a bird and screaming for the ball. Slip it to me and there was just an empty net to knock it into. Not a chance! He calmly knocked the ball past Banksy and into the back of the net. Well, that's how I remember it anyway. A few other players have their own account of the goal and we'll never know who was right as there were no television cameras there to capture Eddie's magic moment. He'd say that was just his luck, but perhaps if other people's version of the event are to be believed then luck was on his side. Then again, others say it's the greatest goal that nobody ever saw. In my mind, he deserved all the applause and plaudits which came his way. Although, when I asked him why he didn't use me, he replied: "I did. I used you for what you were best at being – a dummy."

We won the first leg 3-2. But it was only the League Cup – we had bigger trophies in our sights and we were now well and truly into the business end of the season, with each game seemingly as important as the last.

From a League Cup final to a vital league fixture and then Liverpool awaiting us in an FA Cup semi-final; these were the games every footballer wanted to be a part of, when the stakes are high.

The best part of 70,000 supporters greeted us at Villa Park and they should have been on their feet cheering a Chelsea goal midway through the first half. We were awarded a corner on the right-hand side, from which I would deliver one of my trademark inswinging corners, the type of cross George Graham would always say he made to look like a decent ball. But George wasn't on the end of it for once. This time it was

John Mortimore who was quickest off the mark. The Liverpool keeper, a Scottish chap called Tommy Lawrence, was slow off his line and John had already got his head to it by the time the keeper went clattering into him. The ball nestled in the back of the net, but our joy was quickly curtailed as the referee blew his whistle and signalled for a free-kick. "What the bloody hell has he given that for?" I thought to myself. There was no contact before the header and, anyway, it was the keeper going into John. It was definitely a goal. But the referee, like they do today, decided that the slightest contact between player and goalkeeper should result in a free-kick. It makes me laugh when I think back to a game less than 10 years before that when an incident occurred in an FA Cup final between Aston Villa and Manchester United involving Peter McParland and Ray Woods – no eyes for the ball, just a straightforward shoulder charge which wouldn't have looked out of place of a rugby field. No foul was given, the keeper went off injured and, with substitutes still a few years away from being introduced into the game, Villa went on to win against 10 men.

The decision was a huge blow to us and it was as if the wind had been knocked right out of our sails. Slowly, the Reds got on top of us and eventually they ran out 2-0 winners. Had the referee not ruled out John's goal, I'm certain there would have been a different outcome to the end of this story, but instead we were left with FA Cup heartache. It's a feeling I'd know all too well by the end of my career. There's a picture of me walking off at the end of the game, devastated, while the celebrations went on behind me. If I felt like that I can only imagine what the fans were going through. So close and yet so far, the story of my time at Chelsea.

ONE NIGHT

The only exception to that came in the League Cup, which we won after holding out for a tense 0-0 draw against Leicester. Silverware at last. If you'd told me this would be the only trophy I'd lift in my time as a Chelsea player I'd have said you were having a laugh. We were destined for big things and the championship was there for the taking.

So then, the 1964/65 title race was a three-way fight between us, Manchester United and Leeds United. April was packed with eight matches and with three games remaining we stood at the top of the table, but we didn't quite hold all the aces; we had three matches awaiting us in the North West.

We knew if we could win them all we'd end up as champions, and Docherty's Diamonds would forever be spoken about and immortalised among football connoisseurs in the same manner as the Busby Babes.

There was more than just a championship at stake here.

Travelling up to Liverpool on Easter Monday, we were totally confident of turning over the Reds, because we'd inflicted a 4-0 defeat on them in the league just a fortnight after the FA Cup semi-final loss which helped us gain a measure of revenge for that defeat.

However, at Anfield we lost 2-0. So much for confidence.

They talk about fixture congestion today, but that was our third game in the space of four days over Easter. Can you imagine if that happened today? We were fit sportsmen, though, and tiredness certainly wasn't being offered up as an excuse. We simply hadn't been good enough.

With games against Burnley and Blackpool to come over the course of the next seven days, Doc had decided there was no point travelling back to London and had booked us a hotel in

Blackpool. It's how Italian teams have always loved to do things, blocking out the rest of the world and just focusing on the task at hand. As glum as we were feeling at the loss, which had left us relying on other results if we were to finish as champions, it was a good chance to spend a bit of time away from our families and without distractions as well as letting our hair down before the pressure cooker environment awaiting us over the next week.

Instead, it was in this week that our season and, indeed, the destiny of this potentially great Chelsea team was thrown up in the air – a week in which the squad was blown apart. If only it had been handled with a little more common sense. That team could have grown and grown. You can only imagine what we might have gone on to achieve.

The first thing Doc told us when we got to the Cliffs Hotel was to make sure sure we weren't out late. He was setting an 11 o'clock curfew, which we all found a little strange seeing as it was five nights before our next game. The mood at the dinner table was subdued at best, although I have no doubt that was down to the frustration of letting our title hopes slip rather than annoyance at Doc spoiling our fun. In the end, we decided to go bowling and have a couple of quiet drinks. Most of us stuck together, as we usually did, and there was no chance of anyone coming back any later than 11 after Harry Medhurst warned us that Tommy was in a foul mood and waiting for someone to step out of line.

We arrived back at the hotel in good time to be greeted by the manager, who actually seemed in a pretty good mood by this point. "Lads, there's a snooker room downstairs and it's got a bar," he informed us. "Go down there and relax, stay as late as you like."

ONE NIGHT

Later, there was a noise complaint and someone claimed they had seen a group of people leaving the hotel via a fire escape. Tommy argued that it was none of his boys as there was a rugby team staying in the hotel as well, so it must have been them. Tommy must have been so disappointed when the rooms were checked and eight players were missing: Barry Bridges, Joe Fascione, George Graham, Marvin Hinton, John Hollins, Eddie McCreadie, Bert Murray and Terry Venables.

I went down for breakfast the next morning to be greeted by the sight of the eight lads all dressed in their club suits. Tommy had blown his top; they were being sent back on the first train home and, what's more, he had suspended all eight of them from our final two fixtures of the season. I don't think those of us who hadn't been reprimanded quite realised the severity of the situation as we were all having a laugh about it with them, wanting to know what fun we'd missed out on.

Then it hit us: Blackpool's evening paper arrived with the eight players plastered across the front page. The lads had no idea the storm was brewing the whole time they were on the train back. Suddenly, as they pulled into Euston station, they were greeted by a crowd of reporters and television crews. Perhaps The Beatles had been on this train. No, just eight Chelsea players being treated like naughty schoolkids, hung out to dry. All that had been said was they had broken club rules. Fend for yourselves, fellas.

If the reason for the early departure from Blackpool had been given straight away we all felt the incident would have easily been resolved. That never happened. Reports were rife with what was going on and the hotel was suddenly filled with reporters all looking for a nice, juicy story. It had all got out of hand

and the players were taking stick from all sides. In that short time, the trust, spirit and togetherness had been shattered. Both sides had been in the wrong over this one, in my opinion. Cool heads would have dealt with it better, but none were to be found.

It all blew up in everyone's faces and there were no winners from this situation. We faced Burnley without the eight lads, who, in a farcical turn of events, had actually been put back on a train to come and watch us, and with an even younger side than usual. No plan, no clue, no points – a 6-2 defeat and utter humiliation for us all. Our title dreams gone.

Some of the offending players were back in the team for the trip to Blackpool after their suspensions had been lifted, but the mood in the dressing room was heavy. This whole incident hung over us all and we lost 3-2. Third place in the league would usually have been seen as a fine achievement for the club, but it felt nothing like that. It was a missed opportunity.

There's so much pressure on footballers to win. It was important for us and we wanted to win and play well as much for the fans as ourselves. But we also wanted to win as a team, as a group of friends. You couldn't have separated us as team-mates, and that bond remained intact. But something changed in Blackpool and irreparable damage had been done to the relationship between Docherty and some of his players. There's no two ways about it, in my mind he made a wrong call, a rod for his own back. I think he has since said that he acted a little hastily. I think it was through sheer disappointment and frustration at our title hopes potentially drifting away. He was only a young manager and I think he wanted that success as badly as, if not more than, we did. We were known as Docherty's Diamonds and if we had won it, his name would have been immortalised in English football.

ONE NIGHT

I think if he hadn't been so rash and slept on it, and then sat down and talked with someone, even the players themselves, things could have been better. But he acted before he'd thought.

"I knew I had a serious matter on my hands," he later said, "and that if I faltered I would never again be able to command any respect or discipline." I disagreed with that then and I disagree with it now. The club didn't. Chairman Joe Mears, who was abroad, sent him a telegram saying: "We back your decision 110 per cent." Other clubs congratulated him on his stance. But the simple fact of the matter is that a side which had all the potential in the world and looked to be destined for a big future had the rug whipped out from beneath it by the man who had to have the trust of his players.

We lost so much over nothing at all. A storm in a tea cup. We'd won a trophy, reached another semi-final and finished third. We had shown we were a good side, with 17 different scorers and three players – Bridgo, big George and I – with more than 20 goals. What's more, the side was packed full of players in their early or mid-twenties. We had time on our side and I've no doubt we would have got better and better as time went on.

Football is a game of opinions, though, and not everyone sees it the same way. Indeed, you might be reading this and thinking I'm talking out of my backside. I know Jamie, who is Val's son, certainly does. "It's a closed discussion," he insists. "It was the players' fault. They disobeyed a direct order." He's an officer in the navy now after growing up as a little loveable rogue! He's straight as an arrow and while we all say the Doc acted hastily, he is adamant the players were in the wrong.

11

REBUILDING

Despite our frustration at the events which played out over the final week of the previous season, our League Cup triumph had given us a ticket to travel around Europe as England's representatives in the Inter-Cities Fairs Cup.

Chelsea had competed in European competition seven years earlier and come up against Frem from Denmark and Ville de Belgrade from Yugoslavia. They were both good sides, but hardly the kind of glamorous names you associate with football on the continent. Well, this time we more than made up for that in our latest continental campaign, when our run in the competition took in Roma, AC Milan and Barcelona along the way. Chelsea are more than used to staying in Europe for the that in our latest continental campaign, when our run in the competition took in Roma, AC Milan and Barcelona along the way. Chelsea are more than used to staying in Europe for the long haul nowadays, but for us it was a new experience which we couldn't get enough of.

There was initially a bit of disappointment among the lads, though, as in order to compete in the competition it was decided we'd have to step aside from the League Cup that season. We were all keen to defend our trophy, as you would expect, especially as it was the first piece of silverware our young side had won together. However, it was soon forgotten about. With the World Cup coming to England the following summer, all eyes were on the clubs who were competing in Europe, such was the excitement and interest in these exotic overseas stars who would soon be representing their respective countries in the biggest tournament of the lot. And nobody was more excited about it than our boys.

Our first test was Roma and with it came a rude awakening. They hadn't come to Stamford Bridge to play all of this neat tippy-tappy stuff, they were spoiling for a fight! Things boiled over on more than one occasion and it proved to be one time too many for Eddie McCreadie, who was grabbed around the neck and responded by chinning the fella. Between all the fighting there was five goals, four of which were scored by us, including a hat-trick for Venners. One of his goals gave a perfect example of why he was destined for management. Nowadays, any free-kick around the box will be struck directly at goal and that's that. Back in the Sixties there was a bit more thought put into how you could outwit your opponents. There wasn't the television coverage, so if you had a good free-kick it was only written about and not seen by other teams. As a result, there was a lot more invention.

This one was all down to Terry, the great innovator that he was, and it went like a dream. He counted out the 10 yards to the wall, making out to the ref they weren't 10 yards back, and as he got to the line of defenders he wheeled around the side of them and the ball was played alongside him and suddenly we had scored. Everyone was so surprised and the game got even nastier. Roma had someone sent-off and it was reported over there that he was subjected to crowd trouble. I think all it was was that he was booed off down the tunnel, but when we got over to Italy for the return match we were in for quite a surprise.

I was injured for the game, but I travelled over with the boys and as soon as we arrived at the stadium, which was a smaller venue with the crowd right on top of you, I knew there was going to be trouble. We went out there in our suits and within a few minutes the pitch was covered with rotten fruit and veg! They threw worse at our boys during the game and I'm sure Boylers got knocked over by one missile.

I think the hefty lead from the first leg gave Doc the confidence to play Marvin Hinton as a sweeper, which was the perfect role for Lou. He was cool, calm and collected, and he loved to play out from the back. It was a masterful performance, the kind of display which got him in the running for a place in England's World Cup squad. There was only one problem – Bobby Moore played the same position.

We managed to hold out for a 0-0 draw, but the real battle was awaiting us when we got on the team bus after the game. It had been parked up so we'd go directly from the exit of the stadium onto the coach, and we were told to get under our seats and hope for the best. A load of police motorcycles led us out, but they didn't do much good – all sorts got thrown at the windows, which smashed, and it was like something out of an action movie as our coach driver floored it and led us away from danger.

These thrilling adventures were all part of the European experience, which was brand new to nearly all of us, and we were also getting used to a change to English football as substitutes were introduced for the first time. It was nothing like the modern game, where you can change three players for whatever reason you want. We had one sub and the player coming off had to be injured. We have to take some of the blame for all of the play-acting that goes on nowadays because, if the manager gave you the nod, you'd be straight to the ground and the trainer would be on to take a look at you. "No, he can't carry on – get the sub on."

One day, I found myself in the wrong place at the wrong time. Playing on the left meant that for one half of every game I was right in front of where Tommy Docherty would be in the dugout. In this one game, I got the call to go down – or at least I thought I did. Boomph, down I went, holding my leg. Harry came rushing on. "Bob, how bad is it? Do you think you can carry on."

I said, "Harry, what are you on about? I'm not injured – you told me to do it."

"No, you bloody idiot. We want Bert off. I almost had to get my sponge out then! Make sure you pass the message on to Bert." And that's how it went. Play-acting and diving started with us.

REBUILDING

In case you're interested, Keith Peacock, whose son Gavin scored the goals which propelled Chelsea to the FA Cup final in 1994, was the first substitute in a Football League game when he came on for Charlton Athletic in August 1965. The honour of being the Blues' first replacement went to Boylers, although he would probably argue he should have been starting in the first place.

Our next tie in the Fairs Cup, against Wiener Sport-Club from Austria, was pretty dull in comparison with the previous round, although we had to overcome a first-leg deficit to get through, and then it was Serie A opposition once again as we were drawn to face the mighty AC Milan. Whereas Roma had been content to try and kick lumps out of us, the Rossoneri were exactly what you'd expect of an Italian side. They had some incredible players, with Gianni Rivera standing out from the crowd, and their skill level was unbelievable. While we would hit a straight ball when making passes, they would curl the ball around people and when it reached their player it was on the furthest side away from the defender. We learned a lot from the Italians.

Our game was really all about pace and hitting them on the counter-attack, whereas they kept the ball superbly and played at a slower pace. It was a real clash of styles, but we had benefited from a game we'd played in Milan earlier in that season which was against a mixture of AC's defence and Inter's forwards. We knew what to expect, although I suppose they were well prepared for our hard running and swift counters, and we cancelled each other out with 2-1 wins for the home side in each leg. George Graham scored in both games to go along with a goal in the opening round against Roma and he really seemed to be thriving on the big stage. Ossie was on target, too, the young man coming of age.

At this stage, football had yet to discover a suitable tie-breaker if a two-legged tie finished all square. Penalty shoot-outs were still four years away and so there was to be a third game between the sides, the venue of which was decided by the toss of a coin. Then, if that finished level, the coin would come back into play to decide which side went through. Well, you can guess what happened next.

We went back to Milan for the second time and they seemed pretty content to play for a draw, which seemed quite odd unless they had a double-sided coin up their sleeve. As Sir Alex Ferguson famously said: "When an Italian tells me it's pasta on the plate I check under the sauce to make sure. They are the inventors of the smokescreen."

They should have gone for the jugular as we were dead on our feet in the second half with players carrying injuries and whatnot, and there was 30 minutes of extra-time, too. We were quite happy to play out a draw in the end, but then we were led back into the dressing room while Ron Harris went to the middle of the pitch for the toss. Bridgo snuck out to see if he could find out what was happening and when he saw Chopper jumping for joy in the centre circle, he came rushing back to tell us the good news. We were obviously delighted, but whoever came up with that idea to settle a tie must have been crazy. There are so many ways you could decide matches.

We were having such a great time on these trips and I think the press boys were loving it just as much as we were as they were travelling with us every step of the way. We liked our fun and games and those guys didn't mind being on the receiving end because they wanted to feel part of the team. It was all light-hearted fun, as always. And, obviously, they wanted us to do well, because it meant they got to travel around a bit.

We were playing in Germany next, against an 1860 Munich side who were on their way to winning the Bundesliga title that season, and there was some doubt whether the game would even be played because of the snowy conditions. But it went ahead and I scored twice to help us earn a 2-2 draw, which was a great result as they were a top side. Their marking was so intense, almost man-for-man all over the park, so we were absolutely delighted to come away with that result.

When we got back to our hotel, they'd put aside a private room for us at the back and all of the journos, who would typically stay in the same place as us, were in the main part of the restaurant. Doc was on a real high, as we all were, and he kept ordering more and more bottles of champagne for all the lads. The waiters had to walk past all of the reporters to bring it out to us, and among the press pack was a lad who wasn't a football correspondent. His name was Laurie Pignon and he had his own "Opignon" column in a tabloid paper called the Daily Sketch. He was usually a tennis reporter and he was really very posh, but a lovely chap.

After they brought the umpteenth bottle through to us, Laurie poked his head through the door and shouted: "Hey Ossie, any chance of that champagne reaching the rest of us, old chap?"

"No problem, mate – give me a second and I'll bring one out for you," Os replied.

In front of Ossie was a bottle that was about a quarter full, if that. By the time it reached the press boys in the main restaurant, it was three-quarters full, and it hadn't been topped up with champagne, let's put it that way. A few moments later, Laurie came bursting through the door. "Hey Ossie, you want to get your bloody bladder tested!"

That was just the way we were with the press; we enjoyed them and they enjoyed us. That showed in the way they looked after us in the papers. We got on really with them. And they were by no means the only ones on the receiving end of our unique sense of humour. If someone had been filming most of our antics we'd have ended up on Candid Camera or one of Jeremy Beadle's shows, it was that kind of silly, childish thing. But it always had us in stitches and I really wish someone had captured some of it on camera because it's making me laugh just thinking about what we got up to.

Any visit to the airport was always a recipe for silliness. At Heathrow, we had to deal with a furious Harry Medhurst after Ossie thought it would be funny to pin a condom to his jacket. He walked around like that for ages until someone told him. We were absolutely killing ourselves, but I don't think he saw the funny side of it.

If ever we saw someone running for their plane, at least one of us would have a handful of pennies ready to toss so the fella would stop and start going through his pockets to see what he'd dropped. He'd dash off again and then someone else would chuck some. Wearing our club suits also meant we were dressed like airport employees, so whenever an information booth was left unmanned you could bet your life that Venner would be straight in there to help out. I shudder to think how many people only just made their flight because they'd been sent to the opposite end of the airport by one of the top footballers in the country. It was all harmless fun. We were just a bunch of big kids and it was such a good atmosphere. I can't help but think that however important the football was and how much we wanted to win things, we thoroughly enjoyed ourselves along the way.

Unfortunately, it was around this time that the wheels well and truly fell off. After narrowly seeing off 1860 Munich in the home leg, we were drawn to play against Barcelona and also had an FA Cup semi-final to look forward to. It was a game in which we were heavily fancied against Sheffield Wednesday at Villa Park, but once again the curse of the cup came back to haunt us. They beat us 2-0 on a pitch which didn't have one blade of grass on it, with our old mate Jim McCalliog scoring one of their goals.

It was the second season in a row that we'd fallen at this hurdle and it hit Doc hard. He seemed to take it out on Bridgo, dropping him for our next league game, and the two of them had an almighty row just as we were due to fly out to Barcelona. Barry ended up storming off, leaving his bags on the plane, and he never played for Chelsea again.

The first leg in the Nou Camp was to be Venner's final game for the Blues. In a scenario which is scarcely believable, we were introduced to our newest signing, Charlie Cooke, in the dressing room of the stadium just ahead of the game. What a way to get Venner in the right frame of mind for the biggest game of the season! Good luck out there, Tel. Oh, and by the way, this is Charlie, who is going to be replacing you.

Tommy must have told him there would be a bit of a backlash from the lads as he was coming in to take the place of a player who was the heart and soul of the dressing room. Now, Charlie was a hell of a nice lad – still is – and he came in and I can't remember anyone rushing over to shake his hand. He knew he had to break the ice so he got a ball, flicked it up and started doing keep-ups. After he got to about 30, people started to take notice. He flicked it on his neck, rolled it down, caught it on his finger and was spinning it around. All of a sudden it was: "Oh, hi, Charlie, really nice to meet you, glad to have you in the team." He went on to become a legend. That's how you break the ice! I can laugh about it now, but at the time I really felt for Venner.

One side of football I always found hard to handle was the departure of friends and team-mates with whom I shared so many happy memories. Because of the Blackpool incident, which I have no doubt played a big part in the break-up of our young team, it was a situation I was having to deal with on a regular basis. You get close to people, sharing the ups and downs of life; sweet success or bitter failure, it doesn't matter, it all brings you much closer together. We are normal people, not machines – we feel the heartbreak of losing key matches, letting down the supporters, and for me it was never tougher than saying goodbye to players who I'd been alongside through thick and thin, even growing up with them in many cases. Some of these guys became like brothers to me.

The loss of people like Ken Shellito, Bridgo and Venner hit us all even harder because we'd already waved off some of the old heads who'd played such a vital role in our development by sharing their wealth of knowledge and experience with us young 'uns. Frank Blunstone and John Mortimore had both dropped out of the first team in the previous 18 months – Frank through injury and John had transferred to QPR – and we missed them. Blunners was the perfect example to any young pro. He'd broken his leg twice and come back as good as new each time, with close dribbling skills one could only marvel at and a work rate to match it. Everything he did was for the good of the team.

Out in Barcelona, we conceded a really late goal which gave them a 2-0 lead and, to make matters worse, we were playing every couple of days in the league to try and catch up with the fixture congestion caused by our European run. It was at this time that Tommy Doc came up with his master plan to give us a fighting chance in the return leg. Enlisting the help of the local fire brigade, Doc got them to flood the pitch to cause a temporary postponement, which gave us a bit more time to rest our weary limbs. When the match finally took place, Venner and Bridgo had both been sold and Charlie made his Chelsea debut on a waterlogged pitch which wasn't remotely suited to his playing style. Fortunately, Barcelona were equally ill-prepared to deal with such a surface and two late own goals helped us to a draw. The second of them was scored by their goalkeeper, whose son Pepe Reina would go on to represent Liverpool a good few years later.

Once again, the toss of a coin was used to determine the venue for the decider. Chopper called incorrectly, and so off we went to the Nou Camp, nine days after the Division One season had ended, to see who would face Real Zaragoza in the final, which was scheduled to take place at the start of the following season.

Although not many Chelsea fans were able to get back to Barcelona, we knew we were going to be well supported back home as the club would be "beaming" the game back to Stamford Bridge for a crowd of just under 10,000. What a wonderful idea, so it's a pity we weren't able to give them anything to shout about. We were drubbed 5-0, a real hammering and such an anti-climax to conclude a thrilling journey.

Although it had a disappointing end, we thoroughly enjoyed the run in that competition. Every round seemed to be against a top team and that is what made it exciting for us and for the fans. They were seeing players they had only read about, so the crowds were massive. And we loved playing at Stamford Bridge, especially under lights. It made it more exciting and the Chelsea fans were fantastic and really made themselves heard. We had played friendlies in pre-season against foreign sides but they weren't competitive. This was a different experience.

There was also lot of press at the time about the World Cup coming up and about whether players would be in the squad or not. These games were a great advert for us. A load of us were all in contention for the biggest football event ever to be held in England, and I have no doubt the Fairs Cup run played a huge part in that.

Even so, my disillusionment with life at Chelsea was growing. I've looked back through my old scrapbook and found this quote, which I apparently gave to the Daily Mirror just before the end of the season:

"I shall not be content until I get satisfaction from the club. There are things the club and I have not seen eye to eye about. I don't mind where I go. But I don't want to stay at Chelsea."

It wasn't about the football, it was the club. So many of the lads were moving on and you were left wondering what the atmosphere and the spirit would be like. When Docherty went and bought Alex Stepney, who was a highly rated goalkeeper at Millwall, it was a case of seeing how he settles and if he looks good he can replace the Cat. Well, Doc picked the wrong bloke to mess with and Catty was more than ready to play the game. If that's how he wants to do it, then I'm ready to go.

There wasn't any revolt in the group, but a few of us were perhaps looking at it as a good thing coming to an end and maybe it was time to move. I don't think it was down to wages or anything, as none of us were money seekers. It was disappointment at what had happened and perhaps thinking it was time to seek pastures new. Most of my mates had already flown the nest, for various reasons, so it wasn't as if that was drawing me to stay. I was thinking I could maybe see how I'd do elsewhere.

For all of that, though, I never came close to leaving. Sure, there were whispers that so and so might be interested, but nothing concrete ever came up. I was thinking of trying something new, as it might freshen me up, but then when Catty didn't go it was another incentive for me to stay. He'd been worried he wouldn't be the No.1, but when they sold Stepney just a few months after signing him he was reassured he'd be top dog. Or perhaps that should be top cat! We'd been great mates for eight or nine years, room-mates for a lot of that time, so it was a case of staying together and battling on.

When George Graham left for Arsenal a little while afterwards, it came back to me that they'd be interested in me if I was thinking of leaving Chelsea. There was never an official approach, but often that's how clubs would do business in those days. We always did that sort of thing. For example, when Marvin Hinton joined us from Charlton I'd previously played with him for England Under-23s and I was always on at him to make his way across London to play at the Bridge. Sometimes your club would have no knowledge of it, you'd do it off your own back just to get your mates to join you or to sign someone you thought would be decent.

If Arsenal had come in and made an offer for me, I honestly can't say how I'd have reacted, but I don't think I'd have been interested. They were only just starting to get a decent side together, whereas we were always rubbing their nose in it. I had a great record against them throughout the Sixties. Even so, they were always a glamorous club and they had a great stadium. But Chelsea was the love of my life. It still is. You go through rough patches in any relationship; it got to a stage when things seemed to be piling up on me, especially when we'd just been so close to something really big the year before. I started to question whether success would really happen. But would I have left? Not a chance.

It was a difficult time, make no mistake about that. The atmosphere changed drastically when all the lads went their separate ways. There'd been so many of us who had come to the club in the same 12-month period and the core of that was ripped out in the space of a similar amount of time. It was like leaving school. We'd had such a good time together and when the other lads started coming through, it wasn't as if they weren't fun – it was more a case of me and others growing up and these younger lads having a different sense of humour. That's only natural. But it changed the dynamic.

I never fell out of love with Chelsea. The club has been my whole life and it was definitely the right decision to stay. I know others regretted their decision to move on, but as devastated as I was when I eventually left, I knew then it was the right time to go. This wasn't. I still had unfinished business.

12

ENGLAND

For any footballer, representing the country of your birth is one of the greatest honours there is. I was fortunate enough to do so on three occasions. Writing those words still sends a tingle down my spine. I played for England three times. Me!

Several times in this book I've made reference to the fact that my football career owes plenty to good fortune and I know what you must be thinking: yeah, yeah, that's what they all say. But, genuinely, I was a lucky footballer. The story of how I won my first England cap proves that.

Now, during my career I knew a few players who got out of training any chance they got. I'm not naming any names, but if they are reading this they'll know who they are. Anyway, at the start of an international week in November 1962, I got into training on the Monday morning and I just didn't fancy it. I was known to have problems with my hamstrings, so I decided to go and see Harry Medhurst to let him know I had a slight strain and would need a bit of treatment. After a few minutes, I said to Harry: "It must be tea and biscuit time by now?"

That was the worst-kept secret about spending time in the treatment room. Harry always had a packet of biscuits at the ready, just as he would usually have a fag hanging out of his mouth as he administered the treatment, which usually consisted of little more than light manipulation of the area causing you a bit of concern.

Just as we settled down to our cuppa, Tommy Docherty walked in. He looked surprised to see me. "Hey Bob, I didn't know you had a problem. What's up?"

"It's not too bad, Tom," I replied. "I just want to make sure I'm all right for next week, which I'm sure I will be if I take it easy."

"Oh good, you'll be right for next week, will you?" he said, knowing full well there was nothing wrong with me. "You know, Bob, it's a real pity you're not going to be better before next Saturday. I've just had a phone call from Walter Winterbottom and he wanted you to get yourself to the England team hotel because you were going to be playing against Wales on Wednesday. There's been an outbreak of injury and illness among the wingers. I'd better let him know the bad news that it seems to have spread to here."

I had been lying on my stomach up to that point and you've never seen someone shoot up on to their feet quicker. "You're joking, aren't you?" I said, almost pleadingly.

"No, Bob. I'm deadly serious."

There was still no sign of a smile on his face, but I risked it anyway. "Well, actually, it's not that serious. I think I should give it a go. I'm sure it will hold up."

At that point, he burst out laughing. "Now get yourself off that couch and get home and into your suit – they're waiting for you over at Hendon," he bellowed. "And if they're daft enough to pick you in the team, make sure you enjoy it!"

Sensing I may have outstayed my welcome, I quickly scarpered, not forgetting to grab my boots on my way out. I was going to need them.

When I walked into the hotel, I just couldn't believe it. Looking around and seeing all of these players I'd seen and heard so much about. There weren't many I knew personally; obviously there was Greavsie, but I didn't know many that well. Even so, I didn't feel that out of it and I certainly wasn't completely star-struck or anything like that. I remember seeing Bobby Charlton, who I'd played against before, and he was really good when I walked in.

When you are drafted in like I was, as a replacement player, it's hard to escape the feeling that you weren't as good as the rest of these guys. They'd all been picked first time – I was only there because of injuries and drop-outs. In the whole squad there was one injury and two were ill. What did the three have in common? They all played left-wing! Better to be lucky than good...

There's no doubt I was in the right place – or, should I say, played the right position – at the right time, but I also don't want people thinking I completely fluked it. I was in great form for Chelsea and was among the goals in the early months of our promotion season. All of my team-mates at the Bridge felt it was justified and they were very congratulatory.

When the game itself came around, Wembley Stadium wasn't even a third full for this Home Nations match against Wales, but that didn't matter to me. I'd played at schoolboy level, I'd represented the Under-23s, but now I was a full England international. What a thrill.

We won the game 4-0, which I was obviously delighted about, but I wasn't quite so pleased with my own performance. Sure, I'd done well, but I'd fallen into that old trap of keeping things far too simple rather than playing my usual game. It's a common English trait: step up a level, revert to the basics and don't try anything fancy. I stuck to the left flank, I worked my socks off, but there was really only one moment which stood out, when I sent over a teasing cross which perhaps should have been turned in. I simply didn't get into the game enough.

Even so, I felt good when the full-time whistle was blown, bringing down the curtain on a 4-0 win over our Welsh neighbours on my senior international debut. Everyone in the dressing room was happy and I remember Mr Winterbottom coming over to me and saying: "Thanks for the way you reacted to such a late call-up."

I told him it was an absolute pleasure, but I knew I'd never get the opportunity to play for him again. This was his last match as manager, ending his 16-year spell in charge of the national team, and it's incredible to look back on the criticism he received around that time.

There were some who claimed there was no place for coaching in football and that it was a waste of time! We may have won the World Cup four years later, but is it any wonder English football found itself trailing behind the rest of the world for so long?

The next day's edition of the Daily Mirror ran a report of the game in which they noted I had come in for Mike O'Grady, who had a heavy cold, and that I would "play many more times for England. But that will be in his true position and he will leave behind more glowing, golden memories than this". It was very kind of Bill Holden to write that. Certainly kinder than John Bromley, who wrote under the headline The Man Who Was Out Of Place: "As the game settled, so Tambling became more unsettled. After two full seasons as an inside forward, one felt he was itching to get inside."

I'd obviously done something to impress someone, though, as when the next game against France came around I was in the squad once again, this time on merit rather than a replacement for all the drop-outs. It was the second leg of our European Nations' Cup qualifier against France, which was played in February 1963 after we had drawn 1-1 at Hillsborough in October.

The competition would soon develop into a proper summer tournament, which is now known as the European Championship and features 24 teams, but back then we played two-legged ties similar to the European Cup and it was only from the semi-final stage that the tournament was hosted by only one country.

Alf Ramsey had already been confirmed as England's manager before my debut, but he didn't take charge of the game as Walter was given a fitting farewell at Wembley, so this was his first match in charge. It was a strange situation, as at that time the man in the hot seat didn't select the squad and it was left up to a selection committee to pick the players. And, I may be wrong, but I don't recall any of the men on the panel being ex-coaches or players.

147

Without being rude about committees, unless you've got the right people, people who know football, it can often just be a case of them asking: "Well, who's playing the best? Let's pick them." I suppose that makes sense on one level – this guy is playing well, he's having a great season, let's pick him. And it certainly counted for me because I was having a very good year, as we all were at Chelsea, and I'd been scoring goals for fun until Christmas.

Suddenly, I found myself in the same England team with the likes of Bobby Smith, Jimmy Greaves and Bobby Charlton. If you look at those names, something should hit you: they are all goalscorers. It seemed as though we were all playing well for our clubs and the people in charge of the selection looked at it and said: "He's scoring goals, let's pick him."

As a result, I don't think the team was particularly balanced and players weren't necessarily suited to the role they were given. Something didn't add up – the style didn't match the players. Does this sound familiar? It seems to have been a problem England have had for many, many years. On this occasion, it wasn't down to the manager, so you had to feel sorry for Alf. His first game in charge and he's given a group of players he probably wouldn't have picked himself.

I have to say, I was feeling a lot more nervous for this game than my debut. Nothing had been at stake on the Wembley turf in November, whereas this was a crucial game on which our European Nations hopes rested. However, I also knew I could count on the support of some of my best mates as Barry Bridges, Allan Harris, Ken Shellito and Terry Venables flew over to Paris to cheer me on. That really meant a lot to me and was another indication of the wonderful team spirit we had in the Chelsea squad at that time.

ENGLAND

The game was played at the Parc des Princes, a stadium Chelsea have got to know very well with their recent Champions League tussles against Paris Saint-Germain. On this freezing February day, however, the pitch resembled a concrete pavement. It was absolutely rock solid, far from the best conditions to play a football match.

If it sounds like I'm making excuses, then you've probably already guessed that we didn't win. In fact, we were given quite a going over, although at one stage it was close. In the first half we just didn't adapt to the conditions, whereas they performed so well on it – they were a smaller side than us and big players like Bobby Smith found it near on impossible to turn and keep balance.

We found ourselves 3-0 down at half-time, but we rallied to pull one back through Bobby Smith and then, with 15 minutes to go, came the moment I will never forget.

Despite being given a bunch of players he hadn't picked himself, Alf did his best to mould us into a team, and one thing we spent a lot of time on was rehearsing set-pieces. For some unknown reason, I was to follow the two big fellas in on the run; being a small guy, I thought I should have gone first, but I was hardly going to speak up ahead of only my second international game. The two lads went in and took the players, I went in later and had a free header.

Now, Neil Barnett, Chelsea's matchday announcer, loves telling me: "Well, you didn't score too many with your head." But anyone who gives me any stick about it now knows I scored with my head in a cup final at Wembley and in an international match for England!

My first goal for England – I was walking on air.

I cannot fully explain with words alone my exhilaration. This is every schoolboy's dream: to represent your country and score a goal. The only part of that dream is that you never see yourself scoring and then losing the match, but I can look back on the moment now and see that I am part of an elite group of players to have scored for England. I am part of history. There are not many players that get the opportunity to score for their country and I am so very proud to say that I did.

Suddenly, we were back in the game and in with a shout of progressing. We had a lot of big names in our side: Jimmy Armfield was the skipper and we also had Bobbys Moore and Charlton, as well as Greavsie up front. But there was to be no grandstand finish. We conceded twice more to lose 5-2. With England hosting the next World Cup, that was it for competitive internationals for the next three or so years.

Worse was to follow after the match. In those days, there would be a banquet after the game at which both groups of players would sit down with all of the VIPs from both countries. Suddenly, one of the lads jumped up, suffering from cramp. Another followed suit, then another – there must have been about five or six really struggling. You'd see the chair start to jerk and the player would jump up with a pained expression on his face. It was quite funny to watch who would be the next, but you felt for the lads who were hit by it.

I was really disappointed about the result and the game itself. I really took it to heart that we'd been beaten by such a big score, especially while representing our country. I was listening to the conversations around the table. These were experienced internationals who had probably been through this before, but it was as if it was a Sunday afternoon game. "Oh, we got beat, like.

But they were the better side." There's me heartbroken at how crap we had been! I thought for a long while after that match that if that's how they think about international football...

It was the same for me at club level whenever we lost a game. It would take me two days to get over it, I was absolutely sick about it and replaying how we'd played in my head, thinking of what had gone wrong. And this was a couple of hours after the game, at most, and they lightly dismissed the defeat. Maybe it was just because I was new to the squad, or perhaps the older players didn't want to show they'd been ground down by the defeat. I also think it was a bit of the old stiff upper lip from the British. "Yeah, we can take it. We don't care, we didn't want it anyway!" Even so, it shocked me.

I didn't reappear for England until just before the World Cup in 1966, an absence of three years. I'm not exactly sure why there was this gap. My name was on the scoresheet consistently for Chelsea throughout that time, but then England did have Greaves and Roger Hunt scoring plenty of goals. To displace people like that, especially Greavsie, was no small feat. He was a tremendous goalscorer and, although I was scoring freely as well, I was never in his class. I've always said that. When he left Chelsea, I wasn't the next Jimmy Greaves – I was just Bobby Tambling, as I am now. There could only be one Jimmy Greaves. It's the same for all players. All this talk about so and so being the next Messi or whoever; there will never be another Messi.

So, the caps never came rolling in and, I have to say, I wasn't waiting by the telephone for a call-up in that time, nor would I bother checking the squad in the paper. Deep down, I knew. You've got to be honest with yourself. If you are, you don't expect things that aren't there for you.

There was a preliminary squad of 40 selected for the World Cup about halfway through the 1965/66 season, perhaps even a little later, and there were a few Chelsea players on the list: Bridgo, Catty, Marvin Hinton, John Hollins, Ossie and Venner. I've got to be honest, I did check the papers this time to see if my name would be on it. When it wasn't, I thought that was the end of my World Cup dream. Although it was half-expected, it was still hard to take. Every player would love to play at a World Cup in their own country.

Even so, I continued going along nicely for Chelsea and the press boys – well, the ones that liked me – were always on the phone telling me: "You could make the 28-man squad for pre-tournament training." I was ignorant of the fact England could pick someone from outside the initial 40 among the 28. They kept telling me: "You're the only left-sided player they've got up front." They stirred up the emotions – I started to convince myself I was in with a chance. And I was. I was in! Despite the lads from the press doing their best to convince me I'd make the final 22, I was still unconvinced, but at least I had a chance.

Before the final squad was to be announced we had a game against Yugoslavia and I played down the left-hand side. I wouldn't say left-wing, as such. Alf would go on to win the World Cup without playing wingers – the wingless wonders, as they were known – and he wanted people who would work in that system. Without being boastful, I think I'd have fitted into that category. I was known as a worker, which was another tick next to my name. I thought that if I worked hard and, as the press boys pointed out, there weren't many left-sided players in the squad, I might have half a chance.

We beat Yugoslavia 2-0 and, while I wasn't man of the match

or anything, I felt I'd done well enough. Then we went off to the training camp at Lilleshall, which would be followed by the final squad selection and a two-week tour of Scandinavia. It would turn into a complete nightmare for me.

At Lilleshall, I was sharing a room with four other players: Bobby Moore, Geoff Hurst, Martin Peters and Catty. Bobby was the only established international in the room. Geoff and Martin were in the same boat as me in that they'd been capped a couple of times, but that was it. Geoff actually scored his World Cup final hat-trick on his eighth appearance, believe it or not. And two or three of those games were in the pre-tournament tour. Catty had hardly played, but there was no shame in that – no one was replacing Gordon Banks at that stage.

There was a lot of serious talk in that room, let me tell you. As well as weighing up our own fate as far as the squad was concerned, we chatted about the merits of other players, Alf's tactics, how we might fit into the team, everything. Of course, we had a bit of a laugh as well, but it was certainly more serious than usual.

Obviously, I knew Catty already and he was – and still is – one of my best mates, but it was really nice to get to know the other three. Little did I know they'd go on to become three of the heroes of England's World Cup triumph just a matter of weeks later!

I'd always thought Bobby was a bit of a "nose up" kind of guy, if you know what I mean. Well, it turns out I couldn't have been further from the truth; he didn't think he was better than the rest of us, he was just incredibly shy. Once you got to know him, he was a lovely fella. It was the same with Martin, too.

Hursty, meanwhile, was a typical forward – he'd say it as he saw it. I remember playing with him in the Under-23s squad and we'd had a couple of chats then. It quickly became apparent that he was an intelligent forward player. He would say things that were new to me, so I learned so much from playing with him. I remember thinking how great it must be at West Ham for them to be talking about football like that. That was part of the beauty of playing international football; you were able to learn from players who you would otherwise only have faced when you played against them.

Ironically, one of the nicest guys I met through representing England was someone who became one of the most disliked players of his era because of how he played the game: Nobby Stiles. I first played with him in England schoolboys and we won near enough everything. I got to know him really well from that. Whenever we came up against each other for our club sides, we'd always have a chat after the game and congratulate whoever had won. And everyone else hated him! People called him a "hardman" and said he was dirty. He was tough, sure, but he was an honest footballer who made sure you had to be at the top of your game to get the better of him.

Shortly after we'd arrived at Lilleshall, and before we'd even had a proper training session, the lads decided to play a game of cricket. I was fielding when someone played a tremendous shot and smacked the ball across the grass and straight past me into these fir trees. I tried to chase it down, not realising that on the other side there was a slope which must have gone down about nine feet. I had a split-second decision to make: stop and potentially go head over heels or take flight and try to land without doing myself any damage. Well, I went for the latter and, of course, it all went horribly wrong.

ENGLAND

I had badly jarred my ankle, which required treatment in the morning and caused me to miss my opportunity to really impress Alf. I knew I couldn't afford to miss another session if I was to have any chance of making the final squad, so the following day I pretended I was fine to train. We did the usual ball work and that developed into a five-a-side game and then a full-blown 11-a-side match. I simply wasn't able to do myself justice. As the session wore on, I could feel my World Cup dream slipping away from me with every minute that passed. As we headed back to the dressing room, I knew it was over.

If I'm honest with myself, I don't think it was the wrong decision. If I was to be picked, it would probably have been at the expense of Terry Paine, who played for Southampton, or John Connelly of Manchester United. They were both right-wingers and England didn't have a left-sided player, which is why the press boys were giving me that push. The fact Alf didn't play with wingers, as shown by both of those players making only one appearance each in the tournament, didn't really support their theory.

Alf made the right decision with me and he picked a good squad. He got exactly what he was looking for: a solid squad that played as a team. And then won the World Cup with those players. How could I honestly have any grievances about not being selected? There are still people to this day who question why he left Greavsie out after his injury. Yes, he is one of the greatest goalscorers to ever play the game, but his replacement was in good form and repaid the manager by scoring a hat-trick in the final.

In the years that followed the World Cup, people knocked Alf for various reasons, but I thought he was a great manager.

155

People know about his achievements for England, but how many of you are aware of what a great job he did with Ipswich Town before he took charge of the national team? They had been in the Third Division South when he became manager in 1955, the same year as Chelsea were winning the First Division. They won promotion in 1957 and again in 1961, and then in 1962 the Tractor Boys were champions of England. That was the year we were relegated after finishing bottom of the top flight.

Let me tell you, that Ipswich squad comprised a very ordinary set of footballers. I mean no disrespect by that, but they were simply hard-working and well-drilled, lacking any star quality. They had this one tactic which seemed to catch out near enough every side in the division, and when I tell you what that was, you're not going to believe me.

They had a chap on the left wing called Jimmy Leadbetter. He looked a lot older than he was and he certainly didn't look as if he could run as most wingers could. Alf instructed him to drop deep, which was pretty uncommon for wide players in those days, and it completely threw sides off. Right-backs would move up the field to go and mark him, at which point Ipswich would knock the ball into that space for either of their two centre-forwards, Ted Phillips or Ray Crawford, to run on to. It was usually the latter who benefited from it and I shudder to think how many teams fell for this simplest of tactics.

The manager got the utmost out of that side and it just goes to show how important a top tactician can be if they are able to work out the right set of tactics for the set of players at their disposal. You just have to look at the Leicester City side which became the most unlikely of Premier League champions. Alf did that with Ipswich and won the league and he did it with England and won the World Cup. Although I should probably add that teams seemed to figure Ipswich out the following season. They'd won only a couple of their first dozen or so matches when Alf was given the England job.

I had every respect for him as a manager. He had absolutely no doubt about what he wanted and he knew how to put a team together. I don't think anyone would say England had the best players at that World Cup, but they were certainly the best team and that's really what football is all about. It's a sign of a great manager when he is willing to sacrifice individual brilliance for the good of the team.

What stands out most about Alf was that he was a very honourable guy; he was straight down the line, not the funniest – although, he could come out with the odd wisecrack – and he wanted to beat Scotland with a vengeance! I remember later on playing for him after I received a belated call-up for a game between the best players from the English league against the cream of the crop in Scotland. We won 3-1 and I scored our third goal. That was the last time I worked with Alf.

Like all Englishmen, I was absolutely delighted to see us win the World Cup. I wasn't at Wembley for the final as we'd already started our pre-season tour with Chelsea, which just happened to be in the one place we didn't want to be for that game. You guessed it, we were in West Germany! Obviously, it worked out well in the end, and the Germans in our hotel, where we had watched the game, were gracious in defeat.

Even though I wasn't involved, I still felt part of that success, just as I did when England won the Rugby World Cup in 2003. I'm a proud Englishman and I'll always support the team, which is something I feel we should do more as a nation. Look at Ireland's record at international tournaments under Jack Charlton and see just how far fanatical support can take a team. I've never seen anything like it. When they go to a tournament, they enjoy it. That sums me up in many ways, as I just want to enjoy everything I do. It's great to win, but the journey is the most important thing. You know with all sports you are going to lose at some point, so as long as everyone gives their all, you can't ask for more. The Irish fans have got a little bit of extra fire that they bring to the games. They are only too pleased to be there, whereas perhaps in England we feel as though we belong and the trophy is ours for the taking.

Going back to my international career, the Yugoslavia game before the World Cup proved to be the end of the road for me with England, but I loved every minute of it and learned so much. Spending time with players from all over the country and finding out how things were done at other teams was a real eye-opener for me. If you're a footballer and you think you know it all, then you're going about it completely the wrong way. You can learn something from every single player you come across.

One example I'm going to give you is when Tommy Baldwin signed for Chelsea from Arsenal. "Sponge" had this fantastic way of fooling his marker when the ball was played up to him; the ball would be a yard away from Tommy and you wouldn't know which way he was going to turn, but he'd flick his foot one way or the other and he, along with the ball, would be gone. That's only one little thing, but then you add it to something else you learn from another player and then another, and so on. Suddenly, you've built up this whole stack of tricks.

I sometimes wonder about the game today. Players are incredibly skilful and they've got some fantastic tricks up their sleeve, but they spend hours and hours working on these tricks alone. My nephew sees players do something on telly and then he'll go out in the back garden and do nothing but work on perfecting that. He'll ask me: "What do you think?" I always give him the same response: "Very nice – but how many times are you going to use it in a game? Why don't you learn the things you know you're going to use in a game that will benefit you?"

Fancy keepie-uppies might be good for your confidence, but you've got to transfer it to game skills. You can't run down the wing doing keep-ups, as nice as that sounds. Chopper Harris would have you in row Z!

There's a lot more to this sport than just skill. You've got to be able to read the game. Every match will throw something different at you, and it's how you deal with it. That's the difference between scoring 50 goals for Chelsea and 200. But enough about Frank Lampard...

Back when I was on the ground staff at Chelsea, I'd watch foreign teams warming up before Fairs Cup games at the Bridge and there'd be at least one player who stood out because of all the fancy tricks he was doing. You'd think: "Cor, he must be a good player." But then he'd be crap – he showed you everything he had in the warm-up.

The best advice I could give a kid would be to work on both feet. Bobby Charlton had two incredible feet. Unfortunately, I wasn't the same! But my brother was one of the best two-footed players I ever saw and it all came from practising with a tennis ball. He could hit the old leather footballs like a rocket with either foot. You couldn't tell which side was his strongest. If you can use both feet, you've got a bigger advantage because you're almost doubling your ability.

I was all left side, and I thought I had a very good left foot. I had a right foot for standing on – and would probably have been better off with a wooden foot – and I often thought I should have followed this advice I was given early on: "Put a plimsole on your good foot and a boot on your bad one."

Two-footed players open up the game. Defenders don't know where to go. With all of the stats and knowledge today, I'd have struggled with only one decent foot!

I've always said there is a very fine line between different levels of football. From the top flight to the next level, there's a fine line between the two when it comes to individual players. Some players are brilliant in the second tier but then can't do it when they step up a level, or perhaps they're a star in the Premier League but the Champions League is a bridge too far. It's the same thing when you go up to international level. You've got a level you perform easily at and then the next level might be a step too far. I think I was just the wrong side of that fine line when it came to international football. I don't mind admitting that.

I've got one final story for this chapter about England, which I've somehow managed to string out far longer than my international career itself. Now, anyone who knows me will tell you I was never too fussed about football memorabilia. For me, the memories of being out on the pitch and the camaraderie with my team-mates are just two of the things which count for so much more than old shirts, medals, caps and all of that sort of thing. But something happened a few years ago which made me realise there is far more meaning to these things than I thought.

ENGLAND

At some point in the early 1990s, I lost my England caps. Well, actually, I didn't lose them as such. They were destroyed in a very unfortunate accident by one of my family and I almost didn't put this story in as I don't want to embarrass anyone. But this is a book about my life after all, so here it goes.

My son – I'm not going to say which one – was looking after the caps. He's mad about the memorabilia. When I split up with my first wife, he decided he was going to be the man to look after them. He was so proud of the caps, so proud of what I had done in my career.

Then he met a new girlfriend and they moved in together. I don't think she understood much about football and she certainly didn't understand these fancy caps with tassels on, which must have looked like a grammar school cap to her, and they were put into a plastic bag and kept in the airing cupboard. Unfortunately, the tank leaked and they didn't notice for a few weeks. When she finally discovered them, they had gone mouldy. In the bin they went, destined for the rubbish tip on the Kinsella Road on the outskirts of Cork. You get these people who like to go rummaging through these tips to see what they can find – one man's junk being another's treasure, as the saying goes – and I often wonder if someone discovered them.

I only found out a few years later. It wasn't the type of thing we discussed when we met up and I never knew who had what. I think my son was terribly upset about it, and probably quite embarrassed. I can't remember how I found out about it, but I know I said something like: "You didn't do it on purpose, I know that. These things happen."

Because I hadn't had them for so long, I wasn't all that upset about losing them. If anything, I felt worse for my sons, because

I knew just how much they meant to them and it was obviously something nice for them to remember me by when my life ends.

Over the years, various people would ask to see my caps and I'd have to explain what had happened. "Why don't you have a word with the FA?" they'd ask. "They must give out replacements."

I don't know why, but I never followed that advice until I was attending Chelsea's game against Crystal Palace in the 2013/14 season. I noticed a lad who used to be the assistant secretary of the club, if memory serves, and he was only a youngster when I knew him. I asked him if he was still involved with Palace, to which he replied: "No, I moved on to the FA, but I'm now retired from there."

"Ah, now you're a gent I could ask a question to, then."

I told him the story and then asked the million dollar question: "Do you think there is any chance of getting them back?"

"The best man to ask is right here in this room," he said, pointing over to a Chelsea official. "That's David Barnard, who is the club secretary. He would know the right people at the FA to approach."

I had a quick chat with David and he told me to leave it with him, he'd make enquiries on my behalf. But months seemed to pass by without anything happening and I was making myself miserable just thinking about my missing caps and how important they were for the people around me. But I think it was only so important to them because they knew it would make me happy to be able to show them off to people who visit.

Then, about a year or so later, Chelsea were playing against Crystal Palace again at Stamford Bridge. It was a day many of those reading this will remember fondly as the day Chelsea became Premier League champions for the fourth time, but for me it was made even more special.

Now, I wouldn't really say I have had any football heroes since I was a kid, but there are always players who stand out as someone you'd like to meet because you respect them so much. Gary Lineker was one such person for me. He was the perfect role model for aspiring footballers: never booked in his whole career, scored goals by the bucketload, a consummate professional who appeared to be an absolute gentleman off the pitch.

I'd never met him before, but I noticed him in the directors' lounge at the Palace game. I said to Val: "Oh look – that's Gary Lineker. I wouldn't mind chatting to him later."

The next thing I know, he's presenting me with my England caps! You could have blown me away with a feather. I couldn't speak for emotion. In fact, I honestly can't remember what Gary said to me as he gave them to me because I was so overwhelmed. But I do know what we spoke about afterwards: goals! I had so many questions about his career and I appreciated how much he had done for England. In return, I know he was extremely pleased to have been involved in such a lovely gesture.

I couldn't finish my lunch before the game, I was just so excited. I felt like a little kid again. It was marvellous to have them back and I couldn't believe how much time had elapsed since I had last seen them. They are now proudly on display at home and I can only thank the people at Chelsea and the FA for being so kind as to keep this piece of history alive for me and my family. It was a great moment and I can never thank everyone enough.

13

FINALLY

Ever since I watched Stan Mortensen plunder a hat-trick for Blackpool in an FA Cup final, it was my dream to play beneath the Twin Towers and compete for the most prestigious trophy in English football. It was the showpiece event of every season, the one game most footballers would have given their left arm to play in, and we had come so close in the previous two seasons, falling in the semi-finals both times. I knew if the opportunity came along again we could not let it slip.

It was also in the back of my mind at this time that I was edging ever closer to Roy Bentley's club record tally of goals, which stood at a nice round figure of 150. Maybe I'm alone in thinking this way, but as a kid I never thought about being able to achieve something like this. Most of my dreams were of lifting trophies – although, I must admit, most of them also involved me scoring the winning goal – but I'd be lying if I said it wasn't something that excited me. I was only 10 away from matching Roy at the top of the standings and anxious to do it as quickly as possible. Time was on my side but, as I'd seen with Ken Shellito and was soon to discover with Ossie, you never know what this fickle game has in store for you.

Our season kicked off with a trip to the Boleyn Ground and, judging by the atmosphere in the ground and the build-up from the press, you'd have thought we were facing the team which had won the World Cup. Geoff Hurst, Bobby Moore and Martin Peters were paraded before the game for a lap of honour and there was a real celebratory air about the place. By the end of the game that had all changed as Charlie Cooke, on his First Division debut, made a mug out of Moore and fired in a superb winner. Bobby needn't have felt too bad about falling for the Cooke shuffle and shimmy – he was simply the first of many.

Charlie settled into our side like a dream, which is testament to what a quality player he was. When we signed him he had the unenviable task of replacing Terry Venables, the man who so much of our play went through and the joker in our pack, the life and soul of the dressing room. Wherever we went or whatever we were doing, Terry could get a laugh. Charlie was a bit different – for starters, half of us couldn't understand a word he was saying. But we could all see what he could do with a football. He was a tremendous player, a skilled dribbler and very different in style to his predecessor. Charlie played with his head down so he could dribble, whereas Terry always had his head up, watching for the runners to make their runs or see how he could change the direction of play. Both were excellent players in their own way.

We found out pretty early on that Charlie was quite an easy target for a wind-up. All you had to do to get Cookie going was to tell him he looked as though he was putting on weight. He was constantly on the scales or telling you about the wonder diet he was on, always looking for the best way to prepare for games. Unfortunately, I don't think Charlie was the most disciplined. I remember listening to him explain his strict diet one day on our way to the dressing room before a match. Suddenly, he disappeared into the Bovril shop under the old East Stand and emerged a few moments later with a massive pork pie! And you never wanted to be injured at the same time as him – he could lead you astray, big time.

Charlie wasn't the only change to our side from the previous season. As well as Venner and Bridgo going out, we also lost Bert Murray, although Allan Harris had returned to the club from Coventry City and Alex Stepney came in during the summer to give us a second No.1 goalkeeper. You don't have to be a mathematician to figure out that two doesn't go into one, but Doc's plan was to rotate him and Catty. Alex made one appearance before transferring to Manchester United, where he went on to win the European Cup. So much for that experiment. George Graham was also sold early in the season, traded for Tommy Baldwin of Arsenal, which meant I was the only member of our free-scoring front four of the 1964/65 season remaining at the club. It also meant that half of the eight players involved in the Blackpool incident had now been sold. Don't cross the Doc.

Ossie had made great strides the previous season and was firmly established as our centre-forward and John Boyle was to play more games, which I was very pleased about. He was like Bert, not so much in their style of play or position, but in the amount of work they both got through. The one thing we still seemed short of were big centre-halves, which was a bit of a worry as most sides had a battering ram centre-forward up their sleeve.

In spite of our lack of height, we made a really solid start to the season and everyone seemed to be going along nicely except for me, as I struggled away to two goals from the opening eight games. Was the record playing tricks with my confidence? Was I too anxious in front of goal, knowing I was so close to leaving such a massive footprint at this football club? Perhaps. But all of that was about to be blown away in devastating fashion when we travelled up to Villa Park, which had been the scene of our two FA Cup semi-final disappointments.

Having struggled to hit the proverbial cow's backside in the early weeks of the season, everything came off for me in this game and I just seemed to keep finding myself in the right place at the right time. It was just one of those matches that every striker hopes they have once in their career – except Jimmy Greaves, who made a habit of it – and I scored five times in a 6-2 win. Three of the goals were with my right foot and I love to show the pictures of my goals to people like Neil Barnett. Spy always jokes with me about how many I'd have scored for Chelsea if I'd had a right foot and could head the ball! He reckons that if you've only got one foot, then you can't be a professional footballer, but I reply: "What about Puskas? He never used his right foot but he had probably the best left foot ever and was a world-class player. Should he have not been a pro?" He says there are always exceptions to the rule! Obviously, it's better if you can use both, but that's not to say someone who only has one good foot can't be a footballer. I can understand people who say all pros should be two-footed. But take myself. I was self-trained. Everything was with my left foot.

To give you some idea of how this game went for me, I was supposed to be going off just before I scored the fifth. I've heard people tell the story of how I'd already taken off one of my boots before I scored, but I'm sure I still had it on. I was signalling to the bench that I wanted to come off as I felt a twinge in my knee, and then suddenly we were on the attack again and the next thing I knew the ball was in the back of the net. George Hilsdon, who was known as Gatling Gun and is immortalised at Stamford Bridge by the weather vane which features at the ground, is the only man to have scored six in one game for the Blues and I did have a brief thought after the game that I should have stayed on to try to equal that. We were so dominant and there was still 15 minutes to play. Even so, it equalled the most goals by a Chelsea player in a league game – Gatling Gun scored his double hat-trick in an FA Cup win over Worksop Town – and only three other players have matched that feat. Can you name them all? The answer is at the end of this chapter.

That win took us to the top of the table and everything seemed to be going so well for us, especially going forward, where everything seemed to be clicking into place. Little did we know that after our next game, a win over Arsenal, big George was about to be swapped for The Sponge. He hadn't been at Chelsea that long, but what a player. I think the best football we played during my time at the club came with George in the side. His record doesn't tell the full story of how good he was:

102 games and 46 goals. How well that forward line worked with him in it. That's not to say Tommy wasn't a good player – far from it, in fact. He scored on his debut against Manchester City and went on to be a very successful player for the club, bringing different qualities to the side.

The timing of George's exit couldn't have been much worse, for less than a week later fate was to deal Peter Osgood and Chelsea the cruellest of hands. We travelled up to Blackpool for a League Cup match and, as you'll know by now, few of us had much reason to think highly of the place. I'm sure the Pleasure Beach is lovely, but I wouldn't risk going on one of the rides after the bad luck served up for us in that town.

Ossie was good at looking after himself in the face of some pretty brutal treatment from opposition centre-halves, but there wasn't much he could have done to avoid coming off second best in a challenge with Emlyn Hughes. I could hear his leg crack from where I was standing and it was immediately apparent he'd suffered a horrific injury. In those days, you always worried how someone would be affected by such an injury. I was fortunate to never suffer anything as bad as that, but I knew plenty of others who did; some never returned, others came back a shadow of their former self. We needn't have worried with Os, for he came back bigger and stronger than ever, but not without a lengthy spell out of the side.

Doc acted quickly to add some firepower by making Tony Hateley Chelsea's first-ever £100,000 signing. Tony was one of those big centre-forwards I'd mentioned earlier, the kind who gave our defenders sleepless nights, but he had a tough job to fill Ossie's shoes. We had a good mix of attacking players at our disposal, which allowed us to change things up depending on the situation and the opponents. Os was central to that as he was both an excellent targetman and a skilful centre-forward capable of linking up and playing people in. He was as good outside the box as he was in it. Tony had come straight out of the mould marked "old school centre-forward". He had a great scoring record, but the ball needed to be in the air for Tony to excel, whereas we tended to keep the ball on the deck. As Doc would later remark, rather unkindly, I must say: "Tony could trap the ball further than I can kick it", and that his passes should be marked "to whom it may concern".

I'll always have fond memories of Tony's debut, though, as it was a game of huge personal significance for me. I'd scored my 150th goal for Chelsea on 1 October in the match before Ossie broke his leg, but we were now approaching the end of the month and I still hadn't found the back of the net again when Spurs visited us for a midweek fixture at the Bridge. There was always something special about a London derby played under the floodlights, as if the crowd was somehow being powered by the artificial lighting to produce even more noise than usual. It all made for an electric atmosphere and the perfect stage on which to set a new Chelsea record.

It was a typical derby match in that the tackles were flying in and no quarter was given or, indeed, even asked, and added spice was provided by the return of Venner for his first game back at the Bridge. I could have certainly done with having him back in our ranks because none of our midfielders were looking for that pass in behind; everything was aimed at the head of big Tony. Had it not been for the brilliance of Catty in goal, then Spurs would have been out of sight, even Greavsie couldn't find a way past him.

We'd been playing for just shy of an hour when our tactics finally paid off, although not in the manner you may have expected. Tommy Baldwin, who always had a deceptively high leap on him, got above his man to flick the ball on to Hateley, who just about managed to get on the end of it before he was accidentally taken out by Pat Jennings. Penalty! Finally, the chance I'd been waiting for. I grabbed hold of the ball and placed it on the spot. I'd be fibbing if I told you my heart rate was steady at this point, but something wouldn't have been right if that wasn't the case. I took a few steps back and waited for the referee's whistle. Peeeeeeeep! I wasn't one for checking to see which way the keeper was going, I'd make my mind up nice and early and back my technique. I must have taken thousands of penalties before and I wasn't about to get silly with this one. I hit it cleanly; there was no way Pat was stopping this one. Sheer elation. Finally, the goal I had been waiting for was mine and, boy, did it feel good.

Roy Bentley left Chelsea in 1956, which meant his record had stood for 10 years. I'd have been happy with that, especially with a striker as good as Ossie with plenty of years ahead of him. Never in a million years did I think it would stand for 47 years and that the man to beat it would be a midfielder. Good on you, Frank. I know you enjoyed breaking the record as much as I did setting it, because you phoned me straight after and told me as much! And I had a good run with it, something which kept the fans talking about me years after I'd hung up my boots. Whenever they'd ask me about it, I'd reply that it was my life-time's work. My footprint in Chelsea's history.

When I scored that goal, it helped put us back to the top of the table, where we remained for a few weeks, but by the turn of the year we were suddenly shipping plenty of goals and had slipped down the table. It was clear our best hope of silverware was going to be the FA Cup and, for once, the draw was kind to us.

We beat Huddersfield Town, Brighton and the two Sheffield clubs to reach a third successive semi-final at Villa Park, this time against Leeds United. After a bright start to his Chelsea career, Tony Hateley only seemed to be able to score in the cup and he saved arguably his best for the semi as he powered home a fantastic header to put us in front in a tight and typically hard-fought game. Was there any other type of match against Leeds? We were just as dogged and determined as them, clinging on to our advantage. It was a case of third time lucky and finally I would get a chance to fulfil my Wembley dream with the Blues.

What's more, this wasn't just any FA Cup final. It was the first final of the 20th Century to be contested by two London clubs, which added an extra sprinkling of magic to what was already shaping up to be the biggest day of my life. Spurs stood in our way, but we had gone unbeaten against them in our two league games that season, including the 3-0 win in which I scored my 151st Chelsea goal, so we were confident of making that three matches and walking up those famous steps to collect the trophy.

The final was scheduled to take place in three weeks' time and everybody was looking forward to it immensely. Then it started to inch closer and the nerves began to kick in. Remember, this was just about the only match of the season that English football fans would get to see on television, so you weren't just performing in front of the fans in the crowd. We're talking millions tuning in for the biggest game of your career. Tommy tried to keep us calm with a week away in Brighton.

On the Friday night and Saturday morning, when we were back in London, you would have thought we were on our way to a party because we were so laid back. Everyone was having their hair done, stuff like that, just to make sure they looked their best for the big occasion. But it wasn't a wedding – this was the FA Cup final, the biggest game of the year. The biggest game in Chelsea's history at the time. Are we going to take this seriously or what? Then, when we got to the ground a couple of hours before kick-off, we walked out on the pitch and it hit us how serious this was.

We'd done such a good job of relaxing beforehand, but it had come at the expense of being fully prepared for the game. I think most players are at their most relaxed when they know their role inside and out – get that right and your mind is at ease. I can understand people getting really nervous before a big game, and you need a degree of nerves before any game to give you that edge. I've always believed that. But we went past that. By the time we were out in front of the crowd it was a case of: "Bloody hell – we're here!"

The cup final was what every footballer dreamed about at that time. Everyone remembered the cup winners. Who won the league in 1970? No idea. Who won the FA Cup? Chelsea. The magic of the cup was in full force at that time. It was very glamorous. I remember driving down Wembley Way passing the happiest of Chelsea fans. We'd given them what they had been waiting for – but it would all count for nothing unless we finished the job.

As I said, we were actually feeling pretty relaxed when we arrived at the stadium. This continued as we made our way to the dressing room, with people laughing and joking right up until it was time for us to head out. Something must have happened when we walked out of the tunnel, because it was at this point that our entire side seemed to be hit by FA Cup final jitters.

The poor fans who had waited for this moment for years were about to be let down so badly by the players. Hardly anyone in a Blue shirt performed to their usual standard. We went 2-0 down, deservedly so, when Jimmy Robertson and Frank Saul scored either side of half-time. The game was drifting away from us until I pulled a goal back with about five minutes to go. Boylers sent a cross into the middle and it looked to be a straightforward punch for Jennings, but he completely missed the ball and my header went into an empty net.

I had become the first player to score an FA Cup final goal for Chelsea at Wembley Stadium, a list which, as I write this, still only includes seven other names: Peter Houseman, Ian Hutchinson, Roberto Di Matteo, Eddie Newton, Didier Drogba, Frank Lampard and Ramires. But it would be no consolation unless we could turn the game around. You'd have thought we'd have thrown everything we had at Spurs, giving them the most uncomfortable finale they'd ever had. I'm sorry to say that wasn't the case – the game just fizzled out. It was the biggest disappointment of our lives and I'm sure it felt the same for the fans.

That's what hurt more than anything, the fact we were second best all over the pitch and never seemed to get going, even after the goal. We didn't just lose an FA Cup final, we didn't even show up for it. As I shook the hands of the triumphant Tottenham players, I always figured I'd have another chance to go back and play for that magical trophy. Little did I know it was my one and only shot. And we blew it.

BOBBY TAMBLING

Apart from me, the only other players to score five goals for Chelsea in a league game are Jimmy Greaves (who did it three times), George Hilsdon and Gordon Durie, who did it against Walsall in a Division Two match in 1989. Give yourself a pat on the back if you guessed all three correctly.

14

DOC'S
DOWNFALL

After the Blackpool incident, things were never the same for Tommy Docherty and Chelsea.

Sure, we'd had the Fairs Cup run the next season and then made it through to the FA Cup final at long last, but both of those campaigns ultimately ended in failure. Had we been able to secure silverware then there's every chance he would have been able to paper over the cracks for a little while longer, but everything began to unravel when we headed off for our post-season tour, which took in a stop to Bermuda. I've previously written about how much we looked forward to these tours, but I don't think anyone was best pleased to be on the plane this time. As well as the cup final disappointment there was a big row over bonuses. It all made for a pretty tense atmosphere and by the time we reached Bermuda everything was close to boiling point.

We played against a local side who didn't seem to understand the concept of a friendly match as they really went after us from the first whistle. We won 2-0, but Barry Lloyd was sent off for saying something untoward to the referee, and I could understand his frustration as every decision seemed to go against us even though they were kicking lumps out of us.

Things got even worse when we took on the national side and the referee sent off Tony Hateley for shouting at one of his team-mates! Doc was absolutely livid about this, rightly so, and he took his frustration out on the referee, who was a chap named Carlyle Crockwell.

At one stage it looked as though Tommy wanted to call us all in and be done with the whole thing, but we played out the rest of the second half and finished up winning 4-2. As we left the pitch, Doc really got stuck into the referee again. I don't know exactly what he said as I wasn't privy to their discussion, but, either way, the referee reported him to the Bermudan FA and the whole thing escalated from there.

If his behaviour on the field had been inappropriate, then I can only describe how he acted on the flight home as downright bizarre. We were all on one side of the plane, with the players towards the back and then the directors, club officials and coaching staff at the front. Doc decided he wanted to sit with all of us, so midway through the flight he moved to the back, and it was at this point his behaviour took a turn for the worse. There were loads of empty cola cans lying about the place and Doc decided it would be a good idea to start throwing them at all of us. But then he decided to take it a step further by hurling them in the direction of his superiors at the front of the plane. He was just messing about, trying to get us into trouble. Despite being the manager, he was just as bad as we were for carrying out pranks.

One of the air stewardesses came over and told him that this behaviour had to stop or else she'd tell the captain. Of course, that didn't deter him. If anything he got worse. So, the captain came back and told him we'd be landing as soon as possible, which would be in Scotland, and they would put him off the plane there if he couldn't behave. Little Chico Hamilton, only 16 years old and on his first trip with us, was sat nearby and Doc turned to the captain and said: "I'm sorry about this lad, he's only 16. He's just got into the squad, he's a bit nervous and he's just playing a few jokes." Poor old Chico. He went bright red. The captain said, "Sort him out. If he continues, you're off at Prestwick."

I don't think the club officials were over the moon with Tom at that point, but that sort of behaviour was just in his nature. I remember coming back from an away game up north and the lads were playing cards to pass the time. The club doctor was with us and, while he was not a smart arse as such, he was a police doctor as well, so he was a little bit different to what we were used to. Anyway, he asked if he could play and sat down with the lads. The ticket inspector was coming through to clip the tickets and Doc called him over. "Can you do anything about that guy who has just sat down with my lads? He's a professional gambler and I think he's about to take them to the cleaners."

The railway police got on at the next station and asked the doctor to get off. "I'm the club doctor," he pleaded. It just wasn't funny – Doc took it too far. About 10 steps too far! He was still a player in all but name and he was very young for a manager. But what he did, 90 per cent of the players couldn't even see that line, let alone cross it! He wanted to be one of the boys, he wanted to be accepted as one of us. I'm sorry, but you can't do that when you're the manager.

After the incident in Bermuda, Tommy faced an anxious wait to discover his punishment by the FA and matters weren't helped by a disastrous start to the new season. We had all hoped we were heading for bigger and better things after our run to the cup final a few months earlier, especially with Ossie back in action after his long injury lay-off. His return left us a bit overloaded up top, so Tommy sold Tony Hateley to Liverpool. The story goes that Bill Shankly phoned up Doc to enquire about him to be told: "Bill, 100,000 won't buy him." The Liverpool manager replied: "Aye, and I'm one of them!" I think he managed to knock a few grand off his asking price with that line.

By the end of September we were languishing in 19th place and had just been knocked out of the League Cup by lower league Middlesbrough. When the FA made their decision in the first week of October and Doc was handed a month-long suspension from any football activities, that was it. He handed in his resignation, toasted with a glass of champagne shared with the club's directors. That was Tommy to a tee – extravagant and unpredictable.

I would also like to make it clear that as much as what I have written may seem like me having a go at the Doc, I have so much respect for what he did at this football club and the way in which he pulled us up by the bootstraps when we were down in Division Two. He was a great innovator as a manager and he could make you feel 10ft tall. The only problem, as I say, was that he could take things too far with his banter. On this occasion, I think it cost him his job. It was the right time for him to go, which he knew himself. He still loves Chelsea Football Club and whenever I see him at events we'll have a good old chinwag. He truly is one of a kind. But, then again, so was his replacement.

Dave Sexton and Tommy Docherty were like chalk and cheese. Whereas Tom was dynamic, controversial and back-page material, Dave was a very intelligent coach and a master tactician. Tommy could do so much for you but then turn on you in an instance, but he also worked very hard to promote players, pushing them forward for international caps. We owe him a lot for that, but at the same time a lot of credit must go to Dave for adding skills to our repertoire. The pair harnessed together the energy, desire, cockiness and skill of all these young boys. They worked so well together and we were disappointed, but not surprised, when Dave had branched out on his own a couple of years earlier to take charge at Leyton Orient. It didn't really work out for him so he ended up coaching at Arsenal – and the board decided he was the perfect man to turn Chelsea into a force to be reckoned with.

It was a smart move going back to someone we all respected so much. We had been such a close-knit group in the early years of Doc's reign, so when he started to make changes to the dynamic it had an even bigger impact on the lads who stayed and affected both the team and the spirit within the group. To think it had all happened over a little hiccup in Blackpool, nothing more.

Something Dave always believed in was that, when we didn't have the ball, we should all be defenders. Right from the front men all the way back to Peter Bonetti in goal. He worked hard on this, both in his planning and convincing the players, in order to make it tougher for teams to score against us. He often told us it was the best team without the ball that would win the game. It makes everybody aware that just because they play in an attacking position they still have a duty to work hard off the ball, and that influence was there for all to see throughout his time at the helm

Dave was full of ideas taken from different sports, something that would help us just as much in our game. Once, when he was coaching under Tommy, he came in after training and told us to get ourselves changed because we were all going to Twickenham to watch the Varsity rugby match between Oxford and Cambridge. Before the game, he pointed out a few things for us to look out for. I don't think I was alone in having never seen a live rugby match before, me who had flunked an exam just so I didn't have to attend a rugby school!

The game wasn't the best, but it was tough and hard fought. The next day, Dave showed us how the overlapping runs these lads utilised so effectively was something we should get used to doing. He drilled that into us, over and over. We spent the whole training session working hard on it. Instead of a straight run on the inside or outside of their full-back, he wanted us to go around our man on the ball, which seemed to be the long route. We didn't see any sense in running 10 yards further to try and attack their full-back and I think he was waiting for one of us to bring this point up. He took us through it slowly with defenders in place against us. He said for me to go the way I wanted. So, I went to run inside the full-back who was facing Bert Murray and the man marking me had an easy job to just run alongside me as I tried to cut inside. Dave stopped us and asked if that is how it would happen in a game. Sure it was. They won't let us run in behind without marking us. Then he got us to do what he wanted, with me going around Bert on the outside, and it created a two against one opportunity as my marker was reluctant to come across to cover me.

The overlap was to play a big part in our tactics throughout the Sixties, and it was all thanks to a game of rugby. Our full-backs became experts very quickly and it wasn't long before other teams cottoned on and started trying to use the tactic to their advantage. Watch any game of football today and you'll see the full-back going around the outside to get in behind the opposition defence.

When a new manager comes in it is natural for players to be doubly determined to make a good first impression. That's just the way life is. I'm sure in your own working life there have been times when a new boss has come in and you've been eager to impress. Well, on Dave's first day in the job I was stuck in the treatment room, having struggled on for a good few weeks, and the specialist decided I needed to have an operation on my groin. I was to be out for nine weeks, which might not seem all that long to you, but as any footballer will tell you it feels like a lifetime whenever you are out of the team and can't train.

There are many things players dislike, but I think the worst is being injured. Of course you are missing games, which is probably the biggest downer, but outside of that you are usually off getting treatment on your own, missing out on the fun in the dressing room and all the laughs you have on the training ground. I always felt so sorry for anyone who was out injured, especially if it was a really serious one like Ken Shellito had suffered a couple of years previous which brought an early end to his career. But even if it was just a minor knock, I still moped around feeling sorry for myself.

During my convalescence, Dave Sexton bought Alan Birchenall from Sheffield United. Alan was a big inside-forward who had previously done well against Chelsea and he didn't take long to settle in both on and off the pitch, scoring just five minutes into his debut and quickly making friends with all the lads. Ossie was also doing well up front and looking as strong as ever after his lengthy injury lay-off, and the team was suddenly shooting up the table.

Everything Dave had wanted us to do and that we worked hard at was starting to pay dividends. After a slow start, we were improving all the time and Dave's ideas were really going down well with us all. Players were enjoying their football once more and the team was settling down.

Another astute purchase came in the form of David Webb, who would add strength to our defence. We'd been doing better on that front anyway as Dave had taught us plenty about how we could all be defenders when we were out of possession, as I touched upon previously. Everyone worked like defenders to get the ball back and it became a big thing among the group to hustle opponents when they had the ball. There was no standing back and thinking: "I'm a forward and I don't have to do that." No, it became a real source of pride for us all and it didn't seem to have a huge impact on our goalscoring output as we suddenly had three or four forwards all chipping with their fair share. Ossie led the way and, after seeing how down he was to have missed most of the previous season, I was delighted to see him at the top of both the goals and appearances tables at the club.

I was to have another dose of the injury curse, missing another 10 games at the end of the season, this time with an operation on my other groin. On this occasion, though, watching the games gave me a chance to stand back and see all the good things players are doing; the work rate, the running to make openings for others, always covering for one another. These are just a few of the things that go towards making a solid team and I actually didn't feel as bad as I usually would to be stuck on the sidelines. The future was looking bright again.

It was a real roller-coaster ride of a season. We'd seen a change of manager, which meant new ideas to learn and put into practice and new players to fit into our squad, and the team still finished sixth in the league. Tommy, meanwhile, had since taken the reins at Second Division side Rotherham United and, mirroring his spell at Chelsea, suffered relegation. He'd gone from managing one of the leading clubs in the country to Division Three in the space of eight months.

15

FRIENDS

You don't tend to see too many testimonial matches nowadays.

When I was playing, it certainly wasn't a rarity for an individual to spend a decade or more with the same club and a testimonial was a great way of thanking the player for his loyalty. You'd get to keep the gate receipts from the game, which was a huge amount of money to us and I suppose it went some way to looking after you in later life and rewarding you for missing out on all the signing on bonuses that could have come your way. Nowadays, the players certainly don't need the money from a testimonial match in those rare instances when they stay at the same club for 10 years.

The 1968/69 season was my testimonial year and the club arranged a friendly against Charlton Athletic to mark the occasion. They also produced a publication to celebrate my time at Chelsea, for which I must thank Albert Sewell, who was the programme editor at the time. I'm so grateful he put it together as I can look back on it now and remind myself of just how much I had enjoyed being part of the Chelsea family. In fact, it serves as an abridged history of my time at Stamford Bridge. If you hadn't reached this point of the book, I'd have recommended trying to pick up a copy on eBay and saving yourself the boredom of reading about my life as a footballer, but you've got this far…

As well as some great adverts – including one for a supplier of football club ties, a business run by the Tottenham Hotspur legend Dave Mackay – it also featured a few pearls of wisdoms from yours truly. I took supporters "Behind the dressing-room door", a few passages of which I have reproduced below to give you an idea of what it was like at Stamford Bridge before kick-off.

"You'll always find Peter Bonetti changing just inside the door on the right," I wrote. "Harry Medhurst has set out the kit in No1-12 order on the bench-seat that runs around three sides of the room (the baths, with streamers across the entrance to them, are on the other) and we always keep our same places.

"I like to be stripped and ready to go on the field 20 minutes before kick-off. Other players will while away the time tapping the ball about. Eddie, Ossie and Boylers, the main dressing-room jokers, can be relied on to provide a few bits of nonsense, and occasionally Dave Sexton will produce some new party-piece in the conjuring line. He has quite a touch of magic and it helps to keep the tension from showing.

FRIENDS

"As the buzzer, signalled from the referee's room, sounds and the last boot-laces are tied and socking tie-ups are done, we go round the dressing-room shaking hands and wishing each other luck.

"It began about three years ago. Before the opening game, we shook hands all round, wishing each other a good match and a good season. We won that day, and the handshakes have become a regular thing. I've not heard of anything like this in other clubs.

"The last words as we file out are from Dave Sexton. It's always a bright and cheerful send-off. Short and sweet, something like: 'Come on, my bonny lads. Go out there and enjoy yourselves... you can win this one... good luck.' Suddenly, the longest hour of the week is over. Now for the game. Let's hear those cheers. They really do help."

That handshake ritual really was a funny old thing. Forget shouting and screaming or ranting and raving before kick-off. Just a quick shake of the hands and a "good luck, old boy". It's the perfect image of a gentleman's sport – and then you'd get someone like Chopper Harris kicking lumps out of the opposition!

Speaking of Chopper, he was one of the players I selected in my best-ever Chelsea XI, which I probably wouldn't make many changes to almost 50 years down the line. Here is the team I selected: Catty, Shellito, Mortimore, Chopper, McCreadie, Venner, Cooke, Greaves, Osgood, Baldwin and Blunstone.

I hope some of the fans who turned out for my testimonial match at the end of the season are reading this book as I'd like to thank them for making it such a special occasion. Perhaps the biggest thank you should go to those who worked on my testimonial committee; without their help and hard work it would not have been a success. There was Chris Matthews, who did all the hard work. She was just fantastic, she did it all, really. The others were just providing their expertise and she organised the lot. Then Bill Drummond and George Seymour were always on hand to offer advice and Richard Attenborough was the chairman and, more than that, a good friend. Dickie didn't just lend his name to the cause, he was there for all the meetings and his input was very serious and important.

I really liked Dickie and I can honestly say he was just a really genuine bloke. There was no superiority complex or anything like that, he was a normal guy and he would always stop to have a chat with you. I remember bumping into him in the west end once. We were on our way to the theatre and he was there with his missus and his son, with Jane Seymour in tow. We had a lovely chat. What a surprise to see her turn up a few years later in a James Bond film!

Chelsea fans should be forever grateful for Dickie's input over the years and he was so important in making sure the club stayed at Stamford Bridge in the Eighties, when he refused to sell his shares to the property developers. Chelsea owe him so much and I was really upset when he passed away a few years ago. A true Blue but, more than that, a true gentleman.

The problem most people had with testimonial matches was finding the right team to play against. You needed to find someone who could draw a crowd and all of the top sides were asked so many times by different clubs and players that you had a job to convince them. As I've mentioned, I ended up with Charlton, who were battling with Crystal Palace for promotion, and the committee figured they'd bring fans wanting to see how they'd do against a First Division side. Of course, Charlton then went downhill and didn't get promoted, whereas Palace did! But at least they were a local side.

The game finished 5-1 to Chelsea, but the players did everything to stop me scoring! It's usually the other way round, but even Catty came up to take a couple of penalties! I was just happy to be getting the testimonial. The game wasn't unimportant, as such, but I imagine I was standing there trying to count how many people were in the crowd! That was so important for us. It was a great reward for 10 years' service.

The season as a whole actually went pretty well for the club, continuing on the path laid out by Dave Sexton. We began solidly, but there was an early exit from the League Cup and even worse to follow in the Fairs Cup when we lost to a small Dutch club called DWS Amsterdam on the toss of a coin. What made matters even worse was that I'd missed a penalty in the first leg, but they set out their stall from the very first whistle. I can understand teams playing for penalties as you still control your own fate, although I'm not convinced it's the fairest way of settling a match, but the toss of a coin is just pure luck.

I touched upon the change in the dressing room's dynamic a couple of chapters ago, and there was to be more arrivals during the course of the campaign, two of which would pay dividends over the course of the next few seasons.

One was a tough type of centre-forward and Chelsea fans would grow to love him. He seemed a very quiet type of guy, hard as nails, but with a secret weapon which would turn out to be an FA Cup winner. Those of you who know your stuff will have guessed I was talking about Ian Hutchinson, who could take a throw-in and the ball could reach the penalty spot at head height. But there was more to this fella than this incredible weapon. He would run over big centre-halves like they were lightweights and he never gave up on anything. He formed a partnership with Ossie which no defender looked forward to coming up against. The raw toughness of Hutch, combined with the guile of Ossie – well, that's a match for anyone.

Another player that completed our defence was John Dempsey. Now, where was he five years earlier? Here was a centre-back who was outstanding in the air and could hold his own against all the big centre-forwards doing the rounds at that time. I think if we'd had him in the side earlier in the Sixties we would have won a lot more silverware. It just goes to show you don't need brilliant ball players all over the field. A team is made up of all sorts of players: some very skilful, others hard workers and then a few more who are as tough as teak. You can't all be chiefs – some have to be the Indians. You need some good thinkers. Get the right mix and you have a good team; throw in a support like Chelsea's and you're on the right path.

This season we also had a very unusual thing happen in an FA Cup replay with Preston North End. We were leading 2-0 and the game was well into the second half when suddenly we were in engulfed in darkness. The floodlights went out – and they weren't coming back on. We waited patiently in the dressing room to see if they would be mended or someone would stick their hand in their pocket to pay the bill! Jokes were flying around as everyone thought it would only be a matter of a time before they came back. But no, the game was abandoned and we would have to replay the whole game, despite us leading 2-0 with not long left to play. That was no joke. With our terrible luck in the cup, all sorts of theories were flying around as to why the lights had suddenly gone out. Had someone put a curse on us or what?

Before the replay we played away at Southampton, a game in which Alan Hudson made his debut. Prior to the match it was like the Blackpool incident all over again when a few of the lads decided to go out for a liquid lunch instead of receiving treatment, so Dave dropped the lot of them and we ended up getting hammered 5-0. Great preparation for the replay.

Come the night of the game, Dave kept on telling us to forget what had happened before and just go out and do our jobs and win the game. There was no cup jinx, he insisted. You make your own luck. Mind you, Dave was as superstitious as the rest of us, so what we had lurking at the backs of our minds was probably affecting him as well.

The game was even like the first draw and then our worst fears started to come true – they scored. Everyone was doing their best to gee each other up and make sure heads didn't drop, but deep down this was what we feared the most. At half-time Dave realised what a problem he had to lift us. But there was no better man to do it. He was going around the dressing room talking to all of us, telling us exactly what was required from each of us and reassuring us that if we did that then we would win. There was no talk about fate dealing us a bad hand, it was all focused on how we were playing and how we needed to give our supporters something to shout about.

It worked. We upped our game and put pressure on the Preston defence, which was standing firm and growing in determination and confidence as the minutes ticked by. We hadn't been in a state of panic but suddenly we threw everything at them and defenders were coming forward at every opportunity to add weight to our attacks. Preston must have thought they had done the job and some of the supporters must have thought the same as they started to leave. Well, there was soon to be an almighty roar and I think a fair few tried to make their way back into the ground!

All of a sudden, our effort, endurance and skill bore fruit. We had a corner and David Webb was on the spot to score from it. It wasn't unlike Webby – he'd previously scored a hat-trick for us against Ipswich, playing from centre-half. I should remember that one, really, because I set up his first with a corner and then the second with a low free-kick.

We had overcome our fear of losing with just a few minutes left to play. Preston were shattered, you could see it in their faces. We piled on more pressure, going for the killer blow, and it came from an unlikely source. Cookie will be the first to admit he didn't score enough goals for a man of his talent, and this was the perfect example of his skills as he brilliantly surged through the defence and placed his shot out of the reach of the keeper. We nearly crushed Cookie with our celebrations! We had given our all and overcome the perceived jinx. I realised then that the old saying about making your own luck was true. And some of the fans learned that day that the game isn't over until the final whistle blows.

Of course, we might as well have just gone out to Preston as two rounds later we bowed out to West Bromwich Albion, a side we thrashed home and away in the league. But we finished solidly in the league, a fifth place finish a good indication that we were heading in the right direction, although we were a distant 17 points behind champions Leeds United.

One player I hardly seem to have mentioned from year to year is our goalkeeper, Peter Bonetti. He was so calm under pressure and, other than being well over six foot, he had everything you would look for in a goalkeeper. He was agile, had a safe pair of hands, was a great shot-stopper and could catch crosses as easy as pie. The perfect guy to have as your last line of defence.

The way he would come and catch crosses was a treat to watch. When you looked at him against goalkeepers of today, he was quite small, but he could leap like a salmon. For 10 years I looked after him as his room-mate, doing everything for the room! I know he will have a laugh about that... More like it was the other way round! Catty was a very popular guy, except when playing cards. He was known to be very, very lucky. Generally he was fairly quiet off the field, but he was the best mate you could have. He looked after you and was just a pure gentleman. And what a nickname – The Cat! It's just a pity he was around at the same time as Gordon Banks...

Towards the end of our time at Chelsea we shared a mutual interest in sportswear. The firm also had Frank Blunstone as a partner in its early days, when they started out as a sports shop in Wandsworth. I think they were one of the first shops to put replica boys kits on the market and Peter also had green gloves with his name on, but when they got wet the keeper would end up like the Incredible Hulk with green hands!

I think this chapter is an appropriate opportunity to pay tribute to a few more of my team-mates and I've decided to focus mainly on the 1963 promotion-winning team although there are also players mentioned who were not with us during that season.

Each and every one of us will have different views on players and their value to the team, but these were among my best mates and people who I spent the best part of 10 years with.

Ken Shellito – Cool, stylish full-back who played football that would suit today's game. Passed well, was one of the first attacking full-backs who didn't get a nosebleed when he crossed the halfway line. Perfected the overlap run and a very good crosser of the ball. Many goals came from his side of the pitch. A laid-back person and a gentleman who suffered the worst luck ever. He injured his knee in the mid-Sixties and tried to come back three times. It cut short a great future.

I don't see much of Ken because he lives on the other side of the planet, but we talk on the phone about once a month and we still have a great laugh. One of us will start a story and before we can finish the other one is killing himself laughing!

John Mortimore – A very reliable centre-back, nothing posh (unlike him), did his job well. John was one of the senior players of the squad and he would help anyone and set a good example to all of us. Never seemed worried. Good in the air, our biggest centre-half, but would be one of the players you would not like to sprint with. Very good at card games

Frank Upton – Tough man; started life as a miner, which you could tell when he shook hands with you. You never wanted to upset Frank by playing jokes on him. On the pitch he was steady and straightforward as he would win the ball and give it to someone else. He could upset the opposition very easily and played a strong role in the side. Sure, he didn't make many headlines, but you were glad to have him alongside you.

FRIENDS

Eddie McCreadie – Had everything you would want in a full-back – very fast, quick in the tackle and with the ability to recover, he got forward well on the overlap. Eddie was also a hard man who was afraid of no one, not to mention being good in the air for someone who wasn't the biggest. You didn't upset Eddie. Loads of energy on and off the field, very excitable, and I'm sure he would have liked to have been a forward.

Eddie lives in America now and he sounds very happy and settled out in a ranch, I'm told. I wonder if he still thinks I am a dummy! I would love to see him come back to the Bridge for one big get-together. I hope it can happen one day.

Marvin Hinton – Mr Cool; nothing upset Marvin. Another player who would suit today's game, he liked to play out from defence and was the best sweeper in the game at that time, but he could also play full-back or centre-back. Wasn't the biggest of players so would struggle against old-fashioned centre-forwards, but that was one of his few flaws.

Ron Harris – It goes without saying that Chopper was a hard man. You picked him first in the five-a-sides as it was better to be with him than against. Could man-mark, play full-back or feature in the middle, nothing fazed him. Ron was a better player than most people thought. Well, that's what he told us in the dressing room. Who would disagree? Very quiet off the field. Believe it or not, Ron told us after he finished playing that he was only sent off once in his career. My conclusion is that even the refs were scared of him...

John Hollins – Could run all day, so you made sure you weren't with him on the cross-countries. He looked so young but could do it all. Shoot! One of the hardest shots at the club. A good lad, Holly's got a great sense of humour and he has always got on with everyone. He always looked after himself and was great to have a drink with – you knew you would get home safe.

Terry Venables – Without doubt the funniest guy in the dressing room. You had to have your wits about you when he was in the company. He was the best wind-up merchant in the business and no one was safe in his company. Made the dressing room swing along, he loved a sing-song. Someone once told him he could sing – we are still looking for the guy...

That was off the field; on it he was a great passer who would find you if you made a run. He read the game very well, intercepted loads of passes and would always know what was going on around him.

A thinker who was always going to be a great coach and still should be; he was always thinking about tactics and you could tell he was way ahead of his time. He went on to become the coach we all thought he would be and he did England proud as our manager. He is also still a very funny man with that sharp wit of his.

John Boyle – I have great respect for this man. I often use him as an example for young players today. Why? When he first came down to Chelsea from Scotland, he was very enthusiastic and willing to learn everything Dave Sexton had to give. What a job he did. He had limitations when he started, but he put his head down, learned everything and eventually he could do it better than most. He had a great spirit. He wasn't that fast but he never let that worry him. His Chelsea record: 1964-73, 266 appearances, 12 goals, three cup final appearances and two ending in victory. All of this because he had a great attitude to learning and listening and then applying that to his game. He always had a great spirit and never let what he couldn't do get him down. A good person to hold up to youngsters to show what can be achieved in life with the right attitude.

Graham Moore – A gentle giant and another real good person to have around the dressing room, always good for a laugh. Didn't stay with us long, but what a season he had with us, winning promotion in 1963. For a big man he had good skills, very neat and tidy. Very strong, made a good mix with Terry. Well liked in the dressing room.

Bert Murray – Another unsung hero. Worked his socks off on the right-hand side of midfield, used more like a winger or a wing-back. He and Ken Shellito had a great understanding and worked well together, both in attack and defence. Bert played a big part in our promotion year; scored his fair share of goals, set up plenty, great worker and a very good crosser who knew where to put the ball. Another who was good in the dressing room and always up for a laugh.

Frank Blunstone – Everyone liked Frank. What a man and what a player, he helped all us youngsters along so much. Frank broke his leg twice, came back twice and still thrilled the crowd with his wing skills. His close ball control caused many a full-back problems and even after the broken leg he was never afraid to get stuck in. He was a quiet man who loved playing cards on away trips. Frank, John Mortimore, Harry Medhurst and myself played a game called hearts and let me tell you he was very crafty when it came to the cards. It was a thinking man's game and we would have many a good laugh.

Barry Bridges – I have left a very good mate until last. Never go on a sprint with Barry – he ran like the wind and was naturally a very fast player, someone defenders hated to play against as his movement pulled them all over the place. He scored goals only he could have got to. I think he was unbeaten in sprints – in training that is, certainly not to the bar!

Near-post goals were a speciality and crossing was practised for hours to make sure the wide men and full-backs knew where to put the ball – Barry did the rest.

Barry and his wife Megan are still good friends of Val and I and we always have a very good time whenever we meet up. We usually end up laughing about our younger days and the crazy things we got up to. One is when we went to dance lessons. I can honestly say they didn't do much for me – I still can't dance! Today, Barry will put this female voice on and go, "Quick, quick, slow!" as though I'm having a dance lesson and we always end up laughing together. We visit them whenever we can and it's always nice to get together.

Bobby Tambling – VERY LUCKY.

There are players who came to Chelsea later in the Sixties, who all served the club with great skill and honour. People like Charlie Cooke, David Webb, John Dempsey, Paddy Mulligan. Of course, there was also George Graham, one of the best headers in the game; timing and a good jump would be his style. He was so cool – Gorgeous George off the pitch and Stroller on it.

We traded George for Tommy Baldwin, someone who would go on to play and score in some of the big games Chelsea had in the future. I liked playing with Tommy. He was a worker and very skilful, he could always turn a defender easily enough. We do the hospitality together at Stamford Bridge and I love having a chinwag with him every other week.

I almost missed out another gem of a player: Peter Osgood. Ossie could do everything. He'd beat people, set up team-mates, head, shoot. What a player. I loved playing with him because he could always find you in a packed goal-mouth. For a big man he had a great touch.

I don't see enough of these guys, but a couple of years ago we had a dinner for the 1962/63 promotion-winning side, and George Graham, who was a very welcome gatecrasher! It was one of the best nights I've had. We even had a Beatles tribute band to really take us back. It was so nice to be able to see people after such a long time, in some cases the best part of 50 years like Graham Moore.

Some we will only have our memories to remember them by. That's been one of the nicest things about writing this book. When I think about some of the amazing people I've known and then put that down on paper, it brings things out as though it was only a few years back.

It's been a great honour to know all these players and to play with them. They made Chelsea so very easy to play for, but a big part of the club that has never changed is the supporters. They are just the finest crowd to play for and it's still a great thrill and pleasure to come to the Bridge and meet you all again and have a chat.

It's lovely to write all this down and to remember all of the fun and laughter. It has made it clearer in my mind, bringing a smile to my face and also a tear to my eyes. It makes me realise how my life was truly living a dream.

16

THE END IS NIGH

As the title of this chapter suggests, my time at Chelsea was about to come to an abrupt conclusion. Perhaps abrupt is not the correct word, seeing as it was a bit of a long, drawn-out process, but in other ways it was a pretty dramatic slide out of the first team and onto the scrapheap.

While the previous campaign was by no means my strongest – I'd scored just shy of 20 goals, which is typically the benchmark for any goalscorer – I felt I still had plenty to offer Chelsea. Without knowing it at the time, I was embarking on my final season as a Blue. It's hard to write those words even now, so you can imagine how it felt at the time. Devastated doesn't even begin to cover it, but I'm a proud man and not one for sticking around and outstaying my welcome.

The signs were there as early as pre-season, which was noticeably tougher than in previous years because of the quality players we had throughout the squad. It was pretty clear that Dave Sexton had yet to decide on his best starting XI and I knew I had a real fight on my hands to get in the team. To give you an idea of the uncertainty in Dave's thinking, the Ossie and Hutch partnership that would prove to be so potent later in the season didn't even seem to be in his thinking at this time. Os would usually be utilised in midfield, which shows you just how talented a player he was. There was also a load of promising youngsters all knocking on the first-team door, waiting for their opportunity. A decade ago, that was me. How things change.

When the big kick-off finally arrived with a trip to Anfield on the opening day, I'd been given the nod to start and that alone gave me fresh impetus and bundles of confidence. And then we were drubbed 4-1! Even so, Dave kept faith in me and I started the next three games. It was in the last of these matches that disaster struck – against West Ham United at Stamford Bridge, as fate would have it, the opponents when my first-team career began in earnest. We must have been playing only 10 minutes when I made what I would describe as an ordinary tackle. You'd make a dozen of these – or maybe double that if you're Chopper Harris – in every single game and not think anything of it. This time, however, I knew something was up. At the moment of impact, I felt my knee go and collapsed to the ground.

Footballers of today don't realise how good they have it when it comes to medical care. Harry Medhurst jogged onto the field and over to where I was lying. "What seems to be the problem?" he asked.

"Listen, Harry, this doesn't feel right," I told him. "Something's happened to my knee. I could feel it straight away, I'm going to have to come off."

His response to this was to pull out the magic sponge and give my knee a little rub. That was considered to be advanced medical treatment in those days. Then he helped me to my feet and told me to try and walk on it. I took just one step and started to wobble; straight away it felt like it could give way at any second. Alan Birchenall came on in my place and I was sent home for the rest of the weekend with instructions to keep it iced and not to put any pressure on it.

On Monday, it was into the treatment room nice and early. Harry asked me how the knee was doing. Although there didn't seem to be any swelling, it was still quite sore and so he relayed this message to the manager. Not before we'd had the obligatory tea and biscuit, of course. I'd have given anything – even my last custard cream – to have been out on the training pitch instead of nursing this injury, but after a brief consultation with Harry and Dave we decided I should be fit and raring to go after a fortnight on the sidelines.

Things weren't going great for the lads on the pitch. We won only one of those opening four games when I was involved and then followed that with three consecutive draws. If you look through the team line-ups around that time, you can see we had a very good set of players, of that there was no doubt, but Dave seemed to be caught in two minds as to finding the right formation and the requisite balance in order to get results. At this point, you'd have never guessed how that season would pan out, which is why I struggle to get on with the lack of patience that seems to surround every facet of modern football. Rome wasn't build in a day...

Speaking of patience, I certainly needed plenty of it while I recovered from this injury. Two weeks quickly turned into a month and still the best I could manage was a bit of gentle jogging. A couple of visits to the club doctor had left me none the wiser as to what the next step was and when I could hope to be back on the pitch. I'm not one for sitting around and twiddling my thumbs, so I decided I had to take matters into my own hands if there was to be a quick resolution to my problem. I spoke to Harry and asked him if we could see a specialist, which he was more than happy to arrange for later in the week.

Straight away, I could tell this guy knew what he was doing. He asked me how I'd sustained the injury and he wanted to know how my knee was holding up in various scenarios, such as walking up the stairs. I explained how every time I went up a step I could feel a wobble in that knee. It only lasted a second or two, but it felt like it could give way at any time.

He told me to get up on the bed so he could examine me. This involved grabbing my good leg down at the ankle and shaking it like a whip! Then he did this with the bad leg. "It's cartilage, old boy," he said. "I'm afraid we will have to operate."

I was angry that so much time was wasted before this simple diagnosis, but at the same time I felt a sense of relief that we finally had a resolution that would mean I could get back on the football field as soon as possible. I was only in the hospital for a short time and the operation went as well as could be expected. I couldn't get out of there quickly enough! I started walking as soon as I could and then I was jogging every morning and afternoon. It was like pre-season all over again and soon enough I was out on the training ground partaking in a bit of light ball work. In six weeks, I was looking to get a run in the reserves to regain match sharpness and stake a claim for my place in the first team.

While I'd been out injured, Chelsea had played 11 times and lost only once, albeit drawing seven times. What's more, there was a new name appearing regularly on the team sheet: Alan Hudson. Huddy was a very classy midfielder to add to John Hollins and Johnny Boyle – in fact, the three were very good box-to-box players, making for a fine mix in the middle of the park.

The next 11 games saw only one defeat again, but this time there would be more wins than draws. Huddy's impact was being felt; he wasn't a great goalscorer, but a fine playmaker who read the game like no one else in that Chelsea team. He really did control the game, defending one minute and the next making goals for Ossie and Hutch, who by now were looking quite the partnership. What's more, they had such a close relationship off the field and that was making for spectacular results on it. They were as thick as thieves, just like two brothers.

I was playing in the reserves, slowly regaining my fitness and, I must say, just enjoying being back on the field. It's only when something is taken away from you that you realise just how much you miss it. It might not have been first-team action in front of a packed house at Stamford Bridge, but it was good enough for me at this stage.

Then, an interesting opportunity presented itself. Dave pulled me aside during one training session and told me he'd had a phone call from Bert Head, who was the manager of Crystal Palace and keen to take me on loan. Temporary transfers are part and parcel of the modern game, but back then it was something of a rarity and, so I'm told, I was the first player to be signed by Crystal Palace on loan. Being the forward-thinking gaffer that he was, Dave embraced this opportunity. He thought it would be a good move for me, a chance to get some first-team games under my belt to get back up to speed, which is something he couldn't offer me with the side performing so well. And there certainly wasn't any complaint from me – I was just raring to get back on the field in a proper first-team game.

Boy, were these proper games. Palace had only just been promoted to the First Division and, by the time I arrived in January, they were near the bottom of the table and fighting for their lives. This was going to be tough football, make no mistake about it.

What a great bunch of lads they had there, instantly making me feel at home. Tough as it was for them, considering their plight, they were still enjoying their football, which was lovely to see. There was a good mix of players, some young and others approaching the autumn of their career, a few skilful and the majority your typical English tough guys. I settled down quickly and appeared in three matches without scoring, but I was always waiting to find out what the Chelsea score was each afternoon. Once a Blue and all that...

After a month, I returned to Stamford Bridge all the better for the experience. I felt fitter, for sure, but I was under no illusion as to the battle I had on my hands if I was to get anywhere near the first team. Then, in my first game back, I pulled a hamstring. That was me out for two months. I always considered myself to be a lucky footballer with the opportunities that presented themselves to me over the years, but it was clear I had used up all my good fortune.

While things could hardly be any worse for me, the opposite

Reaching goals: Watching my boots for the 1967 FA Cup against Spurs being made, above, and in action at Wembley, a ground which holds great memories for me

BOBBY TAMBLING

Business pitch: Crowds turn out to the opening of my sports shop in Havant, with a little help from some of my footballing friends, above, and showing a hands-on approach behind the counter, below

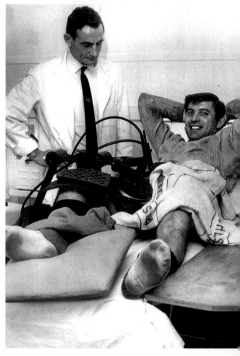

Smiling through the pain: I'm smiling because physio Harry Medhurst has obviously already have given me his famous cup of tea and biscuit

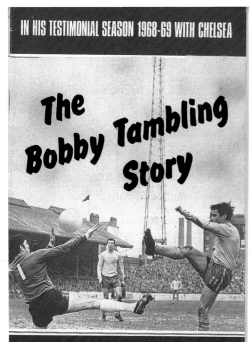

IN HIS TESTIMONIAL SEASON 1968-69 WITH CHELSEA

The Bobby Tambling Story

PRICE TWO SHILLINGS AND SIXPENCE

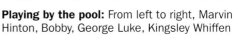

Playing by the pool: From left to right, Marvin Hinton, Bobby, George Luke, Kingsley Whiffen

Tributes: A magazine looking back at my Blues career was released in the 1968/69 season, left, and my testimonial was against Charlton

Portrait: With Kathleen, a five-year-old Gary and 21-month-old Sharon

Palace invite: The early 1970s saw me at Crystal Palace, and here I am having a shot on goal against Manchester United in April 1971, above left, posing for a photo in July 1972, above right, and on a collector card, below left

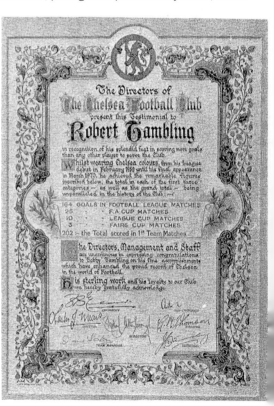

Honour: On a return to play against the Blues, Chelsea presented me with an illuminated address to acknowledge my contribution to the club, right

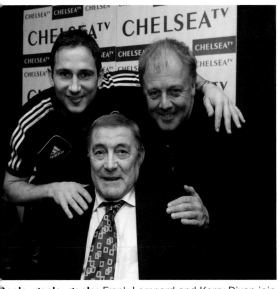

Welcoming: Chelsea owner Roman Abramovich has been so generous to former players like myself

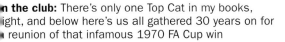

Goals, goals, goals: Frank Lampard and Kerry Dixon join me at the Bridge after a Swansea match in April 2013. Between us we've scored 606 goals for the Blues

In the club: There's only one Top Cat in my books, right, and below here's us all gathered 30 years on for a reunion of that infamous 1970 FA Cup win

Lifelong pals: Me with Charlie Cooke, left, and Ken Shellito. I've enjoyed so many laughs with these guys

Family: On the back row is Bobby, Mick, Ray and Peter with Beryl, Bill and Ivy sat down

Ali B: Dressed as Ali G for a magazine photo shoot which was never used

Strike partners: My friendship with Frank Lampard grew as he closed in on my goalscoring record for Chelsea and it has been a delight to support him all the way

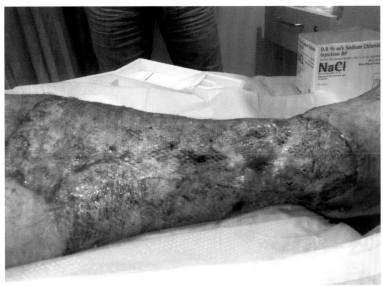

Horror show: The full extent of the Martorell leg ulcer. I make no apologies for showing how graphic it was and if this photo helps diagnose one person then it will have been worth it

The loves of my life: Above, myself with Val, my rock, and below, having the honour of walking on the hallowed turf at the Bridge as the fans cheered my name

could be said for Chelsea at this time. The team was picking itself and the outlook was looking rosier with each passing month. We were going well in the league in third place and, more importantly, in the midst of an FA Cup run which would take us past Birmingham City, Burnley, Crystal Palace and a QPR side featuring my old muckers Venner and Bridgo. Both of them scored in the sixth-round tie at Loftus Road, but an Ossie hat-trick helped us into the semi-finals against Watford. Throughout my time in the first team we'd always seemed to get the toughest draw in the cup, but this time the boys had avoided both Manchester United and Leeds United, who were playing in the other semi. Dave Sexton wouldn't change his suit throughout the cup run and I could see why he wanted to continue this superstition.

The team was in buoyant mood. They had a great spirit and a good laugh at all times, which was showing on the pitch as they strolled past Watford 5-1 to book a place in the FA Cup final against Leeds, a game which would see two of the league's top sides facing each other.

Unfortunately, fate would deal Chelsea and Huddy a cruel hand when he picked up an injury to his ankle ligaments in a game against West Brom, which left him with a real fight to get fit for the final. What a blow to our young star in his first full season in the team. I'm sorry to say it proved to be an uphill battle to get him fit and after such a brilliant season he would play no part in the cup final. How cruel the game can be.

And me? I replaced Huddy in that game at the Hawthorns, one of only four substitute appearances I made during my time at Chelsea, but we lost 3-1 and I'd made little impact on proceedings and ended up hobbling off after pulling my hamstring again. Before the game, I knew I'd had little chance of featuring in the cup final. This merely confirmed that my Wembley dream was over. As upset as I was, the prospect of seeing the club I love and all of my good mates competing for what was then the biggest prize in English football excited me.

It always makes me laugh when I hear players complaining about the Wembley pitch these days, because I can only assume none of them have ever seen footage from the 1970 FA Cup final. Some bright spark had decided Wembley could host the Horse of the Year show in the lead-up to the game and, of course, horses are notoriously nimble-footed creatures so there was no way they were going to leave the pitch looking anything other than pristine. In an era when playing surfaces often resembled mud patches, this one could only be described as a swamp by the time Chelsea and Leeds were to do battle on it.

Eddie McCreadie was left red-faced when he tried to clear an effort off the line and the ball simply skidded off the mud and under his foot, and the Leeds keeper Gary Sprake made a hash of a regulation save from Nobby Houseman which somehow squirmed past him and into the net. When Mick Jones put Leeds ahead late on it looked to be curtains for Chelsea until big Hutch bravely headed home an even later equaliser. A replay at Old Trafford would be needed to decide the destination of the trophy.

As you'll no doubt be aware, this game was one of the most brutal ever seen, with challenges flying in left, right and centre. I was up in the stands and wincing every 30 seconds as players went crashing into one another, ending up in a muddle of limbs on the ground. Perhaps the worst of the lot was the reducer Chopper put on Eddie Gray, having been switched to right-back after Dave Webb had been run ragged by Leeds' tricky winger. Eddie had been Man of the Match in the first game and I think Chopper deserved it in the replay for that challenge alone, which left his opponent limping and ineffective through-out a gruelling contest.

Once again, Leeds took the lead and looked to have their name on the trophy until Ossie equalised with a beautiful diving header from the most sublime cross delivered by Charlie Cooke, the kind of ball he could play in his sleep while most mere mortals could only dream of hitting it so sweetly. It was one of the few moments of class in a game which was con-stantly at boiling point, and how it didn't spill over when Eddie McCreadie did his best Bruce Lee impression on Billy Bremner I will never know. They were team-mates for Scotland, so I can only assume Eddie's eyesight let him down and he fly-kicked the wrong man!

When the winning goal arrived in extra-time, it was certainly in keeping with the rest of the game. Hutch delivered one of his trademark long throws into the box and big Jackie Charlton inadvertently flicked it to towards the back stick, where a mass of bodies descended on the ball. Webby somehow got some-thing on it − he says it was his cheek − but it didn't matter how it happened. The ball had hit the back of the net and we held on to our first lead across the two ties. At long last, Chelsea had won the FA Cup. As much as I'd have loved to have played a part, it was an incredible night to be a Blues fan and an occasion I will never forget. I was going mad with excitement as we finally won the trophy which was central to everything I ever dreamed about. All through the Sixties the fans and players had so many exciting years; two semi-finals, a losing final, good runs that ended abruptly when we thought we could go all the way.

In the days that followed, it really hit me that the year I could not make the team we won the cup. I was sad, really sad, especially when you add in the double whammy of knowing that I'd more than likely run my course at Chelsea. I didn't want to be seen as hanging on to something lost. Just around the corner I was confronted by a decision which would break my heart. In life, sometimes you have to make a big call. You know it is going to hurt like hell, but it simply must be done.

It was obvious that my time at Chelsea was coming to an end. The team was settled, they had players coming up the ranks and, on top of that, they had bought players to add depth to what was already an incredibly strong squad. I decided I needed to speak to Dave about my situation and what followed was an incredibly honest chat for which I will always remain grateful. We both knew the writing was on the wall for me at Chelsea and he'd received another call from Bert Head, who had put in a joint offer for myself and Alan Birchenall. Birch was in a similar position to me and he'd already made his mind up to go. But I'd been at Chelsea for my entire adult life and I had to take a bit of time to make sure I was doing the right thing.

On the one hand, I loved the club dearly. I'd enjoyed 13 great years there, scoring more goals than I could have ever dreamed of but, more importantly, formed friendships with an amazing bunch of lads. During that time I met my first girlfriend, got married and had children. I grew up at the club in so many ways. It had been my life up until that time.

As good as the past had been, though, I knew I didn't have a future at Stamford Bridge. Everything had moved on so quickly during my time out of the team. Just as I had been part of an exciting new generation to come through in the years following the championship win in 1955, replacing lads who had given many years of great service to the club, now the roles had been reversed and it was my turn to step aside. I was still young, only 28, and I thought I had a good few years left at the top level. I didn't want to stay somewhere I would have no chance to play first-team football.

I knew a bit about Palace from my loan spell there. They had been very good to me during that time and I got on well with the players. There was also the added bonus that it was just up the road, so there wouldn't be any upheaval in my personal life. So, with a heavy heart, I told Dave I would talk to them and the next thing I knew I was a Crystal Palace player.

It was a big disappointment to leave behind so many people who had done so much for me over the years. There was the fans who had always treated me with support and kindness, and all the friends and players I had grown up with, the great memories I had in the 13 years I spent growing from a country boy into a man. It was like saying goodbye to my family, but I thought it was the best way to go. I didn't want to outstay my welcome and end up becoming a burden on the club. No, this was the right time to go and the right club to join.

For all the fans who watched us in those days, I hope I've brought back some happy memories of those good days we all enjoyed together. For those too young to remember, I hope I've given you a chance to see how the players felt about the great Chelsea fans of those days and the wonderful support you gave us through thick and thin. In recent years, the players have given you a hell of a lot of trophies to make you feel proud to be Chelsea. Even though we couldn't match them in terms of silverware, I know I speak for all of my team-mates when I say I hope we made you feel the same way. One thing I can say for certain is that you guys made me so proud to be a Chelsea player.

With a lump in my throat and a tear in my eye, it was time to say my farewells and embark on the next chapter of my career.

17

CRYSTAL PALACE

Like so many other people, players and fans alike: once a Blue, always a Blue. That relationship is forever and nothing could ever change the way I feel about Chelsea, which made things a bit strange when I turned up for my first day of training with Palace.

When I'd joined the club on loan, it was a completely different scenario as I knew it was only temporary and I'd be going back to Chelsea in a few weeks' time. Now it was permanent, I felt like a kid going in for his first day at a new school. I could feel the butterflies fluttering in my tummy, but I think that's a good thing because I needed those nerves to give me a bit of an edge. Sure, I had my reputation at Chelsea to fall back on, but I was here to make a good impression. If that wasn't the case, I should have just stayed at Chelsea and turned out for the reserves while picking up my pay packet.

As I wrote in the previous chapter, there was a good feeling around the club at Palace when I arrived there in the midst of a relegation battle, so you can only imagine what a happy place it was after they escaped the drop by just a single point by beating Manchester City on the final day of the season. Mind you, they had to wait over a fortnight for their safety to be confirmed as Sheffield Wednesday, who could still overhaul them, were still to play their final game. That must have been agony for the lads. As we had drawn two of the three games during my loan spell there, I maintain I was the signing of the season!

A lot of the lads who had made me feel so welcome during my brief stay were still at the club and there was also plenty of new arrivals, which made for an interesting environment to begin with. Everyone knew places were at stake, so competition was fierce, but at the same time they were such a great group of fellas so there was always a good vibe around the training ground. I couldn't help but settle in quickly.

Having George Petchey as a coach was also a big help to me personally as he was very much like Dave Sexton in the sense that he was a deep thinker when it came to football. He was in charge of training for the most part and it was quite rare to see Bert Head, the manager, out there unless we were playing a practice match. He was definitely from the old school of thought when it came to management, but he and George worked well together.

Unlike at Chelsea, where we could expect to be among those challenging at the top, it was apparent that mid-table was the best Palace could hope for. After the close escape the previous season, that would have been a good result, although with both myself and Birch coming in and also another lad called Peter Wall, who had been playing for Liverpool, the fans may have expected more. Bert came out with quite a funny quote about his new signings: "We've bought instant footballers, instant goals and instant ability. It's like putting the milk and butter into the pot to get mashed potatoes."

Unfortunately, his instant goals comment wasn't applicable to me as I made the kind of start you'd have nightmares about. Every goalscorer will have runs in their career when you simply cannot buy a goal for love nor money, which is something you learn to accept, even if it leaves you feeling pretty miserable. But when you've just signed for a team and you're particularly eager to get off to a flying start, you don't want to be going a dozen matches without finding the back of the net. When that first goal finally arrived it was a huge weight off my shoulders.

Although I wasn't scoring at the same rate as I had throughout my Chelsea career, I was making up for it by picking my moments and getting goals at big times. One of my first for Palace came in a 1-0 win at Old Trafford, which was Bobby Charlton's 500th league game for the Red Devils, and then I was at it again a few weeks later, converting a late penalty as we beat Arsenal in the League Cup. I'd always enjoyed a pretty good record against them, but for Palace it was their first-ever win over the Gunners and it was a major scalp for us.

I missed out when we faced Chelsea in the FA Cup third round, taking them to a replay after Birch scored in a 2-2 draw, but I was back and in the side for our visit to Stamford Bridge in April.

It was an emotional day when I returned to Chelsea. Obviously I wanted to play my best to show them I was still a worthwhile player, that perhaps it had been a mistake to get rid of me. The whole game was played out with banter flying in my direction, the majority of which came from Ossie. It was all good natured – we may not have been team-mates any longer, but a change of kit wasn't enough to stop us being mates.

We drew 1-1 in a game that was far from exciting, but from my point of view it was pretty perfect as it meant my new team and the club I loved both got a point from it.

It was a pretty quiet season all in all, although we failed to make the most of a strong start and struggled for wins after Christmas. We didn't quite finish mid-table, but at the same time there was no flirtation with the drop and everyone seemed happy enough with how my first campaign had gone. And we had European football to look forward to as the club was taking part in the Anglo-Italian Cup.

The competition was an unofficial summer tournament which was held yearly in the early 1970s, and we were one of the six English clubs to enter that year. It was hardly the cream of the crop: Stoke, West Brom, Huddersfield, Blackpool and Swindon Town, who had won the first tournament. But there were some good sides from Italy, the last two winners of the Scudetto, Inter and Cagliari, among them, as well as Roma.

I have to say, the tournament was a bit of a farce as points in the group stage were awarded for goals rather than victories, which meant we were eliminated despite beating Cagliari and Inter. I scored in both victories, including two wonderful goals in a famous win at the San Siro. The first was a header and then I smashed one in from 25 yards. I don't suppose too many

CRYSTAL PALACE

English teams have won at one of the most iconic stadiums in football, so the tournament did at least give Palace that.

There was still plenty of ambition for the club to improve, which was music to my ears as I was approaching my 30th birthday and still harbouring aspirations to compete at the very top. They also liked to bring through their own, just like Chelsea, and the pick of the bunch was probably Stevie Kember, who was a hard-working midfielder destined for bigger things. As it happened, that meant a move to Stamford Bridge early in the new season.

We'd made a really poor start and the manager clearly wanted to shake things up as Birch and Phil Hoadley, a decent centre-half who was Palace's youngest-ever player when he made his debut, also left the club. Bert brought in six new players: Bobby Kellard, Sammy Goodwin, Bobby Bell, John Craven, Willie Wallace and John Hughes, the latter duo coming down from Celtic. All of this happened in the space of a month and around £500,000 exchanged hands in transfer fees, which was a headline-grabbing figure in those days.

While they were all good players, we still weren't able to bring the success the club craved. I improved my goal output but we actually went backwards as a team and ended up finishing 20th out of 22 teams, which was only one place off the drop zone.

I also fell foul of the manager for the first time this season when I decided to take tactical matters into my own hands. We were playing at Aston Villa in the League Cup and our system was ultra-defensive, with only one man left up front and the rest all mucking in at the back. It was going quite well, but then we conceded early in the second half and time was passing by without any change to the system. I had a quick word with one

219

or two players, thinking we should go for goal, so we changed the system among ourselves and went with three up front. It was much better and we went close to getting an equaliser, but ultimately we lost the game 2-0. In a cup tie, when only the win counts, I thought that it mattered little if we lost by one goal or two, but we had hardly even stepped foot in the dressing room when Bert burst in, shouting and roaring.

"Who was it that changed the system?" he demanded.

Everyone went quiet, but I decided I had to own up. I raised my hand.

"Who told you to do that?" Bert roared.

"I thought it was the only thing to do to get a result," I replied.

"If I'm going to get sacked then it will be because of one of my decisions, not yours," he roared back at me. To be fair to him, it was quite a good line, but I just couldn't understand why we wouldn't have a go. It was not my style to be a trouble-maker, I just thought it made sense.

My old Chelsea team-mates Charlie Cooke and Paddy Mulligan joined me at Selhurst Park for the 1972/73 season and there was renewed optimism that big things were just around the corner, especially with the addition of Don Rogers from Swindon. Now, Don's name doesn't crop up enough for my liking when people are discussing the talents of the Sixties and Seventies. He had a 'tache that was straight out of the great Western movies from that era and it was his feet, not his hands, that were as quick as a flash. He'd go past players in a similar manner to Eden Hazard and he scored plenty of goals, too. I'd certainly rank him among the most talented players I played alongside during my career.

Perhaps his finest hour for Palace came in a thumping 5-0

win over Manchester United, when he scored two goals and ran them ragged. Mind you, they couldn't have been up to much as Paddy also scored twice in that game. No, that's not a mistake: Paddy Mulligan, the Irish full-back who managed about five goals throughout his time in England, scored two in the same game. Against Manchester United, no less. It couldn't have happened to a nicer bloke, although I don't think he's ever stopped talking about it.

Despite that victory, things weren't going particularly well for Palace and my injury problems were starting to rear their ugly head once again. I'd previously been having trouble with a muscle in my left leg. It kept me out for quite a while and I had never had this type of frustrating injury before. It was hard to know when I was fit because I could run with no problems at all, but then as soon as I tried to kick the ball I was in trouble. It was really getting me down, especially when the trainer told me that Bert thought it was all in my head. Rather than let it get to me, I decided to have a bit of fun the next morning at training. I walked into the dressing room with a bandage wrapped around my head and all the lads fell about laughing. The trainer asked me what was wrong. "Well, I heard Bert thought it was all in my head, so I figured I'd put a bandage on it." Bert didn't see the funny side of it.

A worse injury was to follow, one which would effectively spell the end of my playing career at the highest level. I'd been having problems with my right Achilles tendon, so much so that I could hardly run. I went to see the specialist about it and he gave me a cortisone injection, which was pretty standard in those days but actually incredibly damaging to the players. Why do you think so many of my old team-mates and myself have had new hips, knees and who knows what else put in? In some cases, it's a pity they couldn't have brain transplants, mind!

Anyway, this cortisone injection helped a bit, but as soon as I went to run I was in big trouble. I kept having more and more injections, but it was clearly not the answer to my problem. Eventually, it was decided that they would operate so they could see what was causing me grief.

When I came round, the specialist was waiting for me with a bombshell: I should give serious consideration to retiring. I knew it was a bad injury, but I was stunned to receive this news. The first emotion I felt was anger. How dare he tell me when I should stop playing? I was the only person who could make such a massive decision, not some specialist. Surely there was some way I could eke a few more years out of my creaking body?

"Well, there is one thing you could try," said the specialist. "If you can find somewhere the ground is always soft then it might not put such a strain on your Achilles tendon."

Armed with this information, once I was ready to return to training I could think about getting myself a move and pro- longing my career. I wasn't too sure exactly where I should seek out this soft ground, but I was given the opportunity to go and play in South Africa with Durban Celtic for a short while, so I decided to give that a go. It was six-week loan which Bert Head arranged for me, and off I went on a new adventure.

Pause for a moment and think about the climate in Africa. Do you immediately think of soft, wet ground? No. And there's a good reason for that. As you've bought this book, it's already safe to assume you're not an idiot. But the same can't be said for me. As you'd expect, the ground was rock solid for the most part, although actually there was the odd surface to which my

Achilles could hold up to. But it was clear that I couldn't continue in South Africa and I may as well just return to England, where most football pitches were far softer.

Away from the pitch, my residence was located right on the sea front in Durban, a beautiful location spoiled by the underlying racist current of apartheid.

I was stunned by the separate buses for different skin colours and even in football, which is supposed to be a universal sport accepting of all, there was segregation within the stadiums. Worse still, the native people, the Ban-tu, were treated the worst of everyone. I couldn't understand why people who naturally belonged to the area were being shunned by those who had arrived later. I quickly made up my mind that this was not something I wanted to be a part of, hence my trip to South Africa was short lived. I abhor racist behaviour of any kind and cannot understand it.

I remember being at this lovely swimming pool, which was spoiled by only allowing whites. I met this man from the north of England who was there with his young kids, and he told me he had left the north of England because it was being over-populated by black people. I couldn't believe it – the audacity was staggering. What a horrible man.

Another awful moment that stands out is when we all gathered to watch the Roger Moore film The Saint. Nobody I knew in Durban had a TV, so we gathered around to watch a projector beaming the film onto a large white sheet in this courtyard. The owners of the house had a black housemaid and though she was allowed to watch the film, she didn't sit with us.

Instead, she watched it on the other side of the sheet. Totally bizarre and completely unacceptable.

I was feeling fit and raring to go by the time I arrived back at Palace. During my time away there was a change of manager as Malcolm Allison replaced Bert, although he wasn't able to stop the club dropping into the Second Division. Malcolm had a big reputation from his time at Manchester City and he was known as being quite an innovative coach. He was really into his South American football and loved the idea of all the players having nicknames. I'm sure he came up with one for me and all of the players, which he wanted to print in the matchday programme every week! That was just Malcolm, he wanted to stand out from the crowd. That extended to his coaching and tactics, which were different to what we were used to.

When I first spoke with him during the summer break, it actually came as a surprise for him to find me on the books at Crystal Palace. I'd somehow flown under the radar, but he was very much open to the idea of me giving it another go with the club and he told me I had pre-season training to prove that I was back to fitness.

Three weeks before we were due to start back, I started to get going on my own programme. The ankle stood up to the road work I was doing and I was pleased with the progress I was making. When we went back for pre-season I was sharper than the other lads and I looked good in the fives we played. I was called into Malcolm's office and he was absolutely delighted with me. I'd initially been left out of the squad for the pre-season tour, but I'd done so well that he'd changed his mind and I was included on the list.

I scored a couple of goals while we were away and thought I was doing well. So did Malcolm. Come the start of the season, I had played my way into the team. Unluckily for me, the tail end of that summer was particularly dry – so much for it always raining in August – and the grounds became bone dry. My ankle started giving me trouble again and as much as I tried to play through the pain, soon I was back at the stage where I could hardly run.

I was spending more time in the treatment room than out on the pitch and it was starting to get me down. One morning, I arrived in the dressing room and sat next to my old mate Paddy, who is always the first to make a joke about anything, but even he knew I wasn't in the mood for it at that moment. I told him how I was feeling and he replied, quick as a flash: "Cheer up, Bob. I can help you out."

How?

"I know just the place where you can go."

Come on then, tell me.

"What's more, I can fix you up with a club."

Come on, tell me!

He simply smiled and said, "Ireland. It's always soft out there!"

Paddy is as proud an Irishman as you'll find, but this wasn't simply him topping up the tourism trade in his homeland. He was spot on when he said the grounds there were always soft and he was well connected with all the clubs out there.

"Bob. I'll get you a team in Dublin in no time."

"Any chance of Cork instead? I'd prefer to be in the south."

"Leave it to me, I've got a good contact there."

The next morning, I limped into training to be greeted by Paddy. "You don't look as if you can go anywhere," he chuckled.

"Don't worry about that. Did you hear anything?"

"The meeting is all arranged, you need to get yourself over to Cork as soon as you can. They're a good club, I think they're second in the league."

I spoke with Malcolm about the possibility of me going to Ireland and he understood my situation, sending me over there with the club's best wishes and armed with the information that no fee would be required to release me from my contract.

I went to Cork to meet the club officials and things were going well. I got a good feel for the place and was feeling very optimistic about spending the last few years of my career there. We got on to talking about football and I told them I was really excited to be joining a club which is second in the table and competing for the league title.

A few of the officials looked stunned by this comment and it took a while for one of them to pipe up: "I think you may have been misinformed. We're actually second from bottom."

Bloody hell, Paddy! I bet he had a good laugh to himself about that. Still, I wasn't going to be deterred by that minor detail. "Well, you're not going to be second from bottom for long because you've just signed me!"

We shook hands on the deal there and then – I was now a Cork Celtic player and my career in England was officially over. I was right, too, about the club not staying second from bottom for long. We went on a great run and ended up winning the title in my first season, earning a spot in the European Cup. I guess the joke was on Paddy after all...

18

SIMPLY THE BEST

Moving to Ireland proved to be a masterstroke both on and off the pitch. I'll tell you more about the latter a little bit later, but first allow me to focus on the football, which was, after all, what took me across the Irish Sea.

I joined a club largely made up of Irish players, with three English lads and a Welshman mixed in. Thank God they were there, because I just couldn't understand half of what was being said in the dressing room! These lads would be chirping from one side of the room to the other and as far as I was concerned they might as well have been speaking a different language. I'd just smile, laugh when everyone else laughed and try to join in the craic whenever I could figure out what they were talking about. It was clear there was a good spirit in the camp and I was just pleased I hadn't come into a bickering dressing room. I was quite fortunate in that respect throughout my career.

That first season, as I alluded to before, we enjoyed a brilliant turnaround to go from the bottom of the table right up to finishing as champions, thanks in no small part to a run of 19 games without defeat. It was my first league title and, boy, did we celebrate! Nobody does that better than the Irish, let me tell you.

My bad luck in the cup continued, though, but on this occasion it was all down to a sneaky opposition player who got away with one of the worst tricks I have ever seen on a football field.

We were playing against Drogheda but the game was all square when we won a corner which I crossed to our midfielder, Ben Hannigan, who sent a header flying towards the net just by the post. The man who was standing on the line, quick as a flash, yanked the netting up so the ball went through it. He turned to the ref and shouted that the ball had gone through the gap from the other side and it wasn't a goal, to which our players obviously responded with a few choice words and a bit of pushing and shoving broke out. The usual handbags, really. The referee was the best in the league, but it was clear he hadn't been able to see exactly what had happened, so while he spoke with the linesman the arguments carried on. This must have gone on for about five minutes before he finally decided he couldn't allow the goal to stand and pointed for a goal-kick. What a farce! The tie eventually went to a replay, which we lost, and my cup misery continued for another year.

As well as perhaps the most bizarre incident of my football career, my time in Ireland also presented me with an opportunity to participate in the European Cup. I'd previously appeared in the Inter-Cities Fairs Cup with Chelsea, when we took on the mighty Roma, AC Milan and Barcelona along the way, but now for the first time, just past my 33rd birthday, I had a chance to test myself in the biggest club competition in world football. Not only that, I was now the player-coach, so in my first few weeks I was pitting my wits against the best in Europe.

I should actually have done all of that on the day of my birthday, as we were scheduled to play the first leg of our first-round tie against a Cypriot side called Omonoia Nicosia. Instead, a bit of trouble flared up there between the Greeks and Turks, so the game wasn't played and we were given a walkover.

In the second round, we were drawn to face an Armenian club called Ararat Yerevan, who you have probably never heard of, but they were a bloody good side, let me tell you. Back then, they competed in the Soviet Top League and to win that they finished above the best sides from Russia and the Ukraine, to name but two nations. They had six or seven internationals in their side and the USSR had finished as runners-up at the last European Championship. Now you've got an idea of what a tough prospect was awaiting us.

We were on a hiding to nothing, make no mistake about that. Cork Celtic were a semi-professional side and this fixture was a once-in-a-lifetime opportunity for most of our players, as well as offering the club an opportunity to make a few bob. We were due to play the first leg in Armenia, but we managed to switch it so that we'd get a bigger crowd than we would if we played them already trailing by five or six goals. We also played the game at our Cork neighbour's ground, Flower Lodge, which was both bigger than our stadium and had a great playing surface. The money men didn't care that a better pitch would suit the opposition, but I don't think anyone was particularly fussed about that. We were just excited about the game.

When they arrived in Ireland, it soon became apparent what a professional outfit they were. We had been told they were not a typical Soviet team, who at that time were known to play strong and dour football. My contacts said they preferred a more artistic and skilful game. They were very talented.

They were big, strong athletes as well, of course, but I could appreciate how good they were when I watched them in training. They moved around in circles as all teams do while working the ball from one to another, but they did it at great speed and they fired it in quickly.

The contrast couldn't have been more apparent than on the night of the game, when I pulled into the car park and hauled the skip containing all of our gear out of the boot of my car and dumped it on the ground. There were two chaps covering the game for the English papers standing next to me and we had a good chuckle about it.

The game itself was actually a pleasant surprise. As is often the case in football, the underdogs played out of their skin – we chased every ball, hassled them at every opportunity and made the most of our two quick frontmen. We just couldn't get the goal we needed to give us a foothold and something to hang on to. They weren't creating any clear-cut chances, but two long-range shots had given them a comfortable lead and there wasn't much for our fans to shout about as we approached stoppage time. However, I then got half a chance and was determined to make it count.

The ball was played across the edge of the box by Dinny Allen, who was a former all Ireland-winning GAA player and more than capable of putting in a decent cross, and I managed to send a stunning left-foot shot arrowing into the corner of the net. What a feeling! And, putting all personal glory to one side, it was a vital strike. With one swing of my left leg we were back in the tie and in with a chance.

That moment has given me my favourite quiz question to ask Chelsea fans: Did I ever score in the European Cup? They think about it for a while and then say: "No, you couldn't have scored in it because Chelsea and Palace never qualified in your time there." Well, there you have it.

We'd given the fans some hope with that late goal, but we knew a stiffer test followed when we flew out to Armenia a fortnight later. The trip itself was nothing short of a disaster. We arrived in Moscow for our connecting flight and must have spent the best part of nine hours waiting around there. Then, when it was finally time to board, we were led out to this tiny plane which looked like it had about 50 seats. We were joined on the flight by some local folk who were carrying all sorts into the cabin. One fella had the spare wheel from his car with him!

When we arrived, there seemed to be a lot of glum expressions on the faces of the locals, but they certainly admired our clothes – quite a few of the lads had offers to buy their gear, with jeans proving to be especially popular. A few took advantage, although quite what they spent their roubles on I do not know. It wasn't really the place for souvenirs, if you catch my drift.

We were very well looked after by the opposition and they played in the Hrazdan Stadium, which was huge and unlike anything many of our players would have experienced before. The dressing rooms were also completely different to what we were used to. Usually, you'd be happy enough just to have a bench going all around the wall, but here they had armchairs for the players to sit in! You could put your feet up, grab yourself a nice cuppa and read the paper. It's a shame more clubs weren't as thoughtful.

I didn't play in the game, probably sensing we'd have to do a fair bit of running around on a big playing surface, and we ended up losing 5-0. Nobody was too disheartened, though, as we knew what a quality outfit they were, which they showed in the next round by pushing the eventual European Cup winners Bayern Munich all the way. It was just a great experience for me at the end of my career and also for the young lads who were just starting out in the game. I'm sure it stood them in good stead.

I was finding it a bit of a struggle to combine coaching and playing. During the week, it was no problem at all and I was really enjoying the coaching side of things, but when it came to matchday it was so difficult to fulfil both roles to the best of my ability. The title win was, by now, long forgotten and the club was desperate for a big name signing to put a few more bums on seats and add a few quid to the coffers.

I'd heard a few rumours that George Best might be available if the price was right. He'd left Manchester United the year before; Tommy Doc was the manager at Old Trafford and I can only imagine the arguments the two of them would have had! Besty seemed to have entered semi-retirement, turning out sporadically for Stockport County in the Fourth Division, but this was a guy not yet even past his 30th birthday, a European

Cup winner seven years earlier and arguably the greatest British footballer of all time. It was ludicrous to think we could even speak with him, let alone convince him to join, but the whispers were growing increasingly louder and I told the chairman we could be in with a shout of bringing him over.

A deal was quickly struck for Besty to come over and play in our home matches for a fee of £1,000 per game, which dwarfed the salaries of everyone else in the squad, but the money from the gate receipts would have more than covered the expense. For the players and supporters, money didn't even come into it. This was an opportunity to see the great Georgie Best in the flesh.

He was due to play his first game just after Christmas when we took on Drogheda United. Talk about having all your Christmases at once. The lads were beside themselves with excitement. All the talk in the dressing room and around the town was, "Best this, Best that." Father Christmas would have to take a back seat to this superstar.

I knew if he stayed in Cork he wouldn't get a moment's peace, so I arranged for him to stay in a hotel near where I lived in the hope he would get a nice, quiet night. He had a lady friend with him, whom he said was his secretary, and I naively asked if he wanted us to book him two rooms to accommodate the pair of them. Yes, I know what you are thinking, I must have been the greenest tree in the forest.

George just laughed at me and said one room would be fine. George Best and quiet nights don't exactly go hand in hand. I rang him at about 7 o'clock on the evening before the game just to check if everything was okay and he asked if I would like to come down for a chat and a coffee.

I took my eldest son Gary with me and we had a very enjoyable evening. It was very interesting to talk to someone I had respected for such a long time and shared a football pitch with over the years without really ever having a proper chat. Gary couldn't believe what a normal fella he was and we were laughing together as we recalled some of the stories he told us.

The next day, he travelled up to Cork for the match, which was being played at Flower Lodge again to allow for all the extra supporters to attend, and he seemed like he was really looking forward to it. The dressing room was abuzz as the other boys came in and were introduced to George. He was so natural you would have thought he had been their team-mate for years.

Outside, the crowd rolled in waiting to see a player they never thought they would see live. He'd always been a great favourite with the fans wherever he went and Cork was no different. The crowd jumped from about 1,500 to 15,000 – that's what you call a real crowd-puller. Men brought their sons to watch just so they could say they were there when George Best played in Cork. I still get people coming up to me today saying "I remember when Besty came over here in the Seventies. What a thrill." The majority of people in Cork at that time who were into football, it didn't matter who they followed, just wanted to see George Best. Imagine if Pele had come to play for your local team – allegiances go out the window, you just want to see a great footballer. You don't miss that opportunity, and the people of Cork didn't.

The 2-0 defeat was almost irrelevant given all the fanfare surrounding the game, although no one blamed George for the result. Our own players seemed to be so much in awe of him that they forgot to worry about their own games. I don't think anyone played up to their usual standard. Then, whenever the ball got to George, he was immediately confronted by two defenders. It seemed the presence of Besty led to the opposition raising their game. He wasn't at his fittest either, but no one cared – they had seen him play live and that was all that mattered.

They would get another chance a fortnight later when we welcomed the champions, Bohemians, to Cork. This was more like the old Besty and he looked noticeably hungrier. I had a great view of the action as I'd been forced to go in goal when our regular keeper, Bertie O'Sullivan, got injured. With George Best playing and Bobby Tambling in goal, anyone could have been forgiven for thinking they were watching an exhibition game, but it was fiercely contested. George was delighting the crowd and chasing back at every opportunity, perhaps spurred on by me shouting like mad every time the opposition came into our half.

Somehow, we were winning 1-0 going into the last few minutes when the referee pointed to the spot. I was our usual penalty taker, but this was an opportunity for me to do the honourable thing and say to George, "Go on, you put it away." Instead, I foolishly ran the length of the pitch to take the spot-kick, only to put the ball wide. I scampered back to play out time, red-faced and not wanting to make eye contact with anyone. I always think of that as one of the biggest embarrassments of my football career – not missing the penalty, but not giving it to George. But I must have played okay as later on I received the Player of the Month award for the first time!

Though George had really enjoyed himself in this game, and it goes without saying everyone in Cork had been mesmerised by one of the greatest football talents to walk the planet, something they still talk about today, I could see that he wasn't playing to his potential.

I had come up against him in England at his most wonderful and I knew we were not going to be able to sustain these incredible gate receipts. Regretfully we had to let him go but then we were due to play Shelbourne away and they asked if there was any chance that George would be on the team sheet.

I explained the arrangement that he was being paid £1,000 per game and Shelbourne agreed to pay it along with all his expenses. Such was his name; such was his brilliance even when his fitness was letting him down. George pulled on the Cork jersey for the last time in that game, but lives on in the folklore and hearts of everyone in Cork.

George went to Fulham a little while later, playing in Division Two, and he was to torment the Blues once again when he scored against us in a 3-1 win for our neighbours. I certainly didn't thank him for that. Rest in peace, George. Just think of the millions of people you entertained and gave so much pleasure to.

Besty wasn't the only superstar to turn out for Cork Celtic at that time. A few weeks later we signed Geoff Hurst and after I'd left they brought in Uwe Seeler, the former West Germany striker who lined up against Hursty in that fateful game at Wembley Stadium in 1966.

Geoff was only with us for a few games, one of which was the local derby against Cork Hibs. We were a fairly decent side, far from being a bunch of cloggers or anything like that, but our opposition were well known for their robust tactics. Put it this way – if you went near one of their defenders, they'd kick you.

Hursty was waiting by the edge of the box before a goal kick in case the keeper didn't get hold of it and I'll never forget the look on his face as he was booted straight up the backside by one of the opposition centre-backs! He couldn't believe what had happened, he was in a total state of shock. I bet if you asked him now about the time he got kicked up the backside by a defender he'd tell you straight away that it happened in Cork. I think he actually scored in that game and got a couple more in his time with us, but that will be the moment he remembers from his brief stay at Turners Cross.

Bridgo, Venner and John Hollins all came out to play in Ireland at one time or another and it became pretty common for big names to come over and "guest" for Irish teams. I don't think it was just seen as an opportunity for one last big payday, I think a lot of them saw it as a chance to extend their career a bit. The football wasn't as good, sure. Without wanting to be unkind, I'd put it on a par with League Two or possibly even lower. But that's not to say there haven't been some outstanding players to come through the Irish league system. A young lad I tried to take over to Leeds when I was scouting for them was David Meyler, but he was from the same area of Cork as Roy Keane, who was managing Sunderland at that time. I knew I had no chance – Keaney only had to ring the doorbell and that was that. You've got Kevin Doyle and Seamus Coleman, and there's a few others who are doing well in the lower leagues. There's a lot of promising talented youngsters. Our female footballers aren't bad, either – Stephanie Roche was in the running for the FIFA Goal of the Year award a few years back.

Locally, in Crosshaven, the players you see are really talented. It's about getting them when they are young enough. You let them do their schooling here, then it's time to get them over to England. I've spent a bit of time coaching youngsters and it is so rewarding. It's lovely when the lads grow up and they still treat you as something of a father figure because you spent so much time with them. I had a fantastic time with them, real good lads who loved a laugh and took a rollicking well. It wasn't until they got to the age of going to university or jobs taking them elsewhere that we split up. It was just fantastic to train them. I worked with some of the best two-touch footballers I'd come across, better than the fellas who had got into the bad habits and couldn't rid themselves of them. I just loved trying to teach them the things Dave Sexton had taught us in the Sixties.

Anyway, I've gone off on a tangent here and there's still my final years as a player to cover. After four years with Cork, I joined Waterford, whose chairman was Joe Delaney, a great guy, and later on I moved to Shamrock Rovers, the club Paddy had wanted me to join. Both clubs are steeped in Irish history as well as being very successful sides.

It was a pleasure to play for both of them. What great fun these lads had while they were playing their football. Waterford had a mix of experienced lads and youngsters aiming to reach the very top. They were great at taking the mickey out of each other and the chairman was as good as anyone for that. He started a running joke which always makes me chuckle when I think about it. If we stayed somewhere on the night before an away game they would all be going to Mass fairly early in the morning. Near enough every single person would knock on my door when they went past, even though they knew I wasn't a Roman Catholic. "Come on, Bobby, get a move on! Come on!"

During my time at Shamrock I also had the good fortune of

sharing a dressing room with a fellow who I'd come up against throughout my time England. To Chelsea supporters, he formed a key part of one of our great enemies, but for me it was just an absolute pleasure to play under Johnny Giles, who was now giving something back to Irish football by managing Shamrock Rovers. He had been an unbelievable midfielder with Leeds and for the Republic of Ireland, and his knowledge of the game was quite incredible. He was combining his role of player-manager at Shamrock with the same position for the Irish national team, which just shows you his appetite for the game.

As my career was winding down, I was to have one last big game away in Argentina representing the League of Ireland. It was in the lead up to the 1978 World Cup, which they were hosting, and we played the national team in La Bombonera. We had some big names in our team, including Giles, Eamon Dunphy and Ray Treacy, and we were greeted by television crews as soon as we got off the plane. They thought it was the Irish national team coming to play a friendly, so they must have got quite a shock when they heard me speak.

I had such a wonderful time playing football in Ireland. We all took it seriously, of course, but the Irish have such a wonderful sense of humour that you can't help but have a laugh about everything.

And it was while I was playing in Ireland that I met my wonderful wife Val.

I joined Crosshaven as manager of their senior team in July 1985. They had been winners of the Munster Senior League in previous years and had some really decent players in their squad. I need to name check a few or they will never forgive me: the great Buzz O'Connell, Willie Lee, Barry McGovern, Jim and John Mulcahy, Mick Cotter, Kevin Gregan, George Meade, Billy Long, Billy and Alan Curran. We had a great season both on and off the pitch. But I must admit that I felt something big was going to happen – and my goodness was I right.

It was pre-season training and I spotted this lovely little blonde girl picking up one of the team after training. I made enquiries as to who she was as I couldn't stop thinking about her. Her name was Val, but she was married like myself and years younger than me. This was a complete no-go area for me, but no matter how hard I tried she kept coming into my thoughts. I made lots of excuses for the team to meet up for social occasions, hoping Val would be there. She had this lovely bubbly personality and was so easy to chat to.

I was also working as manager of the Johnny Giles Sports Shop in Douglas and one day Val came in. I plucked up the courage to ask her if she had time for a coffee. We got chatting and it was like we had known each other all our lives. Val had married young as well and wasn't in the happiest relationship. Her mum, Ena, who was as sharp as a tack, had copped that I was smitten and told her to watch out, but this just made Val realise that she was falling for me too. The more we met up, the more we realised we just had to be together. Nothing else mattered, although we both had families and we didn't want to cause any hurt. It was almost exactly a year to the day after I had first seen her that we decided it was best we just take off and go to England, to start a new life for ourselves in Hayling Island.

19

LIFE'S
SHORT

When I met Val my life changed.

My marriage ended because of my faults and decisions. I hurt people. I loved my children, but I had to get away.

We moved to Portsmouth, close to where all my dreams had started, but that wonderful dream seemed a long way away. I'd hung up my boots and it was now time to go out and do a proper job. I had worked in Ireland with friends in the building trade, which I really enjoyed. We worked hard but had a good laugh while doing so. Yes, it was a long way from the big crowds at Stamford Bridge but I couldn't cling to that forever. I was just a normal guy earning a living.

I got a job through one of my nephews as a hod carrier. For those who don't know what that involves, let me put it in football terms – it's the Makelele role of the bricklaying trade. I'd be the one to carry all the bricks and other building materials (passing the ball) to the bricklayers (the flair players) to work their magic. It didn't worry me, I was just a normal fellow who just wanted to work to keep his head above water. I linked up with two brickies, Steve and Morrie, and we worked together for a good few years, becoming really good mates. Often they were the only ones on the building site who knew I had played for Chelsea. I wasn't ashamed of that fact. Far from it. But if people didn't know about it, I wouldn't be asked the same stupid question every day: "Why are you working on a building site?" As if such a job would be beneath me. I was a normal guy from a normal family and I've never been one to dwell on the past. A few times I'd been on a site a few months without having to explain myself before a driver, for example, would deliver some gear and recognise me. It would go round the site like wildfire, and there was always one smart alec who would say: "I knew it was you right from the start."

By and large, the sites were good for a laugh. It doesn't matter what the work is or what trade you are in, it always goes down much better if you can have a laugh and a joke. On a building site, the most important lesson was to learn to laugh at yourself with the other guys. You'd be pretty miserable otherwise, because the guys were absolutely ruthless! The wind-ups were just as good as any of the football clubs I had been at. Reading about them now, they might seem childish to you, but we had a good laugh at the time.

LIFE'S SHORT

Once, I was asked to bring the water bucket over to a guy. I was walking past it and I just put my arm through the handle all casual, like, trying not to break stride; as I continued walking it nearly took my arm off. Some smart sod had nailed it to the plank! There were four brickies killing themselves laughing.

I think the best trick played on me was when a brickie told me a site drill had been left up on the third floor of the scaffolding and asked me if I would get it. I shot away up there, found the drill box and lifted it up to make sure it was full. It was heavy so I assumed the drill was inside. When I got back down to him, he wanted to make sure everything was okay, knowing full well that instead of the drill there was a brick. I was just about to go back up there again when, falling over laughing, he pulled the drill out of his bag.

Val, who is the most beautiful and wonderful woman you can find, and Jamie, her son, loved living in Portsmouth. I loved it, too. The years passed quickly and before we knew it the 1980s had become the Nineties. Even though I only lived an hour or so away, I never went back to Chelsea in that time. I followed the club's fortunes, just as I had done when I was playing for Palace and in Ireland, and I'd wait by the radio on a Saturday afternoon to find out who had scored for the Blues. Those of you that know your Chelsea history will be fully aware that one name more than any other would have kept cropping up at that time: Kerry Dixon.

I didn't know Kerry back then, although I've since spent a bit of time in his company and found him to be a lovely fella who is Chelsea to the core, but I knew full well what a devastating goal-scorer he was. With each passing season he was inching closer to my record and it got to a stage when I was convinced it was a case of when, rather than if, he'd pass 202 goals. Then, out of the blue, he was sold to Southampton, nine shy of my record, and had he stayed another six months, I'm almost certain he'd have got there, but the record stood for a bit longer. My family were the only others who seemed to be worried.

As I said, I'd not been back to Chelsea at this time, other than as an opposition player with Palace, and I don't think I was fully aware of just how deep my feelings were for this great football club. My life had moved on and, while I always loved the club where I had made my reputation, I didn't realise just how much. But that was all about to change.

I received an invitation to watch a game as one of Ken Bates' guests. Like everyone else, I'd read and heard so much about Ken, most of it negative, but I've never been one to base my opinion of someone on what others say about them. I take everyone as I see them, and it took about two seconds in Ken's company for me to know we were going to get along.

I have to say, I was very much looking forward to finally meeting the man who kept Chelsea alive, and I remember getting there nice and early before any fans had even contemplated putting down their pre-match pint and making their way to Stamford Bridge. I just stared at this wonderful stadium in a state of awe. It was just how we would have liked it to be in our day. The next thing I knew, Ken was walking towards me. We shook hands and the first thing I said to him was: "Thanks very much for saving my club."

Straight away he fired back: "You mean my club, don't you?"

We both started laughing and that was the start of our friendship. It was a perfect way to break the ice because I was slightly apprehensive about meeting him, having seen him many times on television, when he struck me as being a bit too robust. I would find out in time he was quite the opposite. Unseen by many, he is a very kind and generous person to people he hardly knows. His wife, too, is a beautiful and kind woman. Sometimes I wonder where Chelsea would be but for Ken.

Going back to Stamford Bridge brought back all those wonderful memories of my time at this magnificent club. I imagined the stadium as it was in my day, packed with the best supporters a footballer could ever wish to play in front of. I couldn't help but remember my debut against West Ham United, which seemed like it was only yesterday. Where had the time gone? I'd been too busy having fun to realise I was getting old. But in those moments on the pitch, when time seemed to stand still, I was 17 again. I had come home. How could I ever leave this place again?

Later, I would have the chance to walk the walk at half-time, receiving that oh so generous applause from the supporters, the majority of whom were too young to have seen me play, yet so respectful. They made me so proud to have once been called a Chelsea player. What a thrill.

During our time back in England, Val and Jamie would return to Ireland every summer to see her family. But in 1994, with Val's mother unwell, we returned to look after her. What a woman she was, always laughing and joking with us. She liked being part of our family just as we loved being part of hers, and it was always a lively place to be as she had five boys and two girls. She also loved her football and, in particular, Liverpool Football Club. What can I say, nobody's perfect. It made her day when I played in a charity game at Wembley and she had the chance to walk up the famous steps to where the FA Cup was presented. And she got to meet one of her big heroes, Pat Jennings. It's things like this which make me realise just how lucky I was to live this dream on a daily basis. No matter how many times I come to Stamford Bridge, every time I walk into the stadium I am eternally grateful and thankful for everything.

Since I've returned to Ireland that life seems like a dream. I'm very pleased to say that I see my two sons from time to time and they're both keeping well. We'll go for a drink or play a round of golf, things like that. They've given me some wonderful grandkids, all of them Chelsea mad, but I made them promise me they won't call me grandad as it makes me feel old! Life has certainly been very enjoyable in Ireland and I consider it my home now. But things haven't always been rosy here.

With every dream you fear it's going to be followed by a nightmare. I had a good few of them in the game, but nothing compared with what has happened off the pitch in recent years. I have always tried to live with a smile on my face, enjoy life, see the good in people and have fun. Throughout the time I've been in love with Val, life has sometimes been tough, but we have got through it all. You're going to read all about the worst experience of my life in the next chapter but this nightmare simply did not want to go away. I don't really want to go on about an illness, but I do this hoping I can help others who may have the same problem.

I've been lucky to come through it all, but some of my old team-mates haven't been so fortunate. I was in hospital and waiting for an operation when news reached me regarding my old team-mate and great friend, Peter Osgood. He had been at a funeral when he suffered a heart attack and passed away suddenly. I was crestfallen. In hospital, I had plenty of time to think about the years we had spent together at Chelsea. It was a shock that hit me hard. I had no one there that I could really talk to about football and it wasn't until visiting hours I was able to talk about the last time I had seen Peter, which had been some time during the past year. He hadn't looked as well as usual on that occasion, but I hadn't really thought anything of it at the time.

It was at a do at Stamford Bridge and I think it was celebrating the anniversary of winning the 1970 FA Cup, although my memory could be failing me. What I can say for certain is that it had been a great night. There were about 10 of us staying at the hotel at the Bridge and we were, as usual, talking about the good old days – the games, the jokes, the wind-ups. It was all good fun. As the night went on, talk turned to Ian Hutchinson, who we had sadly lost a few years earlier. Both Tommy Hughes, who was back-up goalie to the Cat, and Ossie were very good friends with Hutch, but at different times during his spell at the Bridge. Tom knew him well in his early days when he first came down to Chelsea and they stayed good mates throughout his stay. Ossie and Ian became as thick as thieves through playing together and opening a pub after their playing days ended. They were both right in saying they had been best mates with Hutch, it was just at different times. So far, so ridiculous. The rest of us, mature adults that we are, wound them up a treat about this.

By now it was getting late, but I was absolutely stunned by what happened next. Ossie decided he'd be the first to head off to bed. It was the first time I ever saw that happen! We sent him off to his room with a few barbs about this, and watched as he went off to the lifts. There are two of them there, with a big plant in between the doors, but Ossie had only noticed one of the doors because the other was obscured from where he was standing. He pushed the button and, inevitably, it was the set of doors he couldn't see that opened up. This kept going on and on, and he was getting madder and madder by the second. We were falling about laughing and that only made him worse. Someone tried to tell him what was happening but he wasn't having any of it, he just kept pressing that button. We were in hysterics and finally someone shouted out again for him to look past the plant, where he was greeted by an empty lift. We gave him an almighty cheer and he returned fire with a victory sign!

I'm sorry to say that was the last time I saw the King alive. He really loved life and was full of banter, but he would always go out of his way to help people out. I remember when we were in Europe he would always go around all the lads to see if anyone had any tickets that weren't being used. Any he could snap up would be passed on to the fans. He really was a man of the people. One of a kind. I also remember when I came back to England after years away and he helped me out whenever he had the chance. It was only things like coaching jobs when he couldn't make it along and the odd hospitality gig, but it meant the world to me. I'm sure he helped others out as well. That's just the kind of guy he was. He certainly made you fans feel welcome whenever he was hosting any dos at Stamford Bridge.

When I had left England, I didn't want to be seen hanging around Chelsea, just a limp rag who wouldn't go away. I don't know why I felt that way. The crowd had always been great to me and I had no reason to think they wouldn't want to see me again. I just had this feeling that I'd be seen as someone hanging on. Ossie helped me realise that wasn't the case. He had a role as a host in one of the executive lounges at the Bridge and he couldn't make it for one game. "Bob, how do you fancy standing in for me?" he asked. "Leave Chelsea to me, I'll explain everything to them and okay it. Will you do it? You'll love it."

I agreed and ended up doing it a couple of times. Os was right – I really enjoyed it. Suddenly, I felt part of the club again. I was a footprint from the past, still am, but it's nice to feel that the fans still want to see you. I'm not really one for regrets, but I know I missed out on so much by not coming back to Chelsea for so long, particularly all of those opportunities to talk to the supporters who were always so great to me and the boys. When I got that back again, it was fantastic and I absolutely love being around the club.

It was during my time filling in for Ossie in his role at Chelsea that I ran into Ken Bates more often. He always kept in touch with me and when he found out I'd hurt my back and been advised to give up work, he put on a special do for me at the Bridge with the proceeds going to Val and I. Friends from Ireland flew over with us, it was a great evening and the money raised helped us through a hard time. We were always made welcome at the Bridge by Ken and Suzannah.

He visited us in Ireland, too, and on one such trip he phoned to invite us out for lunch. Over the meal, we talked about what I was doing, which was nothing, and I told him I was bored. I had been used to working and all I was doing was tending the garden. Ken had left Chelsea at this stage and had taken over at Leeds United, which always struck me as quite a strange move because of the history between the two clubs. We had just finished the meal when he leaned across the table. "Why don't you work for me at Leeds? You can be a talent scout for us in Ireland."

I was in total shock – it took a while for it to sink in. Val gave me a kick under the table to bring me out of it and I immediately accepted. I was working under Gwyn Williams, who I also knew from his time at Chelsea, and my job was to look at any players he wanted to check out. I'd send over my report and if Leeds fancied a closer look at them I'd invite the player over to England to see if they could make their dream come true. There is a young goalkeeper, Eric Grimes, who I got over to Leeds from Cork and has made good progress in his career, earning international recognition at Under-21 level. I had a good chat with his parents to put their mind at ease about moving over to Leeds and I hope he enjoys a fine career as he's a great lad and his family are so thankful to see him doing well.

There is so much in my later life I have to thank Ken for. It was quite a strange feeling to be working for Leeds after so many battles with them in my playing days; it was always funny meeting some of their old players and talking about those tough games against one another, hearing a different side to the story. It always ended up with us having a good laugh about them. That's what sport should be about: a good game, hard, both sides fighting to win, but when it's over, respect that it's a game, not a war. I still keep in touch with Ken and Suzannah but not as often as I'd like. I will never forget what he did for us and what he did for Chelsea.

Post-football, I also enjoyed an all too brief career in television. Every time I think about this it makes me laugh. I tell you, I got a hell of a lot of stick for this one – I was so wooden and I don't think I was cut out for the world of showbiz. The thing is, you see footballers in front of the camera all the time now and some of them struggle with it; well, none of us were used to being filmed or even doing many interviews. Nowadays, I'm a lot more comfortable with that sort of thing because of the hospitality work I do at Chelsea. The more you do it, the more confident you get talking to people. That's natural. You can start to make a laugh of things. Although Val always says to me: "You know when someone asks you a question? I don't think I've ever heard you answer it directly." I always find a way to answer it in a way that I can shoehorn something funny in there!

Anyway, there used to be a television show called Fantasy Football League. I'm sure most of you remember it or, at the very least, have some awareness of it. For those who don't, it was basically two comedians, David Baddiel and Frank Skinner, having a bit of banter with footballers and celebrities. When Chelsea reached the FA Cup final in 1994, they wanted me to appear in a sketch. I honestly cannot remember how it came about, but I'd seen the show and enjoyed watching it, and I especially liked the two lads. They were so funny.

When I arrived for filming, they told me what they wanted to do with me and I didn't believe it. I was to sit on an imaginary magic carpet alongside David Baddiel while he sang his unique version of the Bob Dylan song Mr Tambourine Man, which he had imaginatively turned into Mr Tambling Man.

I picked out a really nice blue shirt to wear for the show, keen to look my best on TV and to show my support for Chelsea, but as soon as I got there they took one look at it and said: "Sorry, Bobby, you can't wear that." Apparently, it wouldn't work with the background or something. So, the shirt you can see me wearing on the YouTube clip actually belonged to one of the guys working behind the scenes!

I asked David exactly what he needed me to do on the shoot, to which he replied: "There's not much to it, just make out that you're looking over the edge of a flying carpet."

All I was looking at was the floor. And, obviously, we weren't moving, so I was just looking down at the same bit of the floor while he sang this song, which was taking the mickey out of Chelsea's struggles when he'd started supporting the club. It was hilarious, really enjoyable, and I certainly didn't think it would turn out as well as it did, in the sense that it really did look like we were on a moving magic carpet. It's not like today, when anyone can make something look believable with all of this CGI nonsense.

That was one of the first times a lot of Chelsea fans would have seen me for a long while. I honestly can't remember how on earth they got in contact with me as I was pretty hard to pin down at that time, which was something that I'd decided myself. Having been out of the spotlight for so long, it also emphasises how much of a Chelsea fan David Baddiel is. He didn't forget about me! I've not spoken to him since filming that sketch, but I read in the Chelsea Magazine a few years ago that it was his favourite Blues moment. I'd love to see him again and thank him for taking the piss out of me – and it would be my pleasure if he'd do it again. Actually, I think he was taking the piss out of himself because he was the one singing along.

While we're talking about making fun of me, I've got another picture to show you all in the photos section of this book. It was taken in 2008 but has never seen the light of day – save for a few of the chaps who work on the Chelsea Magazine – until now. I was due to fly over from Ireland to do a Legends Tour at Stamford Bridge, which is always a great laugh as it's always hardcore supporters who seem to know more about my career than I do. In fact, maybe I should have consulted a few of them over this book! Anyway, a couple of days before my flight I received a phone call. "Hello Bobby, this is Richard from the Chelsea Magazine. I hear you're doing a stadium tour at the weekend and I was wondering if I could grab a few minutes of your time for a piece in the magazine."

"Of course you can, I'd really like that."

"There's just one thing. Now, I feel a bit of an idiot asking you this, but I'm new in the job and my editor has come up with an idea for a feature. Your name is Bobby Tambling. Tam-bling. Bling. Like Ali G. So how do you fancy dressing up in an Ali G costume for a few snaps?"

I couldn't stop laughing! Surely he was taking the mickey? The nervous laughter, followed by silence, on the other end of the phone suggested not. But I'm always game for a laugh.

"See you Saturday," I said, still half-expecting them to be winding me up. I was sure I was being had.

Anyway, I turned up at the Bridge on the Saturday morning and started off the tour. I hadn't seen anyone with an Ali G costume and no one mentioned anything to me, so by this point I was convinced it had been a wind-up.

Then this fella turned up halfway through the tour, holding onto a big bag. "Hi, Bobby, nice to meet you. I've got the costume – it cost £50 just to bloody hire it! Shall we see how it looks?"

See for yourself just how ridiculous I looked, but Val loves the pictures and thinks they are hilarious. She was devastated when the magazine called me to say they wouldn't be using them as it had been decided it was a step too far taking the mickey out of the club's all-time leading scorer. "Nonsense," I told them, but secretly I was feeling relieved. I'd have never lived it down.

The pictures still, to this day, have never seen the light of day. But this is my life story and I feel I'd be letting you all down if I didn't show you at least one of these pics. Go on, have a good laugh. Do you know what's even funnier? The chap who dressed me up as Ali G went on to ghostwrite this very book! Sometimes it pays to be a bit silly – life's too short to be serious all of the time.

And as I was about to find out, all too suddenly and scarily, you have to enjoy every moment – because you never know just what lies around the corner...

20

BIGGEST
BATTLE

There is a photograph in this book of the top three goalscorers in Chelsea's history: Frank Lampard, me and Kerry Dixon. Some of you may remember the day it was taken, for it was when my half-time pitch walk was more of a pitch ride; I was pushed around on a wheelchair, unable to stand on my own two feet.

Believe it or not, that was me looking well compared to what I had been through over the previous couple of years. I wasn't kidding when I named this chapter – it truly was the biggest battle I would face.

Interspersed throughout are the words of Val's brother Gerry, whose nickname for years has been Boo, who was with Val and I every step of the way. He wrote them in the immediate aftermath of my ordeal and I believe they help to explain just what a dire situation I found myself in. Make sure you've got a medical encyclopaedia to hand. While many may find much of this chapter double Dutch, I feel it is important to be thorough as there may be others out there going through the same thing I did. If it can help only one person going through the experience I did, then it will have been a worthwhile exercise.

It all started on our flight to Spain in August 2010. Little did I realise then what was to follow. Now, looking back, it was just as well. If I did know, I don't think I could have carried on.

Initially, it was just like any other flight to Spain. Val and I were both in good form and we were looking forward to a nice bit of sun and a relaxing few days. We were sitting on the plane waiting for take-off and my leg was feeling a little sore.

"I think I nicked my leg while doing some gardening yesterday," I said to her.

"Don't worry, once we're in Spain we'll just go to the chemist and get some cream for it," she replied.

Once we arrived in Spain we collected our car and off we went. I had a bit of pain that night, but it wasn't too bad, and we didn't bother going to the chemist until the next day.

The lady gave me some cream to apply to the wound and advised me to see the doctor upon our return to Ireland.

Throughout the holiday I used the cream as directed, but there was no improvement. If anything, the pain was getting worse, and so I started taking paracetamol to try to ease the pain.

The first thing I did when we returned to Cork was book an appointment – the first of many – with my local doctor. First, they started me off with more cream. No change. Then it was antibiotics and cream. No change. Then more antibiotics. No change.

Boo: It was the beginning of the biggest battle of Bobby's life, far distant from the challenges he faced on the pitch in his younger days. This disease acted like a parasite on his emotional, physical and mental state and brought him to the very brink of life and death. It was going to be an ongoing battle for another two or three years, one which above all put a strain on Bobby's fitness and physical activity. However, being an ex-professional football player may have radically contributed to Bobby's ability to handle the disease.

Well, I say no change, but it was getting more painful by the day and so I was stepping up the painkillers. Before I knew it, we were in September and getting ever closer to a cruise we had booked as a treat for the pair of us.

As lovely as the cruise was, the pain remained and I couldn't really do anything physical. They had excursions to different places but I couldn't walk as it was just too painful. Another trip to the doctor resulted in more of the same. Now I was getting concerned.

I managed to get myself across to Chelsea for the Annual Lunch at Stamford Bridge, which took place at the end of November, and I showed my leg to Paddy Mulligan. His response?

"Bob, the minute you get home you have got to get that checked out by a specialist," he insisted. I think he suspected it was cancerous.

When we got home, Val phoned a good friend of mine, who was also my cardiologist: Dr Gerry Fahy. She explained what had been going on since the end of August and he was brilliant. Gerry asked her to take a photo of my leg and send it to his phone. An hour later he rang back to say he had an appointment for me with Dr John Bourke, a brilliant dermatologist, for the following afternoon.

The next day, Val drove me up and I met with John, who was a very nice, quiet man. He took two biopsies and started me on steroids and told me to come back in a week.

I was well dosed up, having been prescribed some strong painkillers, but I couldn't lie down in my bed because of the pain, which in turn meant I couldn't sleep. I was very lucky my brother-in-law, Buzz, had a fabulous leather recliner. Little did I realise it would be my bed for the next two years.

There was no news from John when I went back the following week. Inconclusive biopsies meant more had to be taken, along with more steroids and painkillers but, frustratingly, no let up in my agony.

The doctors were baffled by this disease and the treatment was mainly trial and error. The diagnosis was hard to pinpoint with the progression of the disease, there were no records to compare it to. Was it simply a muscle degenerating problem caused by bacteria or a dermatitis parasite? There were so many underlying problems that the disease ultimately spread from the back to the front of the right leg. At this stage, Bob found it hard to walk.

The disease now overruled his immune system and kept spreading around his leg. There was viscous fluid coming from the black mass as his skin cells died. The discomfort and pain that came with dressing the leg regularly reminded of how serious this disease was and the long road ahead for Bobby and us.

There was no end in sight. I was getting very down in myself as it appeared there was nothing but pain to look forward to. It was getting near Christmas and John decided he would take me into Cork South Infirmary, better known as the South, as it would be easier for him to treat me this way.

I was in there for about eight weeks and, because it was the festive season, they let me out on Christmas Eve and told me to return on 2 January. It didn't matter where I was, Christmas was a disaster. I was in too much pain to enjoy any of it.

Looking back, I feel sorry for everyone around me as it can't have been easy for them, especially poor Val. We were either up and down to the hospital every day or she was visiting me every day with no signs of improvement.

I realise now that I wasn't the easiest to deal with. Val, her brother Ger and son Jamie all tried their best. In January 2011, John thought he had made a breakthrough: he had found something very similar to what I was suffering with. It was called calciphylaxis, which meant there was too much calcium in my blood, so they started me on infusion treatments.

Now, at this stage I was back in hospital and whenever they changed the dressing on my leg and let the air get at it, the pain was simply unbearable. No matter what they gave me, nothing could ease the pain. I started to dread the doctors coming to take a look at my leg.

Nothing seemed to be working. The wound on my leg was so much bigger since I had been admitted to hospital and my blood pressure wasn't great. I think the drugs must have stopped me panicking, as when I cast my mind back to that terrible time it's a wonder I wasn't screaming as the wound rapidly deepened and increased around my leg.

On this initial stay in hospital I had good days and bad days and, of course, I met some wonderful staff in the South who did their best to keep my spirits up along with Val, who was there every day and sometimes even twice a day.

With no improvement in my condition, John reassessed the situation and believed I was suffering with pyoderma gangrenosum. It appeared to match all of my symptoms and we were just so happy that they had finally come up with what it was. So began a new treatment: lots of steroids, which some days seemed to be working but others not, and I was also started on cyclosporine intravenous.

At this point, I must mention how fantastic John Bourke really was. He never stopped researching my symptoms and was constantly talking with other dermatologists worldwide, bringing my case and study to the fore. He never gave up on me – he was truly fantastic.

It appears word had got out that I was in hospital over Christmas and a flood of mail started to arrive from Chelsea supporters the world over. I couldn't believe the amount of goodwill and support I was getting. Some made special cards for me and wrote beautiful messages. I was very touched by each and every one, and I truly believe your support gave me the strength to continue through these very dark and bleak days.

It was terrible to see Bobby kept to a hospital bed. A man with such vigour and vitality, at one point he could run for 90 minutes

and go home and still have the energy to train for another hour.
He had given so many people hours of pleasure when he played
for Chelsea. His legs stood for his symbol of success; now they
were inflicting so much pain and suffering. All the goals and
medals couldn't keep him from coming face to face with death.

If you have got this far, dear reader, you must be feeling utterly
miserable reading about what I went through. But, as you will
have read elsewhere in this book, I have always tried to make
the best of every situation and not take life too seriously, and
even through this nightmare there were some funny moments.
Val and her brothers have a fantastic sense of humour.

There was one occasion when I met the Bishop of Cork and
Ross, John Buckley, during one of his visits to the South. He
was a very nice man and came over to wish me well and we
said a few words to each other. However, a few weeks later I was
taken into Cork University Hospital (CUH) by ambulance and
I was lying in a cubicle, fast asleep, waiting to see the doctor.
As I started to stir, I could feel someone looking down on me.
When I opened my eyes, there was Bishop Buckley in his dis-
tinctive red pontifical vestments, saying a prayer over me. I
nearly leapt out of the bed with the shock! Had I pegged it and
was he already at the pearly gates waiting for me?! Val and Ger
were crying with laughter – the look on my face, I'm told, was
a picture. Bishop Buckley certainly saw the funny side of it as
well.

On another occasion, I was rushed into A&E and my legs were
in agony. Ger searched around for a wheelchair and spotted
one handy in the corridor, so he popped me in and rushed me
to the nurse. I was too distressed to notice that my knees were

up to my chin. The nurse took one look at me. "Sir, you didn't get that wheelchair here," she said.

Ger and I looked at each other, both sharing the same puzzled expression. Then we noticed this poor man struggling out of the gents' toilet. Yikes! In our haste we had rushed off in another man's wheelchair, and he certainly had shorter legs than me.

A lot of the other funny stories are hearsay as I was too out of it on medication or with a high fever. I was dosed to the eyeballs and apparently I was asking Val's brother Buzz to get me something from the ice cream man in the corner!

It was around this time I had Val worried sick as I would call her several times throughout the night and give out to her for not being outside to take me home.

I would be telling my trusty bedside visitors that I really thought I was on a submarine and that I was down in the bar drinking or trying to escape over a fence with my buddies on the run from bombs. My mind was addled from all the medication. I was even sent for an MRI scan in case I truly had lost my mind.

I was really fed up with being in hospital, so one day I phoned Val and told her to come and collect me as I was being let out of hospital. I should add that at this time I was bedridden following a skin graft and I couldn't even stand up, let alone walk. I just wanted to get home come hell or high water.

Val, being the trooper she is, arrived straight away with Ger and Buzz. I told her I was just waiting on the physio to give me the go ahead and I started to get really cross at the delay. Val asked the nurse why there was this hold up and the nurse explained she had already had this conversation with me and that I knew I wasn't going home. When Val came back to tell me, I was eating ice cream – I developed a major love for it during my hospital stays and it clearly loved me back as my weight ballooned – and I nearly cracked the spoon with temper as she explained that I wouldn't be going home.

I now know that I haven't the greatest of patience and I guess that comes from being a professional footballer for a good span of my life. We were so spoilt, with everything being done for us.

Even though the situation looked grim at times, Valerie and I strived to motivate Bobby towards a purpose he could conquer while in hospital, whether it was to walk a few steps a day or just sit up. We strived to keep the atmosphere light with stories of how Bobby believed the nurses were partying at night in the ward or how he was on a submarine.

Then there was the time he told us vehemently that he was allowed home when we knew this wasn't true. I went to get the matron (oh, behave!) as Valerie had gone to get something to eat. However, when I came back to find an empty bed, I began to panic until I heard a moan coming from the side of the bed where Bobby had managed to get stuck between it and the wall.

Throughout 2012, I think I spent more time doing the rounds of the three major hospitals in Cork than I did at home. I did, however, manage to get out in March as we had planned a trip to see Chelsea's home game against Stoke.

My leg was in agony and I had to use wheelchair assistance at the airport for the first time, but I got through it with a load of painkillers and was able to make it out onto the pitch at half-time to show my appreciation to the fans for their wonderful support and letters. Having watched the footage again, I can see how much of a struggle it was just to walk.

A few weeks later, they decided to try a skin graft at the CUH. Mr Jason Kelly took skin from my thigh and did his best to cover the leg. Initially, I was delighted to have less pain, but that emotion wasn't to last as a small area at the edge of the graft started to get active again and the disease was soon destroying more parts of my leg.

It was now May 2012 and I had been at the CUH for a few weeks when I got an invitation to Chelsea's Player of the Year awards dinner. Val explained that I was in hospital, but they were very anxious to get me over as I was to be presented with a Special Recognition Award.

I hadn't a hope of getting over for it. I was devastated. I couldn't believe I had been selected for this wonderful award by the club so dear to my heart and I couldn't even be there to accept it. If I had been feeling low before, I was now utterly heartbroken. I cried my eyes out.

I wasn't going to sulk about it, though, so I asked Val if she would go and accept it on my behalf. Her and Buzz went along to Stamford Bridge and did a great job, and they presented me with the award upon their return. I was thrilled, but it was tempered with the sadness of not being there myself.

Still, knowing that the club cared for me, along with all the supporters who were still making calls, sending letters and emailing their support, gave me even more strength to keep fighting.

I was so depressed at this time that I didn't even realise how heartbroken Val and her family had been on my behalf. They couldn't bear the idea of me receiving such an amazing award in a hospital bed, so they got together and planned a surprise. Derval, Val's sister-in-law, came up with the idea of putting on a special awards night for me.

I probably should have been suspicious of all the phone calls that were going on at that time, especially as Val had to leave the room each time her mobile rang. The two of them were planning the night to perfection.

They had managed to get my best friends Barry and Megan Bridges, along with Paddy Mulligan and his lovely partner, and even Neil Barnett from Chelsea TV to travel over to Cork.

I knew nothing about it, only that I was going for a meal at the Royal Cork Yacht Club with my friends Don and Christine Slyne. I remember saying to Val as I hobbled in on my crutches that it looked pretty busy as there were loads of cars outside. Little did I know what was waiting inside for me.

When I got to the foyer, I was greeted by Derval and my son Gary, who explained there were a few people waiting inside to see me. It still hadn't clicked with me, but as I walked through the doors of the restaurant everyone stood up and started singing Blue is the Colour! The yacht club was decked out in blue and white balloons and covers on all the chairs. It was spectacular.

Derval guided me to a table and I started to spot friends and family on the way as well as players from local teams I had coached. Then there was Barry and Paddy at the top table with big hugs for me, along with Neil and my great mate Steve Forbes and his buddy Trigg. Even the docs were there; my heart was thumping so much I thought we might soon be needing them in a professional capacity!

I just couldn't believe it. I was gobsmacked. All in all, there was more than 120 people there and every one of them meant so much to me. Even the band was special as it was our next door neighbour Paul Murtagh and his mates. As usual, they were terrific.

My award was there, too, sneaked out of the house by Val and presented to me by Gary. There was a phone call from Frank Lampard to wish me well and Derval presented me with a special This Is Your Life-style photo book, which I treasure so much. Believe me, that night had me floating on air and got me through a very wet and terrible summer.

At this point, I must add something I found out much later after that wonderful night. There had been a mysterious bene-factor who had helped out with the expenses, so that it had been possible to make the night just like a proper Chelsea do. That benefactor was my good friend Frank Lampard. What a gem.

I was invited to spend a week in Miami in August during Chelsea's tour of America and I didn't think I could make it. But the tickets were booked and I was out of hospital, so I felt I should go. Who was to tell at this stage if this could be my last trip on a plane? I didn't want the disease to keep winning, so I kept pushing myself to do what I wanted to do when I could, even though the pain was severe. The Chelsea fans were bril-liant once again and looked after myself and Val brilliantly. It was a wonderful tonic.

There was still no sign of improvement in my condition and my heart was out of rhythm following one of the operations, which meant I was a bucket of sweat trying to move anywhere. I was doing my utmost to use crutches, but even getting to the bathroom was a struggle.

Up until now, the disease had only been in my right leg. I had often commented to Val that at least I still had my trusty left leg that had served me so well on a football field through the years. But I was worried about it spreading across.

It was around this time that John Bourke, who had been relentless in his pursuit to cure this disease, discovered the real cause of my disease. He said it was a hypertensive Martorell leg ulcer, and this time he was 99 per cent sure.

Unfortunately, it is one of the most difficult ulcers to diagnose and often gets mistaken for pyoderma gangrenosum. Their treatments are polar opposites, so the treatment of pyoderma can actually aggravate the Martorell ulcer.

My journey to recovery took on a new course, but as much as I tried to get my hopes up, I honestly felt at this stage that I was fighting a losing battle. Val remained as positive as ever, though, and she was learning as much as possible about my condition and its devastation.

There was more skin grafts and more liver spots as my lower leg resembled a patchwork quilt from a horror movie or even as if a shark had got a hold of it and had a good feed.

To top it all off, I was diagnosed with prostate cancer and my heart was still out of rhythm, so I was out of breath quite a lot. Of course, cancer of the prostate means peeing a lot – and that was one thing that took so much effort for me. I felt I had run the London Marathon every time I got to the toilet.

My two cardiologist friends, Gerry and Carl, were constantly working with John and Mr Kelly, doing their utmost to get my blood pressure under control and to get my heart back in rhythm.

Then, another disaster. On one trip home from the hospital

towards the end of 2012, I caught my left leg on the car door. A tiny nick. Please, no – not my good leg. But alas, yes. It started and it was rampant and faster than it had ever been. I couldn't bear the thought of going through it all again. This time the pain seemed worse as I was probably becoming immune to painkillers, so I had to up the dose and I started to drift in and out of reality.

I have no recollection of Christmas 2012. I had been let out of hospital to be at home, and Val said I am probably better off not remembering. Apparently, at one stage I told her and Jamie that it was the best Christmas I ever had!

I was back into the South on 2 January and at this stage I was too sick to care where I was. I had developed pneumonia. My leg was badly infected. I was hallucinating and Val was at her wit's end.

It seemed as if an anchor was permanently tied to his feet and he was being dragged down further and further. He was isolated but, between his immune system being damaged and the leg disease, he was knocking on death's door with only his inner strength to fight it.

The doctor maintained it would be a 24-hour wait to see if Bob could beat it – and he did. With all his willpower and the strength that made him brilliant on the field, he fought back. He sweated it out and then fell to shivering.

The doctors theorised that had he not been a professional footballer he would not have survived the struggle.

I had often asked John if amputating my leg would end the pain. That's how bad I felt. He said he didn't think that was the answer. Well, what was? And could they come up with it pronto?

I was so sick they moved me to the CUH and a room on my own where they had the best equipment to treat me. I drifted in and out of it for the first four months, but I was receiving the best care imaginable.

There seemed to be no light at the end of our tunnel, we appeared destined for failure, standing on the edge of a ravine without a branch to hold onto. The hospital trips began to take their toll after three months. At the beginning, Valerie and I would visit in the morning or evening. It was soul-destroying at times to see Bobby, a withered man, his mind foggy from such strong medication and unable to register our presence or forget we had visited at all.

They even had to do a skin graft using an epidural as I was too sick to be put under, but thankfully I was oblivious.

The treatment I received from the doctors, nurses and all their wonderful staff saved my life and I know that if it wasn't for them I wouldn't still be here and able to write my story. There are too many to list, but everyone from the girls who brought me my meals, those who cleaned my room, the marvellous patient nurses and the docs: a massive THANK YOU. I know I keep thanking Val and saying how wonderful she was, but I cannot overstate what a rock she was.

The physiotherapist, who I praise to this day as a saint of persistence and patience, helped Bobby walk again with a rota of exercises to be done every day from his hospital bed. After a week or two he was able to sit up in bed with enough strength to do it.

By now, Bobby had also come to recognise the familiar faces of the nursing staff and as he was growing quite partial to a Denny's sausage sandwich, those nurses made sure he had his sandwich of a morning!

All of the nurses went above the call of their duties to ensure Bobby's comfort during his illness. It was like a scene from a Carry On film at times, with Bobby providing the comedic repartee while the nurses mollycoddled him. I never did ask him what the secret was with the nurses, but Austin Powers couldn't have said it any better when he replied: "I still have my mojo!"

After three months of painful physio, Bob was allowed home. His physical and emotional distress had taken a heavy toll on body and mind.

Bobby had to relearn everything as if a child learning to crawl and then walk.

He might never had been a soldier but, by God, his legs had been through the wars, the skin marred as if hit by shrapnel and the faint outline of new skin connecting to old as he healed from the grafts.

When Bobby came home, myself and Valerie were changing the dressings. We became professional nurses and experts in all but name. The last treatment that Dr John Bourke gave Bobby stopped the disease with the grafts that Mr Kelly performed.

It was all worthwhile in the end just to see him getting a standing ovation at the game between Chelsea and Fulham from the people that matter most to him – his longstanding Chelsea fans. Everything else just pales into insignificance.

Well done, Bob. You won the greatest battle of your life and are able to fulfil that one wish you had during those two years of hell. Like the man himself, it was a very modest wish: to *walk with Valerie and their three beloved dogs out to the local Crosshaven walkway with the sun and wind in his face. Without the support network, central to which was his partner Valerie, it might have been a very different story.*

As I began to improve and get my mind back together, it was a chance for me to think of all the people who helped me come through the ordeal. All of the medical staff in all three hospitals in Cork treated me superbly and kept my spirits up throughout. There are so many people to thank; my sons Gary and Glenn, Val and Boo for always being there for me. I was blessed when Val and I got together. Many people told us it wouldn't last because of the age difference between us. The things she had to face up to just in those bad days of the illness, it was so hard for her but she was always there, keeping me going. Some days it was just with a smile and a laugh, but that's all I needed. After 30 years together, I think we have proved age doesn't make any difference.

I've also got to thank the friends who all kept me going, even those who I hadn't seen too often in later life. And, of course, those wonderful fans whose well wishes brought a smile to my face and a tear to my eye. It was a great team effort. I had now turned the corner. It was time to get my life back.

Events like this make you realise what you've got and how fortunate you are to have loved ones. They also make you think and reminisce about your life and, in my case, the joy that being a footballer has brought me.

21

FAMOUS
FIVE

Chelsea supporters know me as the player who was once the leading scorer at this football club and, as a result, the first question many ask upon meeting me is the same: what was the best goal I scored? It's a difficult one to answer for a number of reasons.

There's no problem remembering them – any goalscorer will be able to tell you just about every goal he's ever scored, believe me. The issue is how one decides upon what makes a goal great. For me, it isn't necessarily the one which was the most pleasing on the eye, it's all about how important it was.

Before I give you the list of my favourite goals, I want to give you an example that wasn't scored by me which backs up what I have written so far. It was the goal by Tommy Harmer up at Sunderland which was pivotal in our promotion back to the top flight in 1962/63 and was such a great moment for every single person associated with the football club. I cannot overstate the importance of this goal. Without it, we wouldn't have been promoted, it's as simple as that. But it wasn't much to look at – it went in off his private parts!

So, when I tell you about my best goals and you think: "Well, why's he put that one in there? It was only a tap-in." Now you know why.

5. Liverpool 1-2 Chelsea (FA Cup), 22.01.66

As far as FA Cup draws go, it doesn't get much tougher than getting the holders on their own patch in the third round. Liverpool had won the competition for the first time in 1965, beating us in the semi-final after John Mortimore had controversially seen a goal disallowed for reasons beyond me, and to face them at Anfield was a huge test of our character. But the day you don't want to play in a game like this is the day when you ought to be hanging up your boots.

Even going one goal behind didn't seem to bother us, such was our confidence in one another, and we drew level before half-time with a classic corner routine that we worked ever so hard at: inswinger to Bridgo at the near post to flick on for Ossie to run in behind him and turn the ball in. Textbook.

We carried on our good work into the second half and were keeping the ball well, playing out from the back, which proved to be the catalyst for our second goal. Peter Bonetti threw the ball out to Ron Harris, who played it to Terry Venables. I came in off the left wing to receive the pass and lay the ball on to George Graham down the right; I carried on my run and George sent in a tremendous cross which I got my head to. It wasn't a bullet header by any stretch. In fact, it looped over the defender and dropped just under the bar. What a result!

I'll never forget the feeling in the dressing room after the game. It was absolutely wonderful and that carried on all the way back to London on the train. The fans were on great form, too, and that all played a part in making this goal particularly special.

4. Chelsea 2-0 Sheffield Wednesday (FA Cup), 12.03.68)

I know what you are going to think when I describe this goal to you: what were you saying about importance being everything? Well, allow me this indulgence for a one in a million free-kick.

Johnny Boyle and I loved to practise set-pieces against Peter Bonetti, trying to bend the ball around the wall to catch out Catty. What you've got to bear in mind at this point is that the footballs weren't anything like the balloons players get to use today. These were rock-hard footballs and if you could manage to get any sort of swerve on them at all you were doing well. We could get the odd one to bend around the wall, but it was very much hit and miss – usually the latter, if I'm being honest. We decided to see how it would work if the ball was nudged slightly by the other player. The result, as I was to discover, could be spectacular.

Come the day of the game we got a free-kick about two yards outside the box, just to the left of centre. John looked straight over at me. "Remember what we worked on?" he asked. "Well, just go for it."

He stood over the free-kick and gave it a little nudge. I ran up and caught it so sweetly. It curled around the wall on the left-hand side and Peter Springett in goal didn't even move as it crept inside the post.

The strangest thing about it was that John and I never tried that free-kick again, and I have absolutely no idea why. It was a stunning goal.

3. Chelsea 1-0 Leeds United (FA Cup), 12.02.66

After beating Liverpool in the third round we were drawn at home to Leeds United, who had reached the final the year before. That was our luck in the FA Cup, both finalists in consecutive rounds.

It was another close, hard-fought game of few chances and it was apparent that one goal was all it would take to win it. George Graham was involved again, getting on the end of a free-kick and, although he managed to beat Gary Sprake, the ball came back off the post. I was moving towards goal as it dropped at my feet; Sprake had gone for the first effort, so I had a nice empty net to put the ball in. Better to be lucky than good, eh? I remember the sheer elation I felt, setting off in celebration, and I think I must have made it back to the halfway line by the time any of the lads had caught up with me!

What made this all the more special was the manner in which the lads had to dig in to hold on to the lead, with two wonderful saves from Peter Bonetti to deny Jack Charlton really sticking out in my mind. Yes, I had scored what turned out to be the winning goal, but every single fella on our team stuck his hand up and put in a performance that day. And then we went and blew it in the semi-finals, again.

2. Aston Villa 2-4 Chelsea (First Division), 27.11.65

It's goals like this which make me wish I'd been playing in to-day's era, when there are enough television cameras at foot-ball grounds to bring you replays from every imaginable angle. Even one camera would have been enough, mind.

As you will know by this stage, I'm a keen golfer, a lifetime addiction fuelled by those second-hand clubs given to me as a "signing-on bonus" by Jimmy Thompson. Well, any fellow golf enthusiasts out there will appreciate reading about this goal.

We were playing Aston Villa at Villa Park, which turned out to be a lucky ground for me whenever I was up against the Villans. I'd also add for any younger readers that they were a darn sight better than the Villa side from recent years!

We were in front and playing well when we launched another attack down the left. The ball came to me and I took it into the box at an angle, about 15 yards out, when the keeper came out to close me down. He actually did a very good job, because I could hardly see any of the goal. There was only one thing for it – out came the lob wedge, or perhaps I should call it the leather wedge in this instance. I knew I'd have to hit it perfectly in order to get my shot over him quickly but still manage to drop down into the goal. I stubbed my toe under the ball and managed to stop during the follow-through. It worked like a dream.

I've tried it many a time with a golf club and rarely has it come off quite so sweetly as that.

1. France 5-2 England (European Championship), 27.02.63

This was a no-brainer for me. For all of the 202 goals I scored for Chelsea, I had never grown up dreaming of putting the ball in the back of the net for the Blues. I love the club to bits, but I did not become a fan until the day I signed on the dotted line. However, to score for your country is something just about every young footballer dreams of.

Just to get on the field in an England jersey at schoolboy level was truly wonderful. To do it at senior level was an honour that even today sends tingles up my spine. And to score for them? Wow, just wow. What an honour. When I look back on my career, it is the icing on the cake.

As you will know from the chapter on my England career, the result of our game against France is not one I care to be reminded of too often, but Paris was the scene of my first and only goal with three lions on my chest and I will always cherish that.

In training, we worked hard on our set-pieces. For the corners, despite me being one of our smaller players, I was to be the last of the three to run into the box. The two in front were big chaps and I had to make sure I timed my run a little later. Well, the French took too much notice of the big fellas, because I was free to head it home without even jumping. It flew into the net! Although our plan worked perfectly, not a lot else did that night...

I'm sure I'm like almost all strikers when I say that it doesn't matter how it goes in, a goal is a goal. Ever since I was seven years old I loved to put the ball between the posts. In fact, when helping my father with chickens I'd make the most of any downtime to make a goal with two buckets and shoot from about 20 yards. I would chase after the ball and do the same from the other side of the goal and every time I missed I made doubly sure the next one went between the buckets. It's hard to coach players to be a natural goalscorer, which is why they are so hard to come by.

Quite a few have impressed me over the years. I've mentioned Jimmy Greaves several times, so it will come as no surprise that he is top of the list of my favourite goalscorers. He was a really cheeky chap, but when it came to finishing he was ice cool. He'd always be in the right place and he'd never really power the ball in, seemingly hitting the ball just hard enough.

Another fellow from our time was Denis Law of Manchester United. He was deadly in and around the box and he could turn on a sixpence. Despite not being the tallest, he was very good with his head and he was the quick, darting type of forward who was hard for defenders to get close to. From the same club you had quite the opposite in Bobby Charlton. He was an explosive shooter who scored so many goals from outside the box. He'd make his own openings and he could shoot with the same power and accuracy in either foot. What a nightmare for defenders.

I'm going to sound like a Man United fan here, but George Best is next on my list. He wasn't just a natural goalscorer, he was a natural footballer. He'd score for fun and so many of his goals he made for himself. What a great player Besty was, and I am so honoured to have been able to call him a team-mate for that brief time in Ireland.

Lastly, I'm going to select a player from the modern game: Lionel Messi. I just love watching him play. He is like an artist on the pitch, particularly when it comes to goalscoring and, like Besty, he makes his own; like Greavsie, he always seems to stroke it in. He is a genius.

22

THE WAY I
SEE IT

It has been almost half a century since I last kicked a ball for Chelsea, but the wonderful thing about this football club is the way they look after their old players. That doesn't only apply to the people running the club, it's the supporters who I speak to on an almost weekly basis when I'm back at the Bridge to work for the matchday hospitality team.

As anyone who has met me will know, I love talking about football. It doesn't matter if it's analysing the modern game or reminiscing about life at this great football club or whatever, I'll happily sit for hours chewing the fat with the fans.

There is one question which comes up perhaps more than any other, so I thought it would be a good idea to address it in my book. Would I have rather played in the modern era, when footballers today are among the most famous people in the country and handsomely rewarded for it? I suppose, because of the huge difference in our pay packets, most think the answer would probably be yes. And most of us probably would! You'd have to be an absolute idiot, and my bank manager would never forgive me, to say no. I'd love to. But I honestly don't think I could play today with all the razzmatazz that goes with being a superstar. We were normal guys, and still are, just like any of you. We'd come to games on the Tube and most people wouldn't know us from Adam. Occasionally, someone would notice you and pluck up the courage to ask for an autograph, and then for the rest of the journey all eyes would be on you.

I found my first contract a few years ago, and do you know how much I was on? £9 a week, and nothing in the summer! Oh, and let's not forget the signing on fee: a set of second-hand golf clubs. Roy Bentley was getting £12 a week in 1956 and he was one of the best players in the country.

The financial situation was different in our day. The club's income came mainly through gate receipts on a matchday, so the supporters were really keeping clubs going. They couldn't just pay out all sorts to the players. They had to balance the books somehow and, as we saw at Chelsea in the late 1970s, if they didn't do a good job of it, then the consequences could be dire. There was no big television deal – that didn't come around until Sky Sports and the Premier League in the Nineties – and there wasn't really all that much advertising. In short, the money just wasn't there and players were paid accordingly.

THE WAY I SEE IT

The other factor that a lot of people don't consider is whether we'd even be good enough for the modern game. The aim, of course, has always been to score one more than the opposition and there are still 22 players on the pitch, but it has changed so much in the time since I hung up my boots. I'd like to think I'd have been able to adapt and I'm sure many of my old team-mates would have done as well. Are you telling me Bridgo's pace wouldn't have made him an asset in the modern game? Would Venner's innovative thinking and range of passing suddenly desert him just because it's 50 years down the line? I don't think so.

I never sit around wondering what might have been if I'd played in a different era, but what I do know for certain is that I wouldn't have traded anything from my playing career. I enjoyed my football, the game itself, the camaraderie with the lads and, most of all, I could identify with the fans. The pressure players and clubs are under these days is immense, particularly for the top clubs to finish in the top four. So much so that young players struggle to get an opportunity to go to the top and play for the first team of a Premier League side. If you look through the history of football, teams have typically produced players to go from the youth set-up right through to the first team. Think back to the Sixties and all of the big names at Chelsea – nearly all of them came through the ranks. I think at one point our first team had eight or nine former youth players.

Those days are long gone, and it's a shame. I hope English football can find a solution.

I'd also like to take this opportunity to discuss a few other changes that I believe should be made to football across the world. I've watched, played and followed the beautiful game almost my entire life and there is a rule change that I assumed had passed me by. I even looked in the Laws of the Game just to double check, but the page titled "Wrestling in the penalty area" must have been torn out of the copy I flicked through.

I'm referring to players using their hands and arms to impede players at dead-ball situations. It happens at almost every corner or free-kick and sometimes it is going on right in front of the referee. This certainly didn't occur very often when I was playing, although occasionally your shirt would be tugged just to put you off your step. The Italians were the best – or should I say worst, depending on your point of view – at doing this, but it was hard for the referees to pick up as it was usually just a pinch on the shirt, just enough to put you off at the start of your run. Very subtle and nothing like the wrestling which goes on at set-pieces today. Is the game becoming like American football? Even rugby doesn't let this happen at line-outs.

People often argue that they can't stop it as there would be 10 or 15 penalties every game. I know footballers are often thought of as not being the sharpest, but how stupid do people think they are? If penalties were being given left, right and centre they would soon learn.

Why is this happening? Can the defenders not mark the attacking players as they should do? A lot of the time they are not even watching the ball, their eyes never leave their man.

Who do we blame for this? Well, I ask of the players who do this: do you realise the number of children playing the game who see the professionals doing it and therefore deem it acceptable behaviour? Is this what they are teaching at the top end of the game, coaches turning a blind eye and saying it's all right with them? As for the referee, well, isn't he supposed to run the game according to the rulebook? If someone could point me to the page in the rule book where it says this is acceptable, then I shall say no more about it.

We've seen in the past that referees have been given instructions on how to handle different situations that have cropped up. Take the tackle from behind, which was a favourite in our day, when defenders would kick through the back of your legs. That was clamped down on, albeit a good few years too late as far as I was concerned as it would have been nice if it didn't happen to me every week! And diving in with your feet up has meant the slide tackle has almost been done away with altogether, but it is a challenge that can be very dangerous to the opposition and it's good to see less of it.

This shows that FIFA and the FA do look at the games and instruct referees to act upon certain things that creep into the game. So why is nothing being done about this? I asked that very question to Prince Ali bin Hussein, who you may recall from the FIFA presidential election in 2016.

Val and I were invited to the 2015 Community Shield and I was sat next to him at the pre-match lunch. I whispered to Val: "Isn't he the chap running for the FIFA job?" She wasn't entirely sure, so I asked David Rocastle's son, who was a very nice chap, and he confirmed it was Prince Ali. I decided I'd have a little chat with him.

He seemed like a good guy, so I brought up my feelings about this regular occurrence in football which had been really bugging me. I also told him I don't understand why the poor referees aren't helped out by television replays. I want to see the cheats caught and I want them out of the game. He agreed with me.

Take Diego Maradona's "Hand of God". That's one of many bad decisions which have robbed a side of having a chance to progress in the World Cup, a tournament which comes around once every four years and many players may only have one opportunity to play in it – if they are lucky. What about Ireland losing out to that Thierry Henry handball in qualifying for the 2010 World Cup?

I know they don't want to change football from the top level to grassroots, but this is the pinnacle of the game. You don't want to lose out to cheating. If I'd been in the England team when Maradona cheated us, and then had the cheek to call it "the Hand of God"... well, you can guess where I'd have told him to stick his hand.

We need to decide if this is a sport we are playing or if it's sports entertainment. For me, you only want the right decision. Rugby, tennis, horse racing, cricket – they all use technology to decide the big calls. Horse racing is decided by fractions and there is a hell of a lot of money at stake, just like football, but they make sure they get it right.

All of the clubs at the highest level have the facilities to help out the referees, who have the toughest job in football, especially when you consider the speed of the modern game. Let's embrace technology. They did it at Wimbledon, a British sporting institution which was seemingly set in its ways. You've got to make the top of the tree perfect.

These are not local cup games down the park, but the biggest competitions in world football. Every effort should be made so the cheaters don't win. Fair play for all.

It's also been said it would take too long to make a decision and it would slow down the game too much, but would it really be any longer than the ref marking out where the ball is to go and then marking out the wall at free-kicks? Even if it did, the likelihood of the correct call being made would surely clamp down on all the deception.

We should be able to learn from other sports, there are all kinds of things we can take from them. I think rugby is a game which could help us a good bit. Firstly, the respect players have for the officials and the manner in which the referees talk to the players. They are so clear and concise, telling them exactly what they are doing to upset him. I also feel the yellow card has very little effect in football, whereas in rugby it's a 10-minute spell in the sin bin. That would certainly help, especially if the game is getting out of control. There could be times when we end up watching six-a-side games. But it would soon stop players.

And don't get me started on the offside rule. Can you tell me of a situation when you are on the pitch but not interfering with play? If you are on the field then you are in play as far as I'm concerned. What about the other way around. Say the right-back is playing the forward onside but he holds his hands up and walks in the opposite direction. Would the forward then be offside? Why can't they make it as easy as they can for the officials? It's very difficult to have your eye on the forward riding the line and the player passing the ball, who could be 50 yards away. There's a split second between when the ball is kicked and when the player starts his run, and all the time they are trying to keep in line with the last defender.

Finally, I know elections take place every four years, but I don't think the big bosses in the organisations that run the world game should be allowed to keep running for the top job once they've served in that role.

I'm no political expert, just a simple guy, but I think it's fair if they have a four-year reign then they can't run again. There's no reason they can't serve in an advisory role after this, but they shouldn't be making the big decisions for such a long period of time.

The mess FIFA have been in recently is no flash in the pan and the venue for the World Cup shouldn't be used to improve a country's support for the game. Do we see this happen in other sports? It should go to countries who are in the position to run such a competition, who have supported football for a long while, not just anyone. Some of these countries have never had a World Cup played in their country. What must they feel when they see what has happened recently?

These are just my feelings on a few subjects and, while you may not agree with all of them, I'm sure football fans all over the world would agree that we all just want to see fair play. I hope we can look back on this chapter in a few years time and have a good laugh, but I suspect we'll still be talking about the same old problems.

And so I come to the end of my story.

You may well ask why I decided to write this book now, almost 50 years since I last pulled on that famous blue shirt.

I guess it's because I got a second chance.

When I was very sick in hospital, Val planned a trip to Chelsea with her brother Buzz and Derval, which was something for me to focus on. Derval had made contact with Emma Wilkinson at Chelsea, who was totally brilliant and had arranged everything: our airport transfers, accommodation and for Val and I to be in the directors' box and to be as comfortable as possible.

THE WAY I SEE IT

At the time, I am sure they were thinking I might never get there, but at least it was something I could focus on. I was let out of hospital three days before that trip, wheelchair bound and a total nervous wreck. I was shaking at the airport, thinking I was not even going to be able to get on that flight. Val assured me that everything was going to be fine. Buzz would be there to push the chair. A car was meeting us at the airport. Don't be worried!

We got to Heathrow and into the car and as we started towards the Bridge, a calm came over me. I was coming home; everything was going to be okay.

Chelsea were playing Swansea and Neil Barnett met me before the game and asked if I would go on the pitch at half-time.

Of course – it would be my honour. Buzz pushed me onto the pitch and the crowd erupted like never before. I couldn't believe it. I broke down. Val was crying. Buzz was crying. There was grown men in the crowd crying. But that was the moment... that was the moment my determination came back.

The determination to fight again. To stand again. To walk again.

To live every second. To cherish every moment. And to never let an opportunity pass to meet the Chelsea fans and to thank them for bringing me back to life.

I am eternally grateful to you all.

STATISTICS

Bobby Tambling's Chelsea record

COMPILED BY PAUL DUTTON

CHELSEA CAREER APPEARANCES AND GOALS
SEASON-BY-SEASON

Season (Div)	League		FA Cup		Europe		League Cup	
Goals	Apps	Goals	Apps	Goals	Apps	Goals	Apps	Goals
1958/59 (1)	1	1	-	-	-	-	-	-
1959/60 (1)	4	1	-	-	-	-	-	-
1960/61 (1)	24	9	1	-	-	-	3	3
1961/62 (1)	34	20	1	2	-	-	-	-
1962/63 (2)	40	35	4	2	-	-	-	-
1963/64 (1)	35	17	2	2	-	-	1	-
1964/65 (1)	33	15	5	4	-	-	7	6
1965/66 (1)	26	16	6	5	10	2	-	-
1966/67 (1)	36	21	7	6	-	-	3	1
1967/68 (1)	24	12	5	3	-	-	1	-
1968/69 (1)	36+2	17	5	1	4	1	3	-
1969/70 (1)	5+2	-	-	-	-	-	-	-
Totals	**298+4**	**164**	**36**	**25**	**14**	**3**	**18**	**10**

Overall totals: 366+4 appearances and 202 goals

BOBBY TAMBLING

CHELSEA'S LEAGUE RECORD IN TAMBLING ERA

Division One	P	W	D	L	F	A	GD	PTS	POS	Top League scorer
1958/59	42	18	4	20	77	98	-21	40	14th	Jimmy Greaves 32
1959/60	42	14	9	19	76	91	-15	37	18th	Jimmy Greaves 29
1960/61	42	15	7	20	98	100	-2	37	12th	Jimmy Greaves 41
1961/62	42	9	10	23	63	94	-31	28	22nd	Bobby Tambling 20
Division Two										
1962/63	42	24	4	14	81	42	39	52	2nd	Bobby Tambling 35
Division One										
1963/64	42	20	10	12	72	56	16	50	5th	Bobby Tambling 17
1964/65	42	24	8	10	89	54	35	56	3rd	Barry Bridges 20
1965/66	42	22	7	13	65	53	12	51	5th	George Graham 17
1966/67	42	15	14	13	67	62	5	44	9th	Bobby Tambling 21
1967/68	42	18	12	12	62	68	-6	48	6th	Peter Osgood 16
1968/69	42	20	10	12	73	53	20	50	5th	Bobby Tambling 17
1969/70	42	21	13	8	70	50	20	55	3rd	Peter Osgood 23

CHELSEA'S CUP RECORD IN TAMBLING ERA

	FA Cup	League Cup	Fairs Cup
1958/59	Round four		Round two
1959/60	Round four		
1960/61	Round three	Round four	
1961/62	Round three	Did not enter	
1962/63	Round five	Did not enter	
1963/64	Round four	Round two	
1964/65	Semi-final	Winners	
1965/66	Semi-final	Did not enter	Semi-final
1966/67	Runners-up	Round three	
1967/68	Quarter-final	Round two	
1968/69	Quarter-final	Round three	Round two
1969/70	Winners	Round four	

STATISTICS

RECORD AGAINST EVERY CLUB FACED

Team	Goals	Games	Won	Draw	Lost
Aston Villa	12	13	7	2	4
Arsenal	10	13	10	2	1
West Ham	9 (1 pen)	18	5	6	7
Sheffield United	8	8	6	1	1
Liverpool	8 (1 pen)	15	3	0	12
Sheffield Wednesday	8 (1 pen)	16	5	5	6
Birmingham City	7 (1 pen)	10	6	2	2
West Brom	7	13	8	1	4
Manchester United	7	15	5	3	7
Portsmouth	6	3	2	0	1
Charlton Athletic	6 (1 pen)	4	4	0	0
Tottenham Hotspur	6 (1 pen)	15	6	2	7
Ipswich Town	5	7	6	0	1
Wolverhampton W	5 (1 pen)	7	1	3	3
Newcastle United	5 (1 pen)	10	5	2	3
Leicester City	5	11	6	3	2
Burnley	5	15	4	4	7
Nottingham Forest	5	16	8	4	4
Derby County	4	4	2	1	1
Southampton	4	8	4	0	4
Manchester City	4	8	3	2	3
Sunderland	4	8	4	1	3
Fulham	4 (1 pen)	10	7	3	0
Northampton T	3	2	2	0	0
Brighton and H Albion	3	2	1	1	0
Grimsby Town	3	2	2	0	0
Hull City	3	2	1	1	0
Norwich City	3	3	2	0	1
Cardiff City	3	6	2	0	4
Preston North End	3	6	4	2	0
Blackpool	3	8	3	1	4
Stoke City	3 (1 pen)	14	6	5	3
Peterborough Utd	2	1	1	0	0
Doncaster Rovers	2	1	1	0	0
Notts County	2	1	1	0	0
TSV Munich 1860	2	2	1	1	0
Walsall	2	2	1	0	1
Luton Town	2 (1 pen)	2	2	0	0

BOBBY TAMBLING

Team	Goals	Games	Won	Draw	Lost
Middlesbrough	2	3	1	0	2
Bolton Wanderers	2	3	2	0	1
Coventry City	2	4	2	1	1
Huddersfield Town	2	4	1	0	3
Blackburn Rovers	2	5	3	2	0
Carlisle United	1	1	1	0	0
Workington Town	1	1	1	0	0
Rotherham United	1	1	1	0	0
Greenock Morton	1	2	2	0	0
Tranmere Rovers	1	2	1	1	0
Bury	1 (pen)	2	1	0	1
Swansea Town	1 (pen)	3	1	1	1
Leeds United	1	10	3	4	3
Everton	1	10	2	7	1
Shrewsbury Town	0	1	1	0	0
Crewe Alexandra	0	1	0	0	1
Plymouth Argyle	0	1	0	0	1
Swindon Town	0	1	0	0	1
DWS Amsterdam	0	2	0	2	0
Queen's Park Rangers	0	2	2	0	0
Wiener Sportklub	0	2	1	0	1
Scunthorpe United	0	2	1	0	1
Barcelona	0	3	1	0	2
AC Milan	0	3	1	1	1
Totals	**202 (13 pens)**	**370**	**176**	**77**	**117**

STATISTICS

BOBBY TAMBLING'S CHELSEA MATCH LIST

Season/Date	Opp	Comp	Venue	Result	Att
1958/59					
07 Feb	West Ham	Div 1	Stamford Bridge	W 3-2 (1)	52,968
1959/60					
05 Sep	Burnley	Div 1	Stamford Bridge	W 4-1	36,023
09 Sep	Birmingham	Div 1	St Andrew's	D 1-1 (1)	28,132
12 Sep	Leeds Utd	Div 1	Elland Road	L 1-2	17,011
19 Sep	West Ham	Div 1	Stamford Bridge	L 2-4	54,349
1960/61					
22 Oct	Burnley	Div 1	Stamford Bridge	L 2-6	29,080
24 Oct	Workington	LC2	Stamford Bridge	W 4-2 (1)	5,630
29 Oct	Preston NE	Div 1	Deepdale	W 2-0 (1)	14,174
05 Nov	Newcastle Utd	Div 1	Stamford Bridge	W 4-2	30,489
12 Nov	Arsenal	Div 1	Highbury	W 4-1 (1)	38,666
16 Nov	Doncaster	LC3	Belle Vue	W 7-0 (2)	9,951
19 Nov	Man City	Div 1	Stamford Bridge	W 6-3 (1)	37,346
26 Nov	Nottm Forest	Div 1	City Ground	L 1-2	22,121
03 Dec	WBA	Div 1	Stamford Bridge	W 7-1	19,568
10 Dec	Cardiff City	Div 1	Ninian Park	L 1-2	21,840
14 Dec	Portsmouth	LC4	Fratton Park	L 0-1	13,054
17 Dec	Aston Villa	Div 1	Stamford Bridge	L 2-4	23,805
24 Dec	Man Utd	Div 1	Stamford Bridge	L 1-2	37,601
26 Dec	Man Utd	Div 1	Old Trafford	L 0-6	50,213
07 Jan	Crewe Alex	FAC3	Stamford Bridge	L 1-2	32,574
18 Feb	Everton	Div 1	Goodison Park	D 1-1	34,449
25 Feb	Sheffield Wed	Div 1	Hillsborough	L 0-1	21,936
04 Mar	Birmingham	Div 1	Stamford Bridge	W 3-2 (1)	27,727
11 Mar	Burnley	Div 1	Turf Moor	D 4-4 (2)	19,435
18 Mar	Preston NE	Div 1	Stamford Bridge	D 1-1	22,031
25 Mar	Newcastle Utd	Div 1	St James' Park	W 6-1	28,975
31 Mar	Tottenham	Div 1	White Hart Lane	L 2-4	65,032
01 Apr	Cardiff City	Div 1	Stamford Bridge	W 6-1 (1)	22,697
03 Apr	Tottenham	Div 1	Stamford Bridge	L 2-3	57,103
08 Apr	Man City	Div 1	Maine Road	L 1-2 (1)	27,720
15 Apr	Arsenal	Div 1	Stamford Bridge	W 3-1 (1)	38,233
22 Apr	WBA	Div 1	The Hawthorns	L 0-3	17,691
29 Apr	Nottm Forest	Div 1	Stamford Bridge	W 4-3	22,775
1961/62					
19 Aug	Nottm Forest	Div 1	Stamford Bridge	D 2-2 (1)	20,857
23 Aug	Man Utd	Div 1	Old Trafford	L 2-3 (2)	45,559
26 Aug	Aston Villa	Div 1	Villa Park	L 1-3 (1)	35,840
30 Aug	Man Utd	Div 1	Stamford Bridge	W 2-0 (1)	42,248
02 Sep	Fulham	Div 1	Stamford Bridge	D 0-0	37,998
06 Sep	Cardiff City	Div 1	Ninian Park	L 2-5	20,883
09 Sep	Sheffield Utd	Div 1	Stamford Bridge	W 6-1 (3)	22,026
16 Sep	West Ham	Div 1	Boleyn Ground	L 1-2	27,530
20 Sep	Cardiff City	Div 1	Stamford Bridge	L 2-3	15,804
23 Sep	Blackburn	Div 1	Stamford Bridge	D 1-1	23,301
30 Sep	Blackpool	Div 1	Bloomfield Road	L 0-4	24,191
07 Oct	Sheffield Wed	Div 1	Hillsborough	L 3-5 (3)	28,093
14 Oct	Leicester	Div 1	Stamford Bridge	L 1-3	21,377
21 Oct	Birmingham	Div 1	St Andrew's	L 2-3 (1)	20,079
28 Oct	Everton	Div 1	Stamford Bridge	D 1-1	25,535
04 Nov	Arsenal	Div 1	Highbury	W 3-0	37,604
11 Nov	Bolton	Div 1	Stamford Bridge	W 1-0 (1)	12,404
18 Nov	Man City	Div 1	Maine Road	D 2-2 (1)	16,583
25 Nov	WBA	Div 1	Stamford Bridge	W 4-1 (1)	25,025
02 Dec	Ipswich	Div 1	Portman Road	L 2-5 (1)	22,726
09 Dec	Burnley	Div 1	Stamford Bridge	L 1-2 (1)	33,296

BOBBY TAMBLING

Season/Date	Opp	Comp	Venue	Result	Att
16 Dec	Nottm Forest	Div 1	City Ground	L 0-3	17,419
23 Dec	Aston Villa	Div 1	Stamford Bridge	W 1-0	20,538
26 Dec	Tottenham	Div 1	Stamford Bridge	L 0-2	51,282
30 Dec	Tottenham	Div 1	White Hart Lane	L 2-5	44,630
06 Jan	Liverpool	FAC3	Anfield	L 3-4 (2)	48,455
13 Jan	Fulham	Div 1	Craven Cottage	W 4-3 (1)	35,640
20 Jan	Sheffield Utd	Div 1	Bramall Lane	L 1-3	19,626
03 Feb	West Ham	Div 1	Stamford Bridge	L 0-1	34,259
16 Feb	Blackpool	Div 1	Stamford Bridge	W 1-0 (1)	24,276
24 Feb	Sheffield Wed	Div 1	Stamford Bridge	W 1-0	23,760
09 Mar	Birmingham	Div 1	Stamford Bridge	D 1-1	23,959
20 Apr	Wolves	Div 1	Stamford Bridge	L 4-5 (1)	31,221
23 Apr	Wolves	Div 1	Molineux	D 1-1	14,597
28 Apr	Burnley	Div 1	Turf Moor	D 1-1	29,078

1962/63

Season/Date	Opp	Comp	Venue	Result	Att
18 Aug	Rotherham	Div 2	Millmoor	W 1-0 (1)	11,268
22 Aug	Scunthorpe	Div 2	Stamford Bridge	W 3-0	18,377
25 Aug	Charlton	Div 2	Stamford Bridge	W 5-0	24,683
28 Aug	Scunthorpe	Div 2	Old Showground	L 0-3	11,196
01 Sep	Stoke City	Div 2	Victoria Ground	D 0-0	19,470
08 Sep	Sunderland	Div 2	Stamford Bridge	W 1-0	32,901
10 Sep	Southampton	Div 2	Stamford Bridge	W 2-0 (1)	18,890
15 Sep	Leeds Utd	Div 2	Elland Road	L 0-2	27,620
19 Sep	Southampton	Div 2	The Dell	L 1-2	18,717
22 Sep	Swansea Town	Div 2	Stamford Bridge	D 2-2 (1)	22,693
29 Sep	Portsmouth	Div 2	Fratton Park	W 2-0 (2)	22,627
06 Oct	Cardiff City	Div 2	Stamford Bridge	W 6-0 (2)	25,434
13 Oct	Huddersfield	Div 2	Leeds Road	L 0-1	23,936
20 Oct	Middlesbrough	Div 2	Stamford Bridge	W 3-2 (2)	32,551
27 Oct	Derby County	Div 2	Baseball Ground	W 3-1 (3)	12,653
03 Nov	Newcastle Utd	Div 2	Stamford Bridge	W 4-2 (1)	34,428
10 Nov	Walsall	Div 2	Fellows Park	W 5-1 (2)	8,492
17 Nov	Norwich City	Div 2	Stamford Bridge	W 2-0 (2)	28,816
24 Nov	Grimsby	Div 2	Blundell Park	W 3-0 (2)	10,823
08 Dec	Preston NE	Div 2	Deepdale	W 3-1 (2)	14,487
22 Dec	Charlton	Div 2	The Valley	W 4-1 (4)	21,307
26 Dec	Luton Town	Div 2	Kenilworth Road	W 2-0	11,867
05 Jan	Tranmere	FAC3	Prenton Park	D 2-2 (1)	17,162
30 Jan	Tranmere	FAC3R	Stamford Bridge	W 3-1	20,505
09 Feb	Swansea Town	Div 2	Vetch Field	L 0-2	13,359
23 Feb	Cardiff City	Div 2	Ninian Park	L 0-1	16,108
02 Mar	Huddersfield	Div 2	Stamford Bridge	L 1-2	32,427
06 Mar	Charlton	FAC4	The Valley	W 3-0 (1)	37,907
09 Mar	Middlesbrough	Div 2	Ayresome Park	L 0-1	24,781
16 Mar	Man Utd	FAC5	Old Trafford	L 1-2	48,298
23 Mar	Newcastle Utd	Div 2	St James' Park	L 0-2	39,418
27 Mar	Derby County	Div 2	Stamford Bridge	W 3-1 (1)	19,553
30 Mar	Walsall	Div 2	Stamford Bridge	L 0-1	19,625
01 Apr	Luton Town	Div 2	Stamford Bridge	W 3-1 (2)	21,211
06 Apr	Norwich City	Div 2	Carrow Road	L 1-4 (1)	20,581
12 Apr	Bury	Div 2	Stamford Bridge	W 2-0 (1)	45,069
13 Apr	Grimsby	Div 2	Stamford Bridge	W 2-1 (1)	21,768
16 Apr	Bury	Div 2	Gigg Lane	L 0-2	11,936
20 Apr	Plymouth	Div 2	Home Park	L 1-2	17,027
27 Apr	Preston NE	Div 2	Stamford Bridge	W 2-0	23,770
30 Apr	Leeds Utd	Div 2	Stamford Bridge	D 2-2	24,387
11 May	Stoke City	Div 2	Stamford Bridge	L 0-1	66,199
18 May	Sunderland	Div 2	Roker Park	W 1-0	47,918
21 May	Portsmouth	Div 2	Stamford Bridge	W 7-0 (4)	54,558

1963/64

Season/Date	Opp	Comp	Venue	Result	Att
24 Aug	West Ham	Div 1	Stamford Bridge	D 0-0	46,298

STATISTICS

Season/Date	Opp	Comp	Venue	Result	Att
27 Aug	Burnley	Div 1	Turf Moor	D 0-0	19,674
04 Sep	Burnley	Div 1	Stamford Bridge	W 2-0	31,881
07 Sep	Liverpool	Div 1	Stamford Bridge	L 1-3	38,202
11 Sep	Blackburn	Div 1	Stamford Bridge	W 1-0	27,384
14 Sep	Aston Villa	Div 1	Villa Park	L 0-2	23,720
16 Sep	Blackburn	Div 1	Ewood Park	D 2-2	23,217
21 Sep	Tottenham	Div 1	Stamford Bridge	L 0-3	57,401
25 Sep	Swindon	LC2	County Ground	L 0-3	17,916
28 Sep	Wolves	Div 1	Molineux	L 1-4	20,762
02 Oct	Man Utd	Div 1	Stamford Bridge	D 1-1	45,351
05 Oct	Stoke City	Div 1	Stamford Bridge	D 3-3	29,204
12 Oct	Ipswich	Div 1	Portman Road	W 3-1 (2)	15,703
19 Oct	Sheffield Wed	Div 1	Stamford Bridge	L 1-2	31,948
26 Oct	Fulham	Div 1	Craven Cottage	W 1-0 (1)	32,945
16 Nov	Arsenal	Div 1	Stamford Bridge	W 3-1	47,050
23 Nov	Leicester	Div 1	Filbert Street	W 4-2 (1)	23,175
30 Nov	Bolton	Div 1	Stamford Bridge	W 4-0 (1)	19,969
07 Dec	Everton	Div 1	Goodison Park	D 1-1	39,328
14 Dec	West Ham	Div 1	Boleyn Ground	D 2-2 (1)	21,950
08 Jan	Tottenham	FAC3R	Stamford Bridge	W 2-0 (1)	70,123
11 Jan	Liverpool	Div 1	Anfield	L 1-2	46,460
18 Jan	Aston Villa	Div 1	Stamford Bridge	W 1-0	23,968
25 Jan	Huddersfield	FAC4	Stamford Bridge	L 1-2 (1)	39,036
01 Feb	Tottenham	Div 1	White Hart Lane	W 2-1 (2)	51,007
08 Feb	Wolves	Div 1	Stamford Bridge	L 2-3 (1)	26,131
22 Feb	Ipswich	Div 1	Stamford Bridge	W 4-0 (1)	20,703
29 Feb	Sheffield Wed	Div 1	Hillsborough	L 2-3 (1)	19,416
04 Mar	Stoke City	Div 1	Victoria Ground	L 0-2	21,441
14 Mar	Arsenal	Div 1	Highbury	W 4-2 (4)	25,513
21 Mar	WBA	Div 1	Stamford Bridge	W 3-1 (1)	19,434
23 Mar	Man Utd	Div 1	Old Trafford	D 1-1	43,172
28 Mar	Birmingham	Div 1	St Andrew's	W 4-3 (1)	14,485
30 Mar	Nottm Forest	Div 1	Stamford Bridge	W 1-0	26,086
31 Mar	Nottm Forest	Div 1	City Ground	W 1-0	16,453
06 Apr	Leicester	Div 1	Stamford Bridge	W 1-0	25,315
11 Apr	Bolton	Div 1	Burnden Park	L 0-1	18,868
18 Apr	Everton	Div 1	Stamford Bridge	W 1-0	37,963
1964/65					
22 Aug	Wolves	Div 1	Molineux	W 3-0 (2)	25,181
26 Aug	Aston Villa	Div 1	Stamford Bridge	W 2-1 (1)	30,389
31 Aug	Aston Villa	Div 1	Villa Park	D 2-2 (1)	19,740
09 Sep	Sheffield Wed	Div 1	Stamford Bridge	D 1-1	31,973
12 Sep	Fulham	Div 1	Stamford Bridge	W 1-0	41,472
23 Sep	Birmingham	LC2	St Andrew's	W 3-0 (2)	15,300
26 Sep	Arsenal	Div 1	Highbury	W 3-1 (1)	54,936
30 Sep	Man Utd	Div 1	Stamford Bridge	L 0-2	60,769
03 Oct	Blackburn	Div 1	Stamford Bridge	W 5-1 (1)	34,913
10 Oct	Nottm Forest	Div 1	City Ground	D 2-2	35,320
17 Oct	Stoke City	Div 1	Stamford Bridge	W 4-0 (1)	28,650
24 Oct	Tottenham	Div 1	White Hart Lane	D 1-1	52,927
26 Oct	Notts County	LC3	Stamford Bridge	W 4-0 (2)	6,596
31 Oct	Burnley	Div 1	Stamford Bridge	L 0-1	29,040
07 Nov	Sheffield Utd	Div 1	Bramall Lane	W 2-0	23,505
11 Nov	Swansea Town	LC4	Stamford Bridge	W 3-2	5,979
14 Nov	Everton	Div 1	Stamford Bridge	W 5-1 (1)	30,716
21 Nov	Birmingham	Div 1	St Andrew's	W 6-1	19,803
28 Nov	West Ham	Div 1	Stamford Bridge	L 0-3	44,204
09 Jan	Northampton	FAC3	Stamford Bridge	W 4-1 (1)	44,335
16 Jan	Fulham	Div 1	Craven Cottage	W 2-1 (1)	26,400
20 Jan	Aston Villa	LC SF (1)	Villa Park	W 3-2 (1)	12,022
23 Jan	Leeds Utd	Div 1	Elland Road	D 2-2	47,109
30 Jan	West Ham	FAC4	Boleyn Ground	W 1-0 (1)	37,000

BOBBY TAMBLING

Season/Date	Opp	Comp	Venue	Result	Att
06 Feb	Arsenal	Div 1	Stamford Bridge	W 2-1	46,798
10 Feb	Aston Villa	LC SF (2)	Stamford Bridge	D 1-1	17,425
13 Feb	Blackburn	Div 1	Ewood Park	W 3-0 (1)	16,683
20 Feb	Tottenham	FAC5	Stamford Bridge	W 1-0	63,205
22 Feb	Nottm Forest	Div 1	Stamford Bridge	L 0-1	29,038
27 Feb	Stoke City	Div 1	Victoria Ground	W 2-0	28,005
06 Mar	Peterboro'	FAC QF	Stamford Bridge	W 5-1 (2)	63,635
10 Mar	Tottenham	Div 1	Stamford Bridge	W 3-1 (1)	51,390
13 Mar	Man Utd	Div 1	Old Trafford	L 0-4	56,261
15 Mar	Leicester	LC F (1)	Stamford Bridge	W 3-2 (1)	20,690
22 Mar	Sheffield Utd	Div 1	Stamford Bridge	W 3-0	31,837
27 Mar	Liverpool	FAC SF	Villa Park	L 0-2	67,686
31 Mar	Everton	Div 1	Goodison Park	D 1-1	40,384
03 Apr	Birmingham	Div 1	Stamford Bridge	W 3-1 (1)	28,975
05 Apr	Leicester	LC F (2)	Filbert Street	D 0-0	26,957
12 Apr	West Ham	Div 1	Boleyn Ground	L 2-3	33,288
16 Apr	Liverpool	Div 1	Stamford Bridge	W 4-0 (1)	62,587
17 Apr	WBA	Div 1	Stamford Bridge	D 2-2 (1)	30,792
19 Apr	Liverpool	Div 1	Anfield	L 0-2	41,847
24 Apr	Burnley	Div 1	Turf Moor	L 2-6	15,213
26 Apr	Blackpool	Div 1	Bloomfield Road	L 2-3 (1)	16,008
1965/66					
21 Aug	Burnley	Div 1	Stamford Bridge	D 1-1	34,067
25 Aug	Stoke City	Div 1	Victoria Ground	D 2-2 (1)	28,549
28 Aug	Fulham	Div 1	Craven Cottage	W 3-0	34,027
02 Oct	WBA	Div 1	The Hawthorns	W 2-1	23,049
06 Nov	Leeds Utd	Div 1	Stamford Bridge	W 1-0	39,373
13 Nov	West Ham	Div 1	Boleyn Ground	L 1-2 (1)	31,551
17 Nov	Wiener S	ICFC2 (1)	Sport Club Platz	L 0-1	4,000
27 Nov	Aston Villa	Div 1	Villa Park	W 4-2 (2)	16,355
01 Dec	Wiener S	ICFC2 (2)	Stamford Bridge	W 2-0	28,254
27 Dec	Northampton	Div 1	County Ground	W 3-2 (2)	23,325
01 Jan	Blackpool	Div 1	Bloomfield Road	W 2-1 (1)	14,065
08 Jan	Tottenham	Div 1	Stamford Bridge	W 2-1	48,529
22 Jan	Liverpool	FAC3	Anfield	W 2-1 (1)	54,097
29 Jan	Burnley	Div 1	Turf Moor	W 2-1	23,825
05 Feb	Fulham	Div 1	Stamford Bridge	W 2-1 (1)	34,247
09 Feb	AC Milan	ICFC3 (1)	San Siro	L 1-2	11,411
12 Feb	Leeds Utd	FAC4	Stamford Bridge	W 1-0 (1)	57,847
16 Feb	AC Milan	ICFC3 (2)	Stamford Bridge	W 2-1	59,541
19 Feb	Arsenal	Div 1	Stamford Bridge	D 0-0	48,641
22 Feb	Sunderland	Div 1	Stamford Bridge	W 3-2	20,828
26 Feb	Everton	Div 1	Goodison Park	L 1-2	52,752
02 Mar	AC Milan	ICFC3 (p/o)	San Siro	D 1-1*¹	30,620
05 Mar	Shrewsbury	FAC5	Stamford Bridge	W 3-2	51,144
12 Mar	Man Utd	Div 1	Stamford Bridge	W 2-0 (1)	60,269
15 Mar	TSV Munich	ICF QF (1)	Grunwalder Stadion	D 2-2 (2)	11,000
19 Mar	Newcastle Utd	Div 1	St James' Park	W 1-0	35,118
21 Mar	Leicester	Div 1	Filbert Street	D 1-1	25,363
26 Mar	Hull City	FAC QF	Stamford Bridge	D 2-2 (1)	46,924
29 Mar	TSV Munich	ICFC QF (2)	Stamford Bridge	W 1-0	42,224
31 Mar	Hull City	FAC QFR	Boothferry Park	W 3-1 (2)	45,328
09 Apr	West Ham	Div 1	Stamford Bridge	W 6-2 (2)	35,958
11 Apr	Nottm Forest	Div 1	Stamford Bridge	W 1-0 (1)	39,380
12 Apr	Nottm Forest	Div 1	City Ground	W 2-1 (2)	29,569
16 Apr	Sunderland	Div 1	Roker Park	L 0-2	32,880
23 Apr	Sheffield Wed	FAC SF	Villa Park	L 0-2	61,321
25 Apr	WBA	Div 1	Stamford Bridge	L 2-3 (1)	22,804
27 Apr	Barcelona	ICFC SF (1)	Camp Nou	L 0-2	70,000
30 Apr	Liverpool	Div 1	Anfield	L 1-2	53,754
07 May	Sheffield Utd	Div 1	Stamford Bridge	W 2-0 (1)	23,072
11 May	Barcelona	ICFC SF (2)	Stamford Bridge	W 2-0	40,073

STATISTICS

Season/Date	Opp	Comp	Venue	Result	Att
16 May	Aston Villa	Div 1	Stamford Bridge	L 0-2	16,232
25 May	Barcelona	ICFC SF(p/o)	Camp Nou	L 0-5	40,000
1966/67					
20 Aug	West Ham	Div 1	Boleyn Ground	W 2-1	36,122
24 Aug	Nottm Forest	Div 1	Stamford Bridge	W 2-1	27,501
27 Aug	Sheffield Wed	Div 1	Stamford Bridge	D 0-0	33,489
30 Aug	Nottm Forest	Div 1	City Ground	D 0-0	22,199
03 Sep	Southampton	Div 1	The Dell	W 3-0 (1)	29,479
07 Sep	Leicester	Div 1	Stamford Bridge	D 2-2	29,760
10 Sep	Sunderland	Div 1	Stamford Bridge	D 1-1	31,766
14 Sep	Charlton	LC2	Stamford Bridge	W 5-2 (1)	14,262
17 Sep	Aston Villa	Div 1	Villa Park	W 6-2 (5)	18,259
24 Sep	Arsenal	Div 1	Stamford Bridge	W 3-1 (2)	48,001
01 Oct	Man City	Div 1	Maine Road	W 4-1 (1)	31,989
05 Oct	Blackpool	LC3	Bloomfield Road	D 1-1	13,520
08 Oct	Burnley	Div 1	Stamford Bridge	L 1-3	42,573
15 Oct	Man Utd	Div 1	Old Trafford	D 1-1	56,789
17 Oct	Blackpool	LC3R	Stamford Bridge	L 1-3	20,240
26 Oct	Tottenham	Div 1	Stamford Bridge	W 3-0 (1)	54,191
29 Oct	Fulham	Div 1	Craven Cottage	W 3-1	42,159
05 Nov	Man Utd	Div 1	Stamford Bridge	L 1-3	56,452
12 Nov	WBA	Div 1	The Hawthorns	W 1-0 (1)	28,151
19 Nov	Sheffield Utd	Div 1	Stamford Bridge	D 1-1 (1)	25,976
26 Nov	Stoke City	Div 1	Victoria Ground	D 1-1	28,447
03 Dec	Everton	Div 1	Stamford Bridge	D 1-1	35,495
10 Dec	Newcastle Utd	Div 1	St James' Park	D 2-2 (1)	32,529
17 Dec	West Ham	Div 1	Stamford Bridge	D 5-5 (2)	47,805
24 Dec	Liverpool	Div 1	Stamford Bridge	L 1-2	36,921
26 Dec	Liverpool	Div 1	Anfield	L 1-2 (1)	51,920
31 Dec	Sheffield Wed	Div 1	Hillsborough	L 1-6 (1)	31,032
07 Jan	Southampton	Div 1	Stamford Bridge	W 4-1 (1)	27,719
14 Jan	Sunderland	Div 1	Roker Park	L 0-2	35,839
21 Jan	Aston Villa	Div 1	Stamford Bridge	W 3-1 (1)	30,922
28 Jan	Huddersfield	FAC3	Leeds Road	W 2-1 (1)	36,407
04 Feb	Arsenal	Div 1	Highbury	L 1-2 (1)	52,467
11 Feb	Man City	Div 1	Stamford Bridge	D 0-0	28,633
18 Feb	Brighton	FAC4	Goldstone Ground	D 1-1 (1)	35,000
22 Feb	Brighton	FAC4R	Stamford Bridge	W 4-0 (2)	54,852
25 Feb	Burnley	Div 1	Turf Moor	W 2-1	20,379
04 Mar	Fulham	Div 1	Stamford Bridge	D 0-0	46,784
11 Mar	Sheffield Utd	FAC5	Stamford Bridge	W 2-0 (1)	40,730
24 Mar	Blackpool	Div 1	Stamford Bridge	L 0-2	37,852
25 Mar	Newcastle Utd	Div 1	Stamford Bridge	W 2-1 (1)	26,388
27 Mar	Blackpool	Div 1	Bloomfield Road	W 2-0	16,186
08 Apr	Sheffield Wed	FAC QF	Stamford Bridge	W 1-0	52,481
29 Apr	Leeds Utd	FAC SF	Villa Park	W 1-0	62,378
06 May	Leeds Utd	Div 1	Stamford Bridge	D 2-2	35,882
09 May	Leicester	Div 1	Filbert Street	L 2-3	17,142
20 May	Tottenham	FAC F	Wembley	L 1-2 (1)	100,000
1967/68					
19 Aug	WBA	Div 1	The Hawthorns	W 1-0 (1)	33,283
23 Aug	Newcastle Utd	Div 1	Stamford Bridge	D 1-1	33,634
26 Aug	Fulham	Div 1	Stamford Bridge	D 1-1	38,404
30 Aug	Newcastle Utd	Div 1	St James' Park	L 1-5 (1)	34,809
02 Sep	Southampton	Div 1	Stamford Bridge	L 2-6	32,726
06 Sep	Sheffield Utd	Div 1	Stamford Bridge	W 4-2 (2)	22,742
09 Sep	Liverpool	Div 1	Anfield	L 1-3	53,839
13 Sep	Middlesbrough	LC2	Ayresome Park	L 1-2	30,425
16 Sep	Stoke City	Div 1	Stamford Bridge	D 2-2 (1)	26,614
23 Sep	Nottm Forest	Div 1	City Ground	L 0-3	34,871
30 Sep	Coventry	Div 1	Stamford Bridge	D 1-1	29,800

BOBBY TAMBLING

Season/Date	Opp	Comp	Venue	Result	Att
14 Oct	Everton	Div 1	Stamford Bridge	D 1-1	34,206
26 Dec	Arsenal	Div 1	Stamford Bridge	W 2-1	51,672
30 Dec	Arsenal	Div 1	Highbury	D 1-1	47,157
06 Jan	Southampton	Div 1	The Dell	W 5-3 (1)	27,132
20 Jan	Stoke City	Div 1	Victoria Ground	W 1-0	21,861
27 Jan	Ipswich	FAC3	Stamford Bridge	W 3-0 (1)	42,986
03 Feb	Nottm Forest	Div 1	Stamford Bridge	W 1-0	33,483
10 Feb	Coventry	Div 1	Highfield Road	L 1-2 (1)	36,646
12 Feb	Liverpool	Div 1	Stamford Bridge	W 3-1 (2)	40,670
17 Feb	Norwich City	FAC4	Stamford Bridge	W 1-0	57,987
02 Mar	Man Utd	Div 1	Old Trafford	W 3-1 (1)	62,471
09 Mar	Sheffield Wed	FAC5	Hillsborough D 2-2 (1)		49,186
12 Mar	Sheffield Wed	FAC5R	Stamford Bridge	W 2-0 (1)	55,013
16 Mar	Leicester	Div 1	Stamford Bridge	W 4-1 (2)	35,990
20 Mar	Leeds Utd	Div 1	Stamford Bridge	D 0-0	47,470
23 Mar	West Ham	Div 1	Boleyn Ground	W 1-0	36,301
30 Mar	Birmingham	FAC QF	St Andrew's	L 0-1	52,500
06 Apr	Sheffield Wed	Div 1	Hillsborough	D 2-2	26,773
12 Apr	Man City	Div 1	Maine Road	L 0-1	47,132

1968/69

4 Aug	Nottm Forest	Div 1	Stamford Bridge	D 1-1 (1)	36,515
17 Aug	WBA	Div 1	Stamford Bridge	W 3-1 (1)	33,766
21 Aug	Newcastle Utd	Div 1	St James' Park	L 2-3 (1)	39,048
24 Aug	Man Utd	Div 1	Old Trafford	W 4-0 (1)	55,114
28 Aug	Sheffield Wed	Div 1	Stamford Bridge	W 1-0 (1)	33,402
31 Aug	Tottenham	Div 1	Stamford Bridge	D 2-2	48,412
03 Sep	Birmingham	LC2	St Andrew's	W 1-0	31,560
07 Sep	Everton	Div 1	Stamford Bridge	D 1-1	42,017
10 Sep	Coventry	Div 1	Highfield Road	W 1-0	36,217
14 Sep	QPR	Div 1	Loftus Road	W 4-0	26,358
18 Sep	G Morton	ICFC1 (1)	Stamford Bridge	W 5-0	28,736
21 Sep	West Ham	Div 1	Stamford Bridge	D 1-1 (1)	58,062
25 Sep	Derby County	LC3	Stamford Bridge	D 0-0	26,975
28 Sep	Burnley	Div 1	Turf Moor	L 1-2 (1)	14,762
30 Sep	G Morton	ICFC1 (2)	Cappielow Park	W 4-3 (1)	8,000
02 Oct	Derby County	LC3R	Baseball Ground	L 1-3	34,346
05 Oct	Ipswich	Div 1	Stamford Bridge	W 3-1	31,625
09 Oct	Sheffield Wed	Div 1	Hillsborough	D 1-1	30,445
12 Oct	Wolves	Div 1	Molineux	D 1-1 (1)	27,810
19 Oct	Leicester	Div 1	Stamford Bridge	W 3-0	33,462
23 Oct	DWS Amsterdam	ICFC2 (1)	Stamford Bridge	D 0-0	28,428
26 Oct	Stoke City	Div 1	Victoria Ground	L 0-2	16,799
30 Oct	DWS Amsterdam	ICFC2 (2)	Olympisch Stadion	D 0-0*²	14,000
02 Nov	Man City	Div 1	Stamford Bridge	W 2-0	40,700
09 Nov	Liverpool	Div 1	Anfield	L 1-2	47,248
16 Nov	Southampton	Div 1	Stamford Bridge	L 2-3	31,325
07 Dec	Sunderland	Div 1	Roker Park	L 2-3	21,976
14 Dec	Wolves	Div 1	Stamford Bridge	D 1-1	26,194
21 Dec	Leicester	Div 1	Filbert Street	W 4-1(1)	23,597
26 Dec	Ipswich	Div 1	Portman Road	W 3-1	24,083
04 Jan	Carlisle	FAC3	Stamford Bridge	W 2-0 (1)	37,322
11 Jan	Man City	Div 1	Maine Road	L 1-4	35,605
18 Jan	Liverpool	Div 1	Stamford Bridge	L 1-2 (1)	52,295
25 Jan	Preston NE	FAC4	Deepdale	D 0-0	31,875
01 Feb	Southampton	Div 1	The Dell	L 0-5	28,147
03 Feb	Preston NE	FAC4R	Stamford Bridge	W 2-1	36,522
12 Feb	Stoke City	FAC5	Stamford Bridge	W 3-2	39,191
15 Feb	Leeds United	Div 1	Elland Road	L 0-1	35,789
22 Feb	Sunderland	Div 1	Stamford Bridge	W 5-1 (4)	29,381
01 Mar	WBA	FAC QF	Stamford Bridge	L 1-2	52,285
05 Mar	Stoke City	Div 1	Stamford Bridge	W 1-0	19,856
08 Mar	WBA	Div 1	The Hawthorns	W 3-0	25,137

STATISTICS

Season/Date	Opp	Comp	Venue	Result	Att
10 Mar	Coventry	Div 1	Stamford Bridge	W 2-1 (1)	17,639
15 Mar	Man Utd	Div 1	Stamford Bridge	W 3-2 (1)	60,436
22 Mar	Tottenham	Div 1	White Hart Lane	L 0-1	47,349
05 Apr	Burnley	Div 1	Stamford Bridge	L 2-3 (1)	30,266
08 Apr	Nottm Forest	Div 1	City Ground	W 2-1	30,413
12 Apr	West Ham	Div 1	Boleyn Ground	D 0-0	32,332
14 Apr	Arsenal	Div 1	Stamford Bridge	W 2-1	37,890
19 Apr	QPR	Div 1	Stamford Bridge	W 2-1	41,263
1969/70					
09 Aug	Liverpool	Div 1	Anfield	L 1-4	48,383
11 Aug	West Ham	Div 1	Boleyn Ground	L 0-2	39,003
16 Aug	Ipswich	Div 1	Stamford Bridge	W 1-0	29,613
20 Aug	West Ham	Div 1	Stamford Bridge	D 0-0	43,346
17 Mar	Stoke City	Div 1	Stamford Bridge	W 1-0	28,996
25 Mar	Sheffield Wed	Div 1	Stamford Bridge	W 3-1	29,590
30 Mar	WBA	Div 1	The Hawthorns	L 1-3	31,207

(Bobby Tambling's goals in brackets following result)

KEY:

FAC	**FA Cup**
LC	**League Cup**
ICFC	**Inter-Cities Fairs Cup**
*¹	won on toss of coin after extra time
*²	lost on toss of coin after extra time

CHELSEA RECORDS, FACTS AND FIGURES

(CORRECT TO THE END OF THE 2015/16 SEASON)

TOP ALL-TIME APPEARANCES

R Harris 795, Bonetti 729, Terry 703, Lampard 648, Hollins 592, Cech 494, Wise 445, Clarke 421, Dixon 420, McCreadie 410, Bumstead 409, K Armstrong 402, Drogba 381, Osgood 380, Cooke 373, Mikel 372, G Smith 370, **Tambling 370**, Bentley 367, H Miller 365, J Harris 364, Ivanovic 361, Blunstone 347, Pates 346, Hinton 344, Houseman 343, A Cole 338, Harrow 334, Law 318, Locke 317, Droy 313, Le Saux 312, Zola 312, Crawford 308, McNeil 306

(Substitute appearances included)

TOP ALL-TIME SCORERS

Lampard 211, **Tambling 202**, Dixon 193, Drogba 164, Bentley 150, Osgood 150, Greaves 132, Mills 125, Hilsdon 108, Bridges 93, Baldwin 92, Hasselbaink 87, Gallacher 81, Whittingham 80, Zola 80, Gudjohnsen 78, Wise 76, Tindall 69, McNichol 66, Spence 66, Terry 66, C Walker 65, Hollins 64, Speedie 64, Durie 63, A Wilson 61, Kalou 60, Anelka 59, I Hutchinson 58, B Turnbull 58, Windridge 58, Brabrook 57, E Hazard 55, K Wilson 55, Blunstone 54, Cock 53, Thain 51, Flo 50

BOBBY TAMBLING

TOP LEAGUE APPEARANCES

R Harris 646+9, Bonetti 600, Terry 467+16, Hollins 465, Lampard 404+25, K Armstrong 362, G Smith 351, H Miller 339, Cech 332+1, Dixon 331+4, McCreadie 327+4, J Harris 326, Bentley 324, Wise 322+10, Clarke 321+9, Blunstone 317, Bumstead 314+24, Harrow 305, **Tambling 298+4**, Law 292, Cooke 289+10, Crawford 288, Osgood 286+3, Pates 280+1, McNeil 279, W Ferguson 272, Locke 270+2, Droy 263+9, Barber 262, P Sillett 260, Hinton 257+8, Britton 253+10, Houseman 252+17, Woodley 252, Brabrook 251

TOP LEAGUE SCORERS

Tambling 164, Dixon 147, Lampard 147, Bentley 128, Greaves 124, Mills 118, Osgood 105, Drogba 104, Hilsdon 99, Bridges 80, Baldwin 74, Gallacher 72, Whittingham 71, Hasselbaink 69, Tindall 67, Spence 63, C Walker 60, McNichol 59, Zola 59, A Wilson 58, Gudjohnsen 54, Windridge 54, Wise 53, Durie 51, R Turnbull 51

TOP FA CUP APPEARANCES

R Harris 64, Bonetti 57, Lampard 51+7, Hollins 51, Terry 49+6, Bentley 42, McCreadie 41, K Armstrong 39, J Harris 38, Wise 38, **Tambling 36**, Clarke 34+2, Osgood 34, Cech 33, Cooke 32+2, Barber 32, Bettridge 31, Cudicini 31, Hinton 30+3, Mikel 29+3, Harrow 29, Molyneux 29, Zola 28+3, A Cole 27+1, McNeil 27, Ivanovic 26+1, Ford 26, Gray 26, Law 26, Miller 26, Drogba 25+4, Le Saux 25+3, Campbell 25, Houseman 25, Spence 25, Boyle 24+1

TOP FA CUP SCORERS

Lampard 26, **Tambling 25**, Bentley 21, Osgood 19, Drogba 12, Terry 11, Zola 11, Gudjohnsen 10, Houseman 10, Bridges 9, Gallacher 9, Hilsdon 9, M Hughes 9, Peacock 9, Whittingham 9, Wise 9, Dixon 8, Kalou 8, Anelka 7, Hasselbaink 7, McNichol 7, Mills 7, Oscar 7, Poyet 7, Ramires 7, R Smith 7, Sturridge 7, R Turnbull 7, Cock 6, Ford 6, I Hutchinson 6, Thain 6, Vialli 6, Webb 6

TOP LEAGUE CUP APPEARANCES

Hollins 48, R Harris 46+2, Bonetti 45, Dixon 40+1, Houseman 32+1, Pates 32, Terry 31+4, Osgood 30, Wise 30, Bumstead 29+5, Spackman 27+1, Webb 27, Nevin 25+1, Niedzwiecki 25, Clarke 24+2, Speedie 23+1, McLaughlin 23, Lampard 22+12, Hinton 22+3, Cooke 22+1, McCreadie 21+1, Boyle 21, Locke 21,

STATISTICS

C Lee 20+4, Cudicini 18, **Tambling 18**, Le Saux 17+6, Mikel 17+3, Droy 17+2, F Sinclair 17+1, Townsend 17

TOP LEAGUE CUP SCORERS

Dixon 25, Lampard 12, Drogba 10, Osgood 10, **Tambling 10**, Garland 8, Kalou 8, Durie 7, Hasselbaink 7, Hollins 7, Speedie 7, Townsend 7, Baldwin 6, Fillery 6, Gudjohnsen 6, Vialli 6, Wise 6, Graham 5, Nevin 5, Shevchenko 5, Brabrook 4, J Cole 4, Cooke 4, E Hazard 4, Houseman 4, I Hutchinson 4, K Wilson 4

TOP ALL-TIME PENALTY SCORERS

Lampard 49, P Sillett 19, Wise 18, Law 16, Roberts 16, E Hazard 15, Hollins 15, Leboeuf 15, Hilsdon 14, **Tambling 13**, J Harris 12, Hasselbaink 12, Whittingham 12, Osgood 10, Venables 10

MOST GOALS IN A MATCH

6: George Hilsdon v Worksop (h) FA Cup, 11 Jan 1908. Won 9-1
5: George Hilsdon v Glossop (h) Div 2, 01 Sep 1906. Won 9-2
5: Jimmy Greaves v Wolves (h) Div 1, 30 Aug 1958. Won 6-2
5: Jimmy Greaves v Preston (a) Div 1, 19 Dec 1959. Won 5-4
5: Jimmy Greaves v West Brom (h) Div 1, 03 Dec 1960. Won 7-1
5: **Bobby Tambling** v Aston Villa (a) Div 1, 17 Sep 1966. Won 6-2
5: Peter Osgood v Jeunesse Hautcharage (h) European Cup Winners' Cup, 29 Sep 1971. Won 13-0
5: Gordon Durie v Walsall (a) Div 2, 04 Feb 1989. Won 7-0

BEST SCORING SEQUENCES

Roy Bentley: 9 in 8 consecutive Div 1 games, Sep to Oct 1952. (7 ones and a two)
Mark Stein: 9 in 7 consecutive Premier League games, Dec 1993 to Feb 1994. (5 ones and 2 twos)
George Mills: 8 in 7 consecutive Div 1 games, Apr to Sep 1936. (6 ones and a two)
Bobby Tambling: 12 in 6 consecutive Div 2 games, Oct to Nov 1962. (2, 3, 1, 2, 2, 2)
Bob Whittingham: 6 in 6 consecutive Div 2 games, Mar to Apr 1911. (6 ones)
Joe Payne: 6 in 6 consecutive Div 1 games, Apr to May 1939. (6 ones)
Jimmy Greaves: 6 in 6 consecutive Div 1 and FA Cup games, Jan to Feb 1959. (6 ones)
John Hollins: 6 in 6 consecutive Div 1, League Cup and European Cup Winners' games, Aug to Sep 1971. (6 ones)

BOBBY TAMBLING

Frank Lampard scored 10 or more goals in 10 successive Premier League seasons from 2003/04 up to and including 2012/13 – a competition record

MOST HAT-TRICKS

Jimmy Greaves 13, George Hilsdon (including one double) 9, **Bobby Tambling** and Kerry Dixon 8, Peter Osgood and Frank Lampard 5 and Jimmy Windridge, Joe Bambrick and Didier Drogba 4.

BOBBY'S HAT-TRICKS

Sep	1961	3 v Sheff Utd (h)	6-1	Div 1
Oct	1961	3 v Sheff Wed (a)	3-5	Div 1
Oct	1962	3 v Derby (a)	3-1	Div 2
Dec	1962	4 v Charlton (a)	4-1	Div 2
May	1963	4 v Portsmouth (h)	7-0	Div 2
Mar	1964	4 v Arsenal (a)	4-2	Div 1
Sep	1966	5 v Aston Villa (a)	6-2	Div 1
Feb	1969	4 v Sunderland (h)	5-1	Div 1

INTERNATIONAL CAREER

England 3 caps, 1 goal
-1962/63 v Wales, France (1 goal)
-1965/66 v Yugoslavia
England Under-23s 13 caps, 11 goals
-1962/63 Belgium (1 goal), Greece (3 goals), Yugoslavia
-1963/64 West Germany (2 goals), Scotland, France (1 goal), Hungary (1 goal), Israel (1 goal), Turkey
-1964/65 Wales (sub, 2 goals), Romania, Czechoslovakia, Austria
England Schoolboy 7 caps, 5 goals
Represented Football League v Scottish League in 1968/69 (1 goal)